IT Security Risk Management in the Context of Cloud Computing

D1537213

WITHDRAWN

André Loske

IT Security Risk Management in the Context of Cloud Computing

Towards an Understanding of the Key Role of Providers' IT Security Risk Perceptions

With a foreword by Prof. Dr. Peter Buxmann

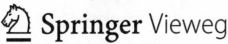 Springer Vieweg

André Loske
Darmstadt, Germany

Dissertation, TU Darmstadt, 2015

Hochschulkennziffer D17

ISBN 978-3-658-11339-1   ISBN 978-3-658-11340-7 (eBook)
DOI 10.1007/978-3-658-11340-7

Library of Congress Control Number: 2015954946

Springer Vieweg
© Springer Fachmedien Wiesbaden 2015

Printed on acid-free paper

Springer Vieweg is a brand of Springer Fachmedien Wiesbaden
Springer Fachmedien Wiesbaden is part of Springer Science+Business Media
(www.springer.com)

Foreword

Cloud Computing is one of the most strongly growing types of IT outsourcing and companies, governments, and non-profit organizations alike are increasingly leveraging this emerging paradigm. For example, SAP recently announced a major strategy change and invests heavily in the expansion of its Cloud business. Most of the SAP applications will be readily available as a service in the near future. However, the acceptance of Cloud solutions by clients lags far behind the predictions of leading market analysts. In the last years, the promised technological and economic advantages of the Cloud were once too often accompanied by serious IT security incidents which not only jeopardized the reputation of the respective service providers but also daunted many clients for the long term. Considering the existence-threatening consequences of IT security incidents in the context of the Cloud, it could be expected that the service providers do everything in their power to mitigate these risks. Nonetheless, a closer look at the security whitepapers of well-established Cloud services in many cases reveals a lack of crucial IT security measures, which are, for example, defined as minimum IT security standards for service providers by the Federal Office for Information Security. Intrigued by this observation, the thesis investigates whether the possibility that the providers' decision makers underestimate their services' IT security risks can explain the failure to implement necessary safeguarding measures in Cloud services.

Therefore, the primary research objective of this thesis is to analyze the effects of decision makers' subjective risk perception on the providers' IT security management. In this thesis's first part, drawing on organizational IT security planning models and findings of previous technology threat avoidance research, a conceptual model of the influence of decision makers' risk perception on providers' IT security risk investment decisions is developed. A quantitative empirical survey is used to examine how the responsible decision makers of the service providers perceive risks and how these risk estimations affect the IT security investment behavior. By transferring well-established approaches from psychological research, Mr. Loske afterwards demonstrates that the decision makers of Cloud providers exhibit a systematic underestimation of the IT security risks that their organizations are exposed to, resulting in underinvestment in safeguarding measures.

The second part of this thesis alters the view and investigates how the providers' assessment of their Cloud services' IT security risk exposure influences the adoption behavior of client companies. Therefore, a theoretical model is developed which integrates the providers' IT security assessments in a technology acceptance model for Cloud services in terms of perceptual incongruence between the providers' perceptions and those of the clients. Based on an empirical survey with potential client companies' executives, Mr. Loske demonstrates that the underestimation of the risks by the providers not only causes an underinvestment in IT security but also facilitates a disagreement among the providers and their clients on the IT security risks of the services. In particular, the perceptual gap between the providers and their clients is shown to both considerably increase the IT security risk perceptions of the clients and significantly inhibit their intentions to use those providers' Cloud services.

Altogether, Mr. Loske makes several significant contributions to information systems science. This thesis offers theoretical explanation and empirical support for the impact of decision makers' subjective IT security risk perceptions on the results of the organizational IT security risk management. Beyond that, the work offers a new perspective on IT security risk perceptions by demonstrating that there are typically two perspectives which are independently associated with downstream beliefs and behavior. Moreover, the thesis adds to the body of knowledge about the formation of IT security risk perceptions by showing that these perceptions are often subject to systematic errors in terms of unrealistic optimism. Additionally, this work advances our understanding of how perceptual differences between providers and their clients concerning IT security risks affect adoption decisions of the clients by transferring the established concepts of perceptual concurrence and cognitive dissonance to the field of IT security. Furthermore, this work highlights the importance for researchers to incorporate both parts of the dyad, i.e. the clients and the providers, when studying questions related to the IT security of modern IT delivery models, such as the Cloud.

Both empirical studies and the statistical analyses show a high degree of methodological rigor and provide numerous interesting results. This thesis will be valuable to readers in both, academia and practice, as it suggests concrete recommended actions for providers and clients that can help to increase the IT security of services and eventually improve the market success of Cloud Computing. Therefore, I wish this thesis a widespread distribution.

Darmstadt, May 2015   *Prof. Dr. Peter Buxmann*

Acknowledgements

This thesis was written during my work as a research assistant at the Chair of Information Systems | Software Business & Information Management at the Technical University of Darmstadt. The progress and completion of my dissertation would not have been possible without the support of many people, whom I sincerely wish to thank with the following acknowledgments.

First, I am especially grateful to my supervisor Prof. Dr. Peter Buxmann, who greatly supported me and made my dissertation possible in the first place. Likewise, I would like to thank and express my deepest gratitude to my advisor Dr. Thomas Widjaja, who challenged me to achieve my highest potential and helped me to deal with those challenges by providing his fullest guidance and support. I sincerely appreciate that he always found the time to devote to our long research meetings, answer all my questions, and provide insightful and prompt feedback despite his busy schedule. I also would like to express my appreciation to my second referee Prof. Dr. Alexander Benlian for his valuable advises and our productive research collaboration.

Furthermore, I would like to thank Prof. Dr. Izak Benbasat and Prof. Dr. Hasan Cavusoglu, who invited me to work as a visiting researcher for the MIS division of the Sauder School of Business at the University of British Columbia. I feel very fortunate that I have had the opportunity to work together with these experienced researchers which did not only broaden my horizon but also enhanced my abilities of conducting good research.

Additionally, I thank the CASED graduate school for granting me a PhD scholarship as well as the numerous CASED postdocs and PhD students with whom I conducted the pre-studies.

My special thanks go to my friends and colleagues Adrian, Alexander, Anton, Christoph, Helena, Hendrik, Jasmin, Jin, Markus, Markus, Martin, Nicole, Nihal, Rabea, Ruth, Stefan, Thorsten, Tobias, and Tobias with whom I have had many interesting and fruitful discussions and who have provided valuable feedback on my research.

Finally, I would like to express a large gratitude to my beloved wife, my family, and to my parents for their invaluable support and thoughtfulness. They all gave me the necessary strength to persist through challenging times.

Darmstadt, May 2015   *André Loske*

Table of Contents

List of Tables

List of Figures

List of Abbreviations

API	Application Programming Interface
ASP	Application Service Provision
AVE	Average Variance Extracted
BC	Bootstrap Confidence
BPO	Business Process Outsourcing
CA	Cronbach's Alpha
CaaS	Communication as a Service
CB-SEM	Covariance-Based Structural Equation Modeling
CDT	Cognitive Dissonance Theory
CEO	Chief Executive Officer
CIO	Chief Information Officer
Cloud	Cloud Computing
CMB	Common Method Bias
CO	Comparative Optimism
CPR	Calculated Protection Ranking
CPU	Central Processing Unit
CR	Composite Reliability
CRM	Customer Relationship Management
CSA	Cloud Security Alliance
ECT	Expectation Confirmation Theory
EDI	Electronic Data Interchange
EFA	Exploratory Factor Analyses
ENISA	European Network and Information Security Agency
EPPM	Extended Parallel Process Model
ERP	Enterprise Resource Planning
HBM	Health Belief Model
HRA	Health Risk Appraisal
HTMT	Heterotrait-Monotrait
IaaS	Infrastructure as a Service
IEEE	Institute of Electrical and Electronics Engineering
IS	Information System(s)
ISO	International Organization for Standardization
IT	Information Technology
ITO	Information Technology Outsourcing

ITSR	Information Technology Security Risk
LISREL	Linear Structural Relations
MIMIC	Multiple Indicators, Multiple Causes
MIS	Management Information Systems
MTMM	Multitrait-Multimethod
NIST	National Institute of Standards and Technology
OLS	Ordinary Least Squares
PaaS	Platform as a Service
PITSR	Perceived Information Technology Security Risk
PLS	Partial Least Squares
PMT	Protection Motivation Theory
PPR	Perceived Protection Ranking
ROI	Return on Investment
ROSI	Return on Security Investment
RQ	Research Question
SaaS	Software as a Service
SD	Standard Deviation
SEM	Structural Equation Modeling
SIEM	Security Information and Event Management
SLA	Service Level Agreement
TAM	Technology Acceptance Model
TTAT	Technology Threat Avoidance Theory
UO	Unrealistic Optimism
VAR	Variance
VIF	Variance Inflation Factor
XaaS	Everything as a Service

Abstract

Although providers' decision makers constantly emphasize a low IT security risk (ITSR) in the Cloud, numerous serious IT security incidents have occurred over the last few years. Considering the theoretical availability of effective safeguards against most of these risks, it seems that in many cases, the Cloud providers' decision makers may have underestimated the ITSRs. The psychological research terms comparable phenomena "unrealistic optimism". While prior research has intensively studied the ITSR perceptions of (potential) Cloud customers, the provider side has been completely neglected. In general, even though correct IT security risk assessments are the foundation for effective IT security risk management in organizations, no research has been dedicated to the effects of organizational decision makers' subjective ITSR perceptions on the implementation of necessary safeguards. Even more importantly, little or no attention has been paid to the existence and consequences of possible systematic errors in ITSR perceptions.

Against this backdrop, the first part of this thesis adds a new perspective to the stream of organizational IT security risk management literature, one that sheds light on the importance of decision makers' ITSR perceptions. Drawing on psychological risk perception theory, we propose an extended theoretical IT security risk management model that explicates how the subjective ITSR perceptions of decision-makers predict the outcome of providers' IT security risk management. Additionally, we transfer established methods of measuring unrealistic optimism to the IT context, which enables us to systematically capture and analyze a potential underestimation of the ITSRs at the provider side. Based on a large-scale empirical study of Cloud providers located in North America, we reveal that in many cases, the providers' decision makers significantly underestimate their services' ITSR exposure, which inhibits the implementation of necessary safeguarding measures.

We also demonstrate that even though the prevalence of ITSR perceptions among customers considering Cloud adoption is widely recognized, providers only pay very limited attention to the concerns expressed by customer companies. In this regard, the specific characteristics of the Cloud and the systematic underestimation of ITSRs by providers' decision makers are likely to cause serious disagreements with (potential) customers about the ITSRs of the Cloud. Drawing on perceptual congruence literature, the second part of this thesis examines matched survey responses of Cloud providers and their (potential) customers located in Germany, showing a consistent pattern of perceptual differences across all ITSRs relevant to the Cloud. In this context, this thesis proposes an extended theoretical model of Cloud adoption that reveals that this disagreement has strong adverse effects on important downstream beliefs of the customer companies' IT managers and, ultimately, on their intentions to adopt Cloud services.

Overall, this thesis extends our theoretical understanding of the role of decision makers' ITSR perception in the providers' IT security risk management. By demonstrating how unrealistic optimism negatively affects ITSR assessments and thus the implementation of necessary safeguards, our work lays the foundation for further studies of the far-reaching consequences of systematic errors in the perception of ITSRs. Moreover, we shed light on the negative effects of the perceptual incongruences between providers and customers concerning the ITSRs in the context of modern IT delivery paradigms, such as the Cloud. Providers' decision makers can use the results of this thesis to understand in which ways and to what extent systematic errors in the ITSR assessments affect the IT security risk management processes, which enables them to make preparations and thus to increase the IT security levels of their Cloud services. Additionally, we recommend actions for providers to ascertain whether their own ITSR assessments agree with that of the (potential) customer companies and to foster a shared understanding of the ITSRs, which in turn make their services more attractive for customer companies. (Potential) customers that are interested in using the Cloud may benefit from our findings, as these will help them identify Cloud services with potentially ineffective IT security risk management.

Zusammenfassung

Obwohl Cloud-Anbieter kontinuierlich das geringe IT-Sicherheitsrisiko ihrer Dienste betonen, gab es in den vergangenen Jahren eine Vielzahl von schwerwiegenden IT-Sicherheitsvorfällen. In Anbetracht dessen, dass effektive Maßnahmen zum Schutz der Cloud-Dienste gegen viele dieser Risiken direkt verfügbar sind, stellt sich die Frage, ob die Entscheidungsträger von Cloud-Anbietern das IT-Sicherheitsrisiko ihrer eigenen Dienste grundsätzlich unterschätzen. Vergleichbare Phänomene werden in der psychologischen Forschung als unrealistischer Optimismus bezeichnet. Während die bisherige Forschung die Wahrnehmung der IT-Sicherheitsrisiken in der Cloud seitens (potentieller) Kunden bereits intensiv untersucht hat, wurde die Anbieterseite jedoch nahezu komplett vernachlässigt. Auch wenn die korrekte Bewertung der IT-Sicherheitsrisiken im Allgemeinen die Grundlage für ein effektives IT-Risikomanagement in Unternehmen darstellt, gibt es zudem bislang keine Forschung über die Auswirkungen der subjektiven Einschätzung der IT-Sicherheitsrisiken durch Entscheidungsträger auf die Umsetzung von IT-Sicherheitsmaßnahmen in Unternehmen. Darüber hinaus existiert bisher keine Forschung über die Existenz von systematischen Fehlern bei der Bewertung von IT-Sicherheitsrisiken und deren Folgen.

Vor diesem Hintergrund bietet der erste Teil dieser Dissertation eine neue Perspektive auf das IT-Risikomanagement in Unternehmen, welche die Bedeutung wahrgenommener IT-Sicherheitsrisiken von Entscheidungsträgern hervorhebt. Auf Grundlage psychologischer Theorien zur Risikowahrnehmung wird zunächst ein theoretisches Modell des organisationalen IT-Risikomanagements erarbeitet, welches die Auswirkungen subjektiv wahrgenommener IT-Sicherheitsrisiken auf das IT-Risikomanagement von Cloud-Anbietern konzeptualisiert. Die Übertragung etablierter Messmethoden des unrealistischen Optimismus auf den IT-Sektor ermöglicht in diesem Zusammenhang die systematische Erfassung und Untersuchung einer möglichen Unterschätzung der IT-Sicherheitsrisiken durch die Entscheidungsträger. Anhand einer großzahligen, empirischen Studie mit Cloud-Anbietern in Nord-Amerika wird gezeigt, dass die Entscheidungsträger der Anbieter das IT-Sicherheitsrisiko ihrer Dienste in vielen Fällen drastisch unterschätzen, wodurch die Implementierung von notwendigen IT-Sicherheitsmaßnahmen in der Cloud verhindert wird.

Auch wenn die negativen Auswirkungen der wahrgenommenen IT-Sicherheitsrisiken auf die Nutzung von Cloud-Diensten im Allgemeinen bekannt sind, zeigen die Ergebnisse der vorliegenden Ausarbeitung, dass die Anbieter nur sehr eingeschränkt auf die IT-Sicherheitsbedenken der Kunden eingehen. Die speziellen Charakteristika der Cloud sowie eine systematische Unterschätzung der IT-Sicherheitsrisiken auf Anbieterseite führen dabei oftmals zu Differenzen mit (potentiellen) Kunden im Hinblick auf die IT-Sicherheitsrisiken der Cloud-Dienste. Im zweiten Teil der Dissertation wird in einer großzahligen, empirischen Umfrage die Wahrnehmung der IT-Sicherheitsrisiken von Cloud-Anbietern und deren (potentiellen) Kunden in Deutschland untersucht, wobei sich erhebliche Wahrnehmungsunterschiede hinsichtlich aller relevanten IT-Sicherheitsrisiken der Cloud zeigen. Darüber hinaus wird verdeutlicht, dass sich diese Wahrnehmungsunterschiede sehr negativ auf die Evaluierung der Cloud-Dienste seitens der (potentiellen) Kunden auswirken und letztendlich eine Nutzung der Cloud in vielen Fällen verhindern.

Die Konzeptualisierung der Rolle wahrgenommener IT-Sicherheitsrisiken im IT-Risikomanagement von Cloud-Anbietern trägt zum aktuellen Stand der organisationalen IT-Sicherheitsforschung bei. Mit dem Nachweis, wie unrealistischer Optimismus sich negativ auf die Bewertung von IT-Sicherheitsrisiken und damit auf die Implementierung von notwendigen Sicherheitsmaßnahmen auswirkt, legt die Arbeit darüber hinaus den Grundstein für weitere Forschung über die weitreichenden Folgen der systematischen Unterschätzung der IT-Sicherheitsrisiken. In diesem Zusammenhang werden auch die negativen Konsequenzen von Wahrnehmungsunterschieden zwischen Anbietern und Kunden bezüglich der IT-Sicherheitsrisiken im Bereich neuer Formen der IT-Bereitstellung, wie z. B. der Cloud, hervorgehoben. Die Ergebnisse dieser Dissertation ermöglichen es Cloud-Anbietern die negativen Auswirkungen systematischer Fehleinschätzungen der IT-Sicherheitsrisiken auf das IT-Risikomanagement nachzuvollziehen und entsprechende Vorkehrungen zu treffen, die den IT-Sicherheitslevel der Dienste erhöhen können. Außerdem werden Handlungsempfehlungen vorgeschlagen, die es Anbietern ermöglichen, Unterschiede ihrer Bewertung der IT-Sicherheitsrisiken gegenüber denen ihrer (potentiellen) Kunden zu erkennen und zu reduzieren, wodurch sie die Attraktivität ihrer Cloud-Dienste erhöhen können. Durch das Aufzeigen von Verfahren zur Erkennung von Cloud-Diensten mit eventuell unwirksamem IT-Risikomanagement unterstützt die vorliegende Ausarbeitung gleichzeitig (potentielle) Kunden bei der Auswahl geeigneter Cloud-Dienste für ihre Unternehmen.

1 Introduction

1.1 Problem Description and Motivation

During the last several decades, a majority of companies, governments, and nonprofit organizations have outsourced at least part of their information systems (ISs) to external suppliers. Cloud Computing (the Cloud) represents an advancement of classical information technology (IT) outsourcing (ITO) by means of modern communication technologies. The U.S. National Institute of Standards and Technology (NIST) defines the Cloud as "a model for enabling ubiquitous, convenient, on-demand network access to a shared pool of configurable computing resources (e.g., networks, servers, storage, applications, and services) that can be rapidly provisioned and released with minimal management effort or service provider interaction" (Mell and Grance 2011, p. 2). Although the Cloud promises a variety of technical and economic advantages over classical ITO concepts (e.g., Marston et al. 2011), its acceptance lags far behind the expectations. For example, in 2010, leading market analysts forecasted that more than 16% of the worldwide market share of enterprise software in 2014 would be accounted for by Software as a Service (SaaS) solutions (Gartner 2010). By the end of 2014, SaaS services were found to have a share of less than 6% of the combined enterprise software market, almost the same level as in 2009 (IDC 2014). Nevertheless, the software industry still holds high hopes for the Cloud. For instance, SAP recently announced a strategy shift along with a considerable expansion of their Cloud service portfolio (SAP 2014a). However, despite the quest today to be ever more efficient and productive, IT managers of (potential) customer companies are often highly skeptical about the Cloud. In particular, recent studies show that most (potential) customers' IT managers are especially concerned about the higher complexity IT security risks (ITSRs) in the Cloud due to the ubiquitous and on-demand network access of resources. Therefore, they demand higher IT security levels on the part of providers as a precondition for using the Cloud as a delivery model (e.g., Ackermann et al. 2012; Benlian and Hess 2011). While providers constantly emphasize their services' level of high protection against ITSRs (e.g., Amazon 2014; SAP 2014b), frequent IT security breaches may not only prove the customers right but also make the vulnerability of the Cloud evident. In this context, for example, an independent industry database lists 1,241 serious IT security incidents for Cloud services in the US in the year 2013 alone (Cloutage 2013). In addition to the directly affected clients, the mainstream media's broad coverage of the major IT security incidents also reached a large number of potential customer companies and had devastating effects not only on the reputation of the providers involved but also on Cloud technology in general (e.g., Armbrust et al. 2010; Vaquero et al. 2010). Considering the theoretical availability of effective IT security safeguards against most Cloud ITSRs (see, e.g., Federal Office for Information Security 2011) and the accumulation of IT security incidents that can threaten the very existence of providers it seems plausible that in many cases, critical miscalculations are made in the providers' IT security risk management.

Organizational IT security risk management is typically conceptualized as a strategic planning process with five key phases, including the assessment of identified ITSRs and the evaluation of available safeguards (e.g., Cavusoglu et al. forthcoming; Straub and Welke 1998; Warkentin and Johnston 2008). However, as with all new technology developments, the lack of historical data regarding the impact and probability of ITSRs frequently hinders an objective quantification of the Cloud's risks with traditional tools (e.g., Hopkin 2012). Additionally, IT security incidents in the Cloud often go undetected or unreported or are not systematically documented, so that typically, no quantitative data about ITSRs are available (Kankanhalli et al. 2003). Accordingly, outcomes of the IT security risk management phases in the context of the Cloud are predominantly determined by the more or less subjective perceptions of the decision makers in charge of a provider's IT security. Yet errors in the risk assessment phase are directly responsible for misspecifications of a provider's IT security risk management. Psychological research has demonstrated that in other, comparable situations, people tend to interpret ambiguous information or unknown situations in self-favoring ways. Additionally, research has identified a predisposition that people have to attribute to themselves various desirable characteristics that they do not necessarily possess and consequently to overestimate their own capabilities (Weinstein and Klein 1996). As a consequence, they considerably underrate their own vulnerability to risks both in comparison to others (e.g., a smoker thinks that his or her risk of serious disease is 10% lower than that of average smokers, while it is actually the same) and in an absolute sense (e.g., a smoker thinks that his or her risk of serious disease is 20%, when it is actually 30%). The psychological research terms this underestimation of absolute and comparative risks "unrealistic optimism" (UO) (Shepperd et al. 2013). UO has been demonstrated to have an important impact on protective behavior – for example, smokers have been found to be less motivated to take precautionary actions such as quitting smoking or having regular medical check-ups, due to their underestimation of their risk (e.g., Weinstein 1987; Weinstein et al. 2004). Similarly, a provider's decision makers' ITSR assessments concerning the provider's own services are likely to deviate significantly from the actual risks. Underestimation of the ITSR exposure of a provider's Cloud service by its decision makers can have adverse effects on the outcomes of the IT security risk management process and subsequently inhibit decisions to implement necessary security controls.

A growing stream of research in the field of IT security indicates an increasing interest in understanding threat avoidance, compliance, and information protection behaviors (Anderson and Agarwal 2010; Johnston and Warkentin 2010; Liang and Xue 2009; Liang and Xue 2010; Vance et al. 2012). Yet little is known about the cognitive processes through which organizational decision makers cope with ITSRs associated with their company's IT systems. Even though previous IS research has highlighted the importance of decision makers' ITSR assessments for effective organizational IT security risk management (e.g., Straub and Welke 1998), previous IT security studies are predominately focused on the perceptions of end users and largely neglect decision makers at the organizational level. Accordingly, little is understood about the decision makers' subjective assessments of ITSRs and how these influence the outcomes of organizational IT security risk management processes. Furthermore, as noted earlier, psychological research has shown that people's perceptions of their own risk generally incorporate two different perspectives: an absolute perception and a comparative perception of their own risk in relation to the risk of others (e.g., Dillard et al. 2012). Although the psychological research has conclusively shown that the two perspectives are principally independent and can influence people's behavior in different ways, previous IS research has focused only on absolute ITSR perceptions and has neglected the impact of comparative risk perceptions. Even more importantly, prior research has paid no attention to the existence and far-reaching consequences of UO with respect to an organization's evaluating its own exposure to ITSRs.

Moreover, possible underestimation of their own service's exposure to ITSRs by the provider's decision makers not only places the service at risk of possible IT security incidents; it also enlarges the gap between ITSR assessments made by providers and their (potential) customers, which reduces providers' ability to understand their (potential) customers' desires and expectations regarding their services' IT security. According to the organizational IT security risk management literature (e.g., Cavusoglu et al. forthcoming; Straub and Welke 1998), if an organization's risk assessment phase concludes that certain ITSRs, such as disclosure of data by the provider or data manipulation on the provider side (Ackermann et al. 2012), pose no considerable threat to the organization, the providers' decision makers will typically not decide to invest in (cost-intensive) safeguards against those ITSRs. However, (potential) customer companies may assess the same ITSRs as critical for their systems and data and consequently expect the implementation of appropriate safeguards against these risks when they use a Cloud service as a delivery model. In this regard, the non-availability of quantified data about the ITSRs of the Cloud is a huge challenge not only for the providers but also for (potential) customer companies. Similar to the providers' decision makers, the customers' IT managers have to rely on other, less objective, sources such as trading association recommendations, reports of other organizations in the industry, and even mass media reports to estimate which ITSRs are relevant for their organization. Moreover, the specific characteristics of an ITO relationship in general and with respect to the Cloud in particular, such as asymmetry in information and different degrees of controllability, are likely to lead to providers and customer companies having divergent perceptions about ITSRs (e.g., Kishore et al. 2003; Shepperd et al. 2002). For example, when a customer company uses Cloud services, some or even all of its data will be stored in the provider's data center. Therefore, customers give providers control over their data, which in many cases constitute a critical company asset (e.g., Jurison 1995), without having direct influence over how the providers will secure their data – for example, which backup and disaster recovery procedures they have in place. Due to feelings of a loss of control, a potential customer company's IT manager is likely to be disproportionately concerned regarding the data's security (e.g., Heng et al. 2011) and to expect very high levels of protection against ITSRs of the Cloud providers. In this regard, previous research studies have consistently shown that most customers' IT managers perceive the Cloud's ITSRs to be critical (e.g., Ackermann et al. 2012; Benlian and Hess 2011). These studies have thereby revealed that the high ITSR perceptions on the part of customers' IT managers are also their most salient reason for not using the Cloud as their delivery model. Accordingly, it is generally not the actual ITSR but the risk as perceived by the decision maker that determines the decision about adopting a Cloud service (Gigerenzer 2004). In light of the importance of the ITSR perceptions of customers' IT managers, providers' unresponsiveness to customer demands for increased IT security levels suggests that there may be fundamental differences between the ITSR perceptions of providers' decision makers and customers' IT managers. These differences are likely to have inhibiting effects on (potential) customer company adoption of Cloud services that reach far beyond those of the actually perceived ITSR.

As described above, previous research has investigated only the ITSR perceptions of customers, and no attention has been paid to the ITSR perceptions of provider decision makers. However, a number of empirical studies in IS research have investigated the existence and consequences of disagreements between IS users and providers regarding IS service quality factors (e.g., Benlian 2011; Boyd et al. 2007; Jiang et al. 2003). This research has found that the cognitive dissonance and gap between users' expectations of a service and IS providers' ability to understand those expectations is tied to lower user satisfaction and to lower adoption levels (e.g., Pitt et al. 1998; Tesch et al. 2005). Similarly, when (potential) customers' IT managers are confronted – e.g., through sales pitches or a provider's customer communications – with the fact that their ITSR perceptions are not matched by the providers' perceptions (e.g., Pring 2010), their satisfaction with the Cloud service and consequently their intentions to adopt the service are significantly reduced. In particular, the disagreement regarding ITSRs is likely to shake the confidence that (potential) customers' IT managers have in providers' capabilities and thus to increase their perceptions of ITSRs associated with the Cloud – which in turn has further inhibiting effects on customers' intentions to use Cloud services (Jiang et al. 2003; Tesch et al. 2005). Nevertheless, despite the fact that protection against ITSRs is generally regarded as crucial for IS service, prior IS research has focused only on the perceptual incongruences regarding traditional SERVQUAL factors and has neglected IT-specific factors (e.g., Benlian 2011; Boyd et al. 2007; Jiang et al. 2003).

1.2   Objectives and Benefits

To meet the challenges presented by the current state of IT security risk management and ITSR perception research and practice, this thesis pursues three major goals with five main research questions (RQs). This section briefly presents the research questions and discusses the associated implications for research and practice.

The first major goal of this thesis is to contribute to a better understanding of organizational IT security risk management by highlighting the importance of decision makers' subjective ITSR perceptions at the organizational level. As described in Section 1.1, organizational IT security risk management is typically viewed as an entirely rational cost-benefit analysis of the implementation of safeguarding measures (e.g., Cavusoglu et al. forthcoming; Straub and Welke 1998). However, considering the frequent non-availability of quantified data regarding the risks in the IT sector that would allow an objective quantification of actual ITSRs and thus an objective assessment of the suitability of safeguards taken against the ITSRs, in many cases the providers' IT security risk management processes are based on less objective sources, the first of these being the perceptions of the decision makers in charge of the IT security. Despite the rapidly growing importance of effective IT security risk management for organizations, little is understood about the nature and the effect mechanisms of decision makers' ITSR perceptions at the organizational level.

To enrich our understanding of organizational IT security risk management, we propose a theoretical framework that integrates three distinct but related streams of literature: organizational IT security risk management, coping, and institutional theory. Drawing on the organizational IT security risk management literature, the first part of the theoretical model explains the roles of the IT security risk management phases – especially the ITSR analysis and safeguard evaluation phases – in determining a provider's IT security risk management. Based on coping theory (Lazarus 1993), technology threat avoidance theory (Liang and Xue 2010), and protection motivation theory (Rogers 1975), the second part of the theoretical model postulates that key phases of organizational IT security risk management are instigated by two perceptual processes of the decision makers that partly influence each other: the ITSR appraisal (e.g., the decision makers' perceptions of the financial damage that can result from IT security incidents) and the coping appraisal (e.g., the decision makers' assessments of the effectiveness of the available safeguards). Based on institutional theory (Scott 1995), the third part of the theoretical model posits that mimetic, coercive, and normative pressures that exist in an institutionalized environment (e.g., the enacted customer power to implement additional safeguards as perceived by the providers' decision makers) have significant influences on decision makers' intentions to increase an organization's IT security level.

Moreover, we draw on psychological risk perception research to add a new perspective to IT security research by demonstrating that there are two different and largely independent aspects of ITSR perception: absolute and comparative ITSR perception. Previous IT security studies have focused only on absolute ITSR perceptions, thereby neglecting the important implications of comparative ITSR perceptions. As such, a deeper understanding of the complex nature of ITSR assessments has the potential to explain a greater degree of variance in behavioral intentions in a wide range of IS research areas, such as the implementation of safeguarding measures or the adoption of new technologies. In order to analyze the effects of decision makers' absolute and comparative ITSR assessments in depth, we integrate both perspectives in technology threat avoidance theory and eventually in the proposed model of Cloud providers' IT security risk management. Based on the developed theoretical model and a large-scale empirical study with 177 SaaS providers, we address the following research question:

RQ1:   In what ways and to what degree do the absolute and comparative IT security risk perceptions of Cloud providers' decision makers predict the outcomes of the providers' IT security risk management?

The thesis then focuses on the irrational aspects of ITSR perceptions, namely, the systematic underestimation of a provider's own exposure to ITSRs. The goal, comprising two research questions, is to enhance our understanding of the causes and consequences of systematic errors in decision makers' ITSR assessments – which may, for example, lead to misspecifications of the organization's IT security risk management or to the non-implementation of necessary safeguarding measures. This is particularly important at the organizational level, where IT security risk management models are typically based on the assumption of a rational risk-benefit analysis (e.g., Cavusoglu et al. 2004b; Sonnenreich et al. 2006). Thus, this study has various implications for IS research related to ITSR perceptions. In particular, when investigating the behavioral consequences of ITSR perceptions, future research should incorporate the possibility that a significant number of people unconsciously underestimate their own absolute and comparative vulnerability (e.g., Liang and Xue 2010; Vance et al. 2012).

Drawing on UO research and the findings of previous psychological literature, we investigate whether the decision makers in the obtained sample systematically underestimate the absolute and/or comparative ITSR exposure of their own organizations' services, in order to comprehensively address the following research question:

RQ2:   Do Cloud providers' decision makers systematically underestimate the ITSR exposure of their own organizations' services?

In addition to capturing and measuring UO, the second major goal also concerns the consequences of providers' decision makers' systematic underestimation of ITSRs. In particular,
we build on the theoretical model described above and the UO literature to examine in what
ways and to what degree the potential underestimation of the ITSR exposure of a provider's
own services by its decision makers affects the provider's IT security risk management, as
reflected in the following research question:

RQ3:   *What are the impacts of the potential systematic error in the decision makers' ITSR*
          perceptions on the outcome of the providers' IT security risk management?

However, potential systematic errors in the ITSR perceptions of providers' decision makers
not only place the providers' services at risk of being compromised by ITSRs, but also inevitably enlarge the gap between providers' ITSR assessments and those of (potential) customer
companies. While a number of empirical studies in IS research have investigated the existence
and consequences of a perceptual incongruence regarding IS service quality (e.g., Benlian
2011; Boyd et al. 2007; Jiang et al. 2002; Jiang et al. 2003; Tesch et al. 2005), no attention
has been paid to the role of disagreement between providers and their (potential) customers
regarding perceptions of ITSR. The third major goal of this thesis is to contribute to IT security research by introducing the well-known concepts of perceptual concurrence and cognitive
dissonance to this field and thus deepening our understanding of perceptual differences regarding ITSRs in the context of the Cloud. To enrich our understanding of this perceptual
incongruence, we conducted an empirical study with 73 Cloud providers and 304 of their (potential) customer companies that investigated ITSR perceptions from both perspectives. This
study attempts to fill the research gaps with regard to the perceptual incongruence concerning
ITSRs by addressing the following research question:

RQ4:   *Is there a significant gap between the ITSR assessments of providers and (potential)*
          customer companies in the context of the Cloud?

The third major goal also concerns the effect mechanisms and behavioral consequences of the
perceptual incongruence concerning ITSRs between Cloud providers and (potential) customer
companies. To this end, the study adopts the perspective of Cloud providers' (potential) customer companies. Drawing on cognitive dissonance theory, the study argues that the perceptual incongruence regarding ITSRs will – similarly to IS quality factors – reduce customer
companies' satisfaction with Cloud services. At the same time, based on expectation confirmation theory, we expect that the gap between the expectations of (potential) customers' IT
managers concerning Cloud services' protection and the ability of providers to understand the
customers' demands (e.g., Pitt et al. 1998; Tesch et al. 2005) will negatively impact important
downstream beliefs (i.e., perceived ITSRs) that affect customers' adoption decisions. Therefore, this research offers various ways for researchers to better understand the formation of

customers' ITSR perceptions and concerns in various fields of application. Moreover, the study underscores the importance of incorporating both parts of the dyad (i.e., the provider and the customer perspectives) when studying questions in the context of modern IT delivery models such as the Cloud. The study therefore addresses the following research question:

RQ5:   *In which ways and to what degree does the gap between the ITSR assessments of providers and those of their (potential) customers influence the intentions of customer company IT managers to adopt Cloud services?*

By answering these five research questions, this thesis makes important theoretical contributions to the emerging body of knowledge about the behavioral and organizational issues surrounding IT security.

In addition to these theoretical contributions, this thesis makes several practical contributions. In particular, answering our five research questions will enable Cloud providers' decision makers to improve their IT security risk management processes and thus the IT security of their organizations' services. Additionally, we recommend actions to reduce the perceptual incongruence between providers and their (potential) customers, which was found to be an important inhibitor of Cloud sales. Moreover, the findings in this thesis can support (potential) customer companies' decision making with respect to Cloud adoption by helping them identify which Cloud services might be more weakly protected than others against ITSRs.

The primary practical contributions are based on the empirical evidence that decision makers' subjective perceptions of ITSRs have a substantial influence on the outcome of providers' IT security risk management. Even though decisions to implement safeguarding measures against ITSRs at the organizational level are often viewed as involving a completely rational comparative weighing of costs and risks, the findings of this thesis highlight the fallibility of the IT security risk management process. In this regard, as decision makers have in many cases been found to substantially underestimate the ITSR exposure of their organizations' services due to UO, which in turn was revealed to considerably inhibit the implementation of necessary safeguards, the findings should especially motivate providers' decision makers to improve their organizations' IT security risk management processes for their Cloud services. In this regard, this thesis not only offers a deeper understanding of the nature of ITSR perceptions and their effects on the outcome of IT security risk management, but also demonstrates in which ways and to what degree the decision makers' ITSR assessments actually affect each of the IT security risk management phases – which will enable providers' decision makers to develop targeted strategies for reducing the potential systematic errors in their ITSR perceptions (e.g., by involving external IT security experts in certain phases of the IT security risk management or by implementing certified IT security risk management systems). Therefore, as the ITSRs associated with the Cloud have also been shown to be an important inhibitor of

potential customers' adoption intentions, the findings of this thesis will help providers' decision makers not only to increase the level of their services' IT security, but also to facilitate
sales of their Cloud services.

At the same time, errors in the providers' IT security risk management also put the IT security
of the customers' systems and data in jeopardy when the Cloud is used as delivery model.
Thus, the results of this thesis should motivate (potential) customer IT managers not to implicitly trust the ITSR assessments of providers and to continuously challenge the IT security
promises made by Cloud providers. Thus, for example, the approaches to measuring the UO
of providers' decision makers proposed in this study can be used by (potential) customers' IT
managers to identify Cloud services whose ITSR assessments may be subject to systematic
errors, indicating ineffective IT security risk management on the part of those providers.

The combined results of our studies presented in this thesis not only stress the need for accurate ITSR assessment but also highlight the importance of a shared understanding of ITSRs
between providers and their (potential) customer companies. Since the mismatch between
customers' expectations regarding the IT security of Cloud services and the ability of providers' decision makers to understand customer requirements was found to be tied to lower satisfaction and eventually to inhibit customer intentions to adopt Cloud services, providers' decision makers should strive to better incorporate customer concerns regarding the ITSRs associated with the Cloud and to bring their ITSR assessments into congruence with those of (potential) customers' IT managers. Therefore, this thesis offers various recommended actions
for providers and (potential) customers of Cloud services.

Further implications for research and practice will also be discussed.

1.3   Structure of the Thesis

The remainder of this thesis is structured as presented in Figure 1-1. Table 1-1 shows which
sections are related to our five research questions presented in Section 1.2. The foundations of
relevant technologies and the theoretical background of our studies are introduced in Chapter
1. Since we focus on ITSR perceptions and IT security risk management in the context of
Cloud Computing, an important and growing field of IT but still a rather new technological
development, Section 2.1 describes the essential characteristics (Subsection 2.1.1), the different delivery models (Subsection 2.1.2), and the major deployment models (Subsection 2.1.3)
along with key technological concepts and terminology of Cloud Computing. Section 2.2 presents the theoretical background concerning the nature of perceived ITSRs (Subsection 2.2.1)
as well as the literature related to ITSR perceptions in the context of IT outsourcing and
Cloud Computing (Subsection 2.2.2). Finally, Section 2.3 describes the organizational IT security risk management process and its five key phases in detail (Subsections 2.3.1 - 2.3.5).

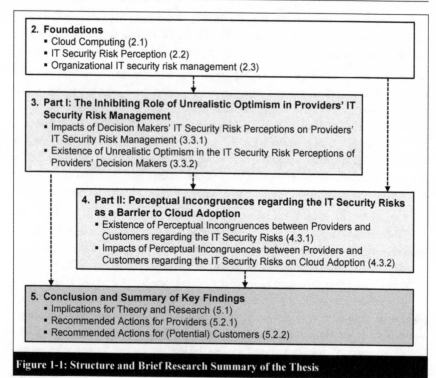

Figure 1-1: Structure and Brief Research Summary of the Thesis

Based on these foundations, the main part of thesis is divided into two parts: Part I (Chapter 0) concerns the effects of decision makers' ITSR perceptions on the outcome of Cloud providers' IT security risk management and the consequences of a potential underestimation of the ITSRs by the providers' decision makers. Part II (Chapter 1) deals with the effects of the providers' decision makers' ITSR perceptions on (potential) customers' intentions to adopt the Cloud by explicating the detrimental effects of perceptual incongruences between the providers and their (potential) customers regarding the ITSRs.

In the first section of Chapter 3 (Part I), we present the theoretical background regarding the organizational IT security risk management and systematic errors in the risk perception and develop our research hypotheses of the first study (Section 3.1). Specifically, we develop a theoretical model of Cloud providers' IT security risk management in three steps: In the first step, based on an integration of an established organizational IT security risk management model (Subsection 3.1.1) and an adapted version of the technology threat avoidance theory (Subsection 3.1.2), we explicate the role of decision makers' perceptions in all stages of the organizational IT security risk management processes. Then, drawing on institutional theory (Subsection 3.1.3), the organizational IT security risk management framework is extended by the influence of relevant external factors (i.e., the stakeholders of the providers) on the providers' IT security risk management decisions. In the final step, we draw on risk perception research (Subsection 3.1.4) and present absolute and comparative assessments as two largely independent perspectives on ITSR perception. Based on findings of previous psychological studies, we integrate both perspectives in the proposed theoretical model in order to in-depth analyze the impact of decision makers' subjective ITSR perceptions on the IT security risk management of providers.

Afterwards, Subsection 3.1.5 presents the theoretical background of the phenomenon of unrealistic optimism (UO), which is a systematic underestimation of people's own vulnerability to risks. Drawing on findings of psychological research, we transfer the effect mechanisms of UO to the field of IT security to investigate the impact of a potential underestimation of the ITSRs by the decision makers on the outcome of the providers' IT security risk management.

We conducted an empirical survey to investigate the effects of the decision makers' subjective ITSR perceptions on the providers' IT security risk management, which is presented in Section 3.2. In this Section, we first present the measurement model along with the developed approaches to measure the degree of UO in the ITSR assessments of the Cloud providers' decision makers (Subsection 3.2.1). Then, the administration of the empirical study (Subsection 3.2.2) and the characteristics of the obtained sample of 177 SaaS providers' decision makers are presented (Subsection 3.2.3). Afterwards, we show the data analysis techniques that were utilized in this study (Subsection 3.2.4).

The results of the analyses of the data collected are presented in detail in Section 3.3. Based on the proposed theoretical model, we first demonstrate how the decision makers' assessments determine the outcome of the providers' IT security risk management process, answering research question 1 (Subsection 3.3.1). We answer research question 2 by demonstrating that the decision makers' in many cases underestimate the ITSR exposure of their organizations' services both in the absolute and in the comparative sense (Subsection 3.3.1.2). By combining the results of these subsections, we then demonstrate in which ways and to what extent the underestimation of the ITSRs by the decision makers affects the outcome of the providers' IT security risk management, thus answering research question 3. The findings of this part are summarized and discussed in Section 3.4.

In the first section of Chapter 1 (Part II), we present the theoretical background of the second study and develop our research hypotheses (Section 4.1). We first give a brief summary of previous IS research regarding perceptual incongruences between IS providers and their (potential) customers (Subsection 4.1.1). Then, in Subsection 4.1.2 we provide an overview of the perceived ITSRs in the context of the Cloud and develop the basic hypothesis concerning the existence of perceptual incongruences between the Cloud providers and their (potential) customers regarding the ITSRs of the Cloud. Drawing on cognitive dissonance theory (Subsection 4.1.3) and expectation confirmation research (Subsection 4.1.4), we derive our research hypotheses regarding the impacts of the possible incongruences on the formation of (potential) customers' intentions to adopt the Cloud. Therefore, we propose a variance model that integrates the hypothesized effects of the perceptual incongruences in an extended technology acceptance model (Subsection 4.1.5).

We conducted two empirical surveys to investigate both the ITSR assessments of Cloud providers and those of (potential) customer companies (Section 4.2). First, we present the measurement models of the provider and the customer studies (Subsection 4.2.1). Then, we describe the survey administration of the provider study and the customer study (Subsection 4.2.2) followed by the characteristics of the obtained samples of 73 decision makers of Cloud providers and 304 IT managers of (potential) customer companies (Subsection 4.2.3). The analyses of the collected data are described in Subsection 4.2.4.

The results of the conducted data analyses are presented in Section 4.3. Based on the analysis of the matched survey responses of providers and their (potential) customer companies, we demonstrate the existence of a large disagreement regarding the ITSRs of the Cloud services, answering research question 4 (Subsection 4.3.1). Additionally, based on the proposed variance model, we show that the perceptual incongruence not only has direct adverse effects on the customer companies' intentions to adopt Cloud services but also negatively affects other beliefs related to the adoption, further inhibiting Cloud sales (Subsection 4.3.2). The findings of this part are summarized and discussed in Section 4.4.

Chapter 1 combines the results of Part I (Chapter 0) and Part II (Chapter 1). First, we present a summarization of the key findings of both parts and discuss important implications for theory (Section 5.1) and practice (Section 5.2). Based on the results of the first part, we develop recommended actions for Cloud providers to improve their IT security risk management processes and mitigate the negative effects of UO (Subsection 5.2.1). Based on the results of the second part, Subsection 5.2.1 also provides recommended actions for Cloud providers to reduce disagreements with their (potential) customers concerning the ITSRs, thus increasing the attractiveness of their Cloud services. Additionally, we recommend actions to (potential) customer companies that will help them to identify Cloud services with potentially ineffective IT security risk management processes (Subsection 5.2.2). We discuss limitations of our studies and present opportunities for future research to enrich the findings of this thesis (Section 5.3). Finally, we conclude with a brief résumé of the findings of this thesis in Section 5.4.

Table 1-1: Mapping of Research Questions to Parts and Chapters

	Part I			Part II	
	3.3.1 Impacts of Decision Makers' IT Security Risk Perceptions on Providers' IT Security Risk Management	3.3.2.1 Analysis of Absolute Unrealistic Optimism	3.3.2.2 Analysis of Comparative Unrealistic Optimism	4.3.1 Existence of Perceptual Incongruences between Providers and Customers regarding the IT Security Risks	4.3.2 Impacts of Perceptual Incongruences between Providers and Customers
In what ways and to what degree do the absolute and comparative IT security risk perceptions of Cloud providers' decision makers predict the outcomes of the providers' IT security risk management? (RQ1)	✓				
Do Cloud providers' decision makers systematically underestimate the ITSR exposure of their own organizations' services? (RQ2)		✓	✓		
What are the impacts of the potential systematic error in the decision makers' ITSR perceptions on the outcome of the providers' IT security risk management? (RQ3)	✓	✓	✓		
Is there a significant gap between the ITSR assessments of providers and (potential) customer companies in the context of the Cloud? (RQ4)				✓	
In which ways and to what degree does the gap between the ITSR assessments of providers and those of their (potential) customers influence the intentions of customer company IT managers to adopt Cloud services? (RQ5)					✓

2 Foundations

In this chapter, we present the theoretical foundations of this thesis. First, we introduce the paradigm of Cloud Computing, along with its core technological concepts and terminology (Section 2.1). Then, we present the work related to the nature of ITSR perception and perceived ITSRs in the context of Cloud Computing (Section 2.2). Finally, the organizational IT security risk management and its five key phases are described (Section 2.3).

2.1   Cloud Computing

Cloud Computing (the Cloud) has recently emerged as a new paradigm for the provision of computing resources, which has the potential to transform large parts of the IT industry (Armbrust et al. 2010; Smith 2014). It is based on the principle that large groups of remote servers are networked to allow centralized access to computing resources, such as data storage, central processing unit (CPU) capacity, and software applications. However, the variety of technologies in the Cloud makes the overall picture confusing (Vaquero et al. 2008). Besides, there is a number of inconsistent definitions of the Cloud (e.g., Armbrust et al. 2010; Buyya et al. 2008; Vaquero et al. 2008; Wang et al. 2008b).

The definition provided by the U.S. National Institute of Standards and Technology (NIST) is most frequently used in IS research and practice. It has also been adopted by the European Network and Information Security Agency (ENISA). NIST universally defines the Cloud as a model "for enabling ubiquitous, convenient, on-demand network access to a shared pool of configurable computing resources (e.g., networks, servers, storage, applications, and services) that can be rapidly provisioned and released with minimal management effort or service provider interaction" (Mell and Grance 2011, p. 2).

By shifting the location of the infrastructure from the users' side to a central provider, the paradigm reduces the costs associated with the deployment and management of hardware and software resources (Vaquero et al. 2008). In this regard, the development of the Cloud is closely related to the advancements in virtualization technologies, which enables the allocation of IT-based resources to worldwide distributed computers (Buyya et al. 2009). Therefore, the providers have the economic advantage that they can use available resources more effectively and realize provider-sided economies of scale (Wang et al. 2008c). However, the Cloud is also attractive to customer companies as it eliminates the requirement to plan ahead for provisioning, and allows organizations to start from the small and increase computing resources only when there is a rise in capacity demand (Zhang et al. 2010). Hence, it is not surprising that leading market analysts forecast that the Cloud will grab a large share of the overall IT market in the next years (e.g., Gartner 2013). Beside the large providers such as Amazon, Google, and Microsoft, an increasing number of organizations tap into the Cloud market.

Today, industry databases already list thousands of different services (Cloud Showplace 2014).

In general, the "cloud model is composed of five essential characteristics, three service models, and four deployment models" (Mell and Grance 2011, p. 2).

2.1.1   Essential Characteristics

The essential characteristics are:

On-demand self-service: The Cloud technology enables customers to request resources, such as computing and storage capacities, independently from the service provider, so that they can be efficiently adjusted to their current needs without having to depend on interaction with the provider (Mell and Grance 2011). In particular, the use of service management software typically allows customers to scale the provided resources with minimal provider interaction (Marston et al. 2011).

Broad network access: The Cloud model is based on network-access of the provided resources and services in real-time, utilizing standard technologies and mechanism, like the Internet and web interfaces (Mell and Grance 2011). The accessibility by heterogeneous thin or thick client platforms (e.g., mobile phones, tablets, laptops, and workstations) makes the Cloud universally usable for customers (Weinhardt et al. 2009).

Resource pooling: By utilizing a multi-tenant model, the providers' computing resources, such as storage, processing, memory, and network bandwidth, are pooled in order to enable parallel use by multiple customers. The different physical and virtual resources dynamically assigned to fulfill current consumer demands (Mell and Grance 2011). In particular, the multi-tenant model allows customers to share the same provider-sided hardware resources by offering them a shared application and database instance, which can be configured to their needs as if it runs on a dedicated environment (Bezemer and Zaidman 2010). In this context, a specific characteristic of the Cloud is that the user has neither knowledge nor control over the actual location of the service provisions. However, customers are often able to specify the location of the data processing at a higher level of abstraction (e.g., country, state, or datacenter) (Takabi et al. 2010).

Rapid elasticity: The Cloud technology leverages an elastic provision and release of computing resources, so that provided services can be dynamically reconfigured and quickly scaled to changed customer demands (Mell and Grance 2011). The capability available for provisioning oftentimes create the impression that infinite resources are accessible at any time (Mather et al. 2009; Owens 2010).

Measured service: The Cloud model allows for an automatic control and optimization of the resource use by offering metering (e.g., pay-per-use or charge-per-use) capabilities at some level of abstraction that is appropriate to the type of provided service (e.g., used storage, processing time, bandwidth, or active user accounts) (Mell and Grance 2011). In this context, the exact monitoring, controlling, and reporting of the resource usage creates transparency for customer companies as well as providers (Fouquet et al. 2009; Weinhardt et al. 2009).

2.1.2   Delivery Models

According to the NIST definition, the Cloud is structured into three consecutive layers, representing different service delivery models (Mell and Grance 2011):

Infrastructure as a Service (IaaS): The resources provided to the customers on the IaaS layer are computing infrastructure, such as storage, networking and processing capabilities (Mell and Grance 2011). In particular, the providers allow the customers to deploy and run arbitrary software – ranging from operating systems to individual software – on their infrastructure by offering a virtual instance of the physical hardware. This virtualization enables the providers to automatically split and dynamically assign their computing resources to customers (Prodan and Ostermann 2009; Vaquero et al. 2010). In this regard, even if the customers do not have direct control of the computing infrastructure, they are typically able to manage and control selected network components (e.g., firewall of the host), operating systems, and storage devices along with the deployed applications (Mell and Grance 2011). However, due to the virtualization of the underlying computing resources, the customers have typically no knowledge about the actual location of the servers and the data processing (Takabi et al. 2010). Widely used examples for IaaS services are Amazon's EC2, GoGrid's Cloud Server, SAP HANA Enterprise Cloud, and Microsoft's Windows Azure (Buyya et al. 2008).

Platform as a service (PaaS): The service provided to the customers on the PaaS layer is the deployment of customer-built or acquired applications onto the Cloud infrastructure (Mell and Grance 2011). In this context, the providers typically offer development tools and application programming interfaces (APIs), which enable the customers to interact with the execution environment and to deploy applications by using the provided programming environments (i.e., programming languages, libraries, services, and tools) (Lenk et al. 2009; Youseff et al. 2008). In particular, due to the ubiquitous network access of the resources, the PaaS layer allows customers to efficiently deploy their own web applications and services (Prodan and Ostermann 2009). When utilizing PaaS services the consumers do not need to invest in the computing infrastructure (e.g., network, servers, operating systems, or storage) nor manage its complexity but have the control over the developed applications and can usually configure the execution environment to their individual needs (Marston et al. 2011). Cloud services on the PaaS layer are typically provided based on Cloud infrastructure services on the IaaS layer (Foster et al. 2008). Examples of established PaaS services include Amazon's Elastic Beanstalk and Simple DB, Google's App Engine, SAP HANA Cloud Platform, and Salesforce's application development platform Force.com (Buyya et al. 2008).

Software as a Service (SaaS): The capability provided on the SaaS layer is the usage of standard software solutions running of the providers' Cloud infrastructure (Mell and Grance 2011). In contrast to traditional software installations, SaaS services typically utilize multi-tenancy architectures, which allow creating multiple instances of software, running on a single (virtual) server. These instances can be used by multiple customers at the same time (Mather et al. 2009). In this regard, services on the SaaS layer are in many cases provisioned based on services on the PaaS or IaaS layer (Prodan and Ostermann 2009). Moreover, SaaS services in general eliminate the need to install the software on the client devices as the provided application is typically accessibly over the Internet through a thin client interface (e.g., a web browser) or a dedicated program interface. Accordingly, the applications can be used by the customers from a wide variety of client devices ranging from mobile phones to workstations (Marston et al. 2011). When using SaaS services, the customers do not have to take care of managing the operation and maintenance of the underlying computing infrastructure, such as networks, servers, operating systems, or application resources. However, customers are usually, to a certain extent, able to configure the SaaS services according to their specific needs (Lenk et al. 2009). In comparison to traditional software delivery models, SaaS solutions offer many possibilities for flexible pricing strategies (e.g., pay-per-use approaches), which, for example, allow small and medium-sized businesses to benefit from efficient enterprise resource planning (ERP) software (Al-Roomi et al. 2013). Examples of SaaS services are Apple's iWork, Google's Apps, Microsoft's CRM Online, and SAP BusinessByDesign, or salesforce.com.

Other definitions of delivery models in the context of the Cloud range from specific technology-driven views (e.g., Communications as a Service (CaaS)) to broad business model perspectives (e.g., Everything as a Service (XaaS)) (e.g., Armbrust et al. 2010; Youseff et al. 2008).

2.1.3   Deployment Models

Following Mell and Grance (2011)'s definition, Cloud services can be provisioned using four different deployment models:

Private Cloud: The Cloud infrastructure of a Private Cloud is operated exclusively for a single organization, serving multiple business units as internal customers. Private Clouds are owned and managed by the organization or an external provider, and hosted either internally or externally (Mell and Grance 2011). Similar to the internal data processing centers, the Private Cloud is only accessible by well-defined user groups (e.g., the organization's business units or partner organizations). Accordingly, Private Clouds are frequently said to entail a higher level of IT security than Public Clouds (e.g., Armbrust et al. 2010; Buyya et al. 2008). Undertaking a Private Cloud project usually requires long-term planning and considerable efforts virtualize the existing infrastructure and business environment but also offers various opportunities to reevaluate and thereby improve current business processes (Takabi et al. 2010). However, regardless whether Private Clouds are hosted internally or not, the cost-intensive computing infrastructure is provided solely for a very limited group of users, so that the model usually does not enable organizations to realize significant economies of scale (Armbrust et al. 2010).

Public Cloud: The Cloud infrastructure of a Public Cloud is rendered over a network that is open for public use (i.e., the Internet). Public Cloud are generally owned, managed, and oper-ated by an external provider. The computing infrastructure is located in data processing cen-ters on the provider premises (Mell and Grance 2011). In general, the Public Cloud enables customers to quickly use and release service capabilities without the need of complex contract negotiations with the provider organizations (Armbrust et al. 2010). Moreover, services in the Public Cloud are in many cases free to use or offer flexible pricing strategies, like pay-per-use models (Al-Roomi et al. 2013). As the Cloud infrastructure is accessible through a public network, the potential ITSR exposure of these services is generally significantly higher than that of Private Cloud models. In particular, the customers have typically no direct control and influence on the safeguarding measures, which are implemented in the Cloud services by the providers (Ackermann et al. 2012). However, efficient sharing (e.g., through virtualization technologies) of the computing infrastructure with many organizations resulting in higher load factors, create in many cases considerable economies of scales, which may significantly reduce the costs of the provided service capabilities (Armbrust et al. 2010).

Community Cloud: The Cloud infrastructure of Community Clouds is provided for the exclu-sive use of a specific group of customers with similar requirements, i.e., organizations with the same goals, legal frameworks, security concerns, policies, and/or compliance considera-tions. Community Clouds are owned, managed, and operated on or off premises by one or more of the organizations in the group or by an external provider (Mell and Grance 2011). Since the Community Cloud is only accessible by members of the group through a private or secured network, the level of ITSR is oftentimes considered as lower than in Public Clouds (Zhang et al. 2010). However, as organizations with similar goals in the market are in many cases also potential competitors, there may be additional security and compliance risks asso-ciated with the use of Community Clouds (Takabi et al. 2010). Nevertheless, as the members of the group concentrate their resources and share the same infrastructure, the costs of the IT capability provision are oftentimes considerably lower, in comparison with the internal data processing centers of the organizations (Armbrust et al. 2010).

Hybrid Cloud: The Cloud infrastructure of a Hybrid Cloud is composed of the Cloud infra-structures provided by two or more distinct delivery models (i.e., private, public, or communi-ty Clouds), which are bound together by standardized or proprietary technology that enables data and application portability (Mell and Grance 2011). This combination enables to com-bine the benefits of the Private Cloud with those of the Public Cloud, for example, by offering data isolation, high availability, and load balancing at the same time (Buyya et al. 2009). For instance, a Private Cloud service is generally less cost-intensive when the underlying compu-ting infrastructure is only designed for the typical workload of an organization. When the ser-vice is operated as Hybrid Cloud, it additionally uses infrastructure of external Public Cloud services to economically handle peaks in demand. However, when data is temporarily swapped to Public Cloud services, it may be exposed to a higher level of ITSR (Takabi et al. 2010).

2.2   IT Security Risk Perception

In economic research, the risk exposure is typically defined as the product of the probability of the occurrence of a negative event and the amount of the losses caused by this event (Boehm 1991; Cunningham 1967; Erb et al. 1996). The definition is primarily focused on the possible damage or potential loss of an investment and does not take potential profits into account. As such, it is categorized as a shortfall-oriented view of risk. The definition is often-used by IS research when the focus is on organizational and behavioral aspects of IT security (e.g., Johnston and Warkentin 2010; Liang and Xue 2010; Vance et al. 2012). Another short-fall-oriented risk measure is the Value at risk, which is widely used in financial mathematics and financial risk management to measure the risk of loss in a specific portfolio of financial assets. Related to economic decision-theory, it is based on the knowledge of probabilities and probabilistic distributions of uncertain events in the future. The risk is considered to be higher when the uncertainty of an expected value increases, independent of whether the deviation is positive or negative. The deviation from an expected outcome is usually measures by the characteristics of the distribution, like standard deviation or the variance (see overview of economic risk measures in Ackermann 2013). In IS research, risk distribution characteristic based measures are frequently used by studies, which develop mathematical models to opti-mize the organizations' IT security levels and investments (e.g., Ackermann et al. 2013; Cavusoglu et al. 2008; Sonnenreich et al. 2006).

Psychological research is usually based on similar shortfall-oriented risk definition but the studies are frequently focused on the probability of a certain negative event, thus neglecting potentially different losses for different persons (see also related psychological research in Subsection 3.1.4 and Subsection 3.1.5) (Weinstein et al. 1990). In contrast to economic re-search, most of the psychological studies concern general life and health risks (e.g., likelihood to have a coronary or a car accident), which can be assumed to be associated with comparable potential losses for everyone (e.g., Dillard et al. 2012; Rose 2010; Shepperd et al. 2013).

However, whenever the utilized risk measures are not based on long-term historical data, they generally capture the risk perceived by a person (e.g., the risk perception of a study participant) and not the actual risk of a negative event (Slovic 1987). Therefore, it is also not the actual risk that is central to risk related decisions (i.e., protection behavior) but the risk perceived by a person (Gigerenzer 2004).

2.2.1   The Nature of Perceived Risks

Risk perception is the subjective judgment that people make about the likelihood and the severity of a risk (e.g., natural hazards and threats to the environment or health risk). Psychological research generally distinguishes between two different measures of risk perception, which were found to be independently associated with behavioral intentions and other downstream beliefs (Dillard et al. 2012). In particular, absolute risk perceptions (e.g., a person's perception of his/or her risk to get a serious disease) were in many studies found to directly predict behavioral intentions, whereas comparative perceptions (e.g., a person's perception of his/or her risk to get a serious disease in comparison to the average person) were revealed to have more indirect effects (e.g., influence downstream beliefs, which facilitates protection behavior) on people's behavior (Shepperd et al. 2013). Absolute and comparative risk perceptions are frequently measured using numerical (e.g., from 0% to 100%) or categorical (e.g., from low to high) scales (Dillard et al. 2012). Besides, Weinstein et al. (2007) recently proposed a feeling-of-risk measure (e.g., a person's feeling to get a serious disease), which is measured on a verbal scale (e.g., from disagree to agree), and according to the authors represents a more intuitive and thus accurate measure of the personal risk exposure (see a detailed description of the different perspectives on risk perceptions in Subsection 3.1.4).

However, independent from the utilized risk measures, the risk perceived by a person or group of persons often considerably deviates from the actual risk of a negative event. In particular, previous research has found people generally to be very incongruent in their risk perceptions in a wide range of areas (e.g., Slovic 1987). The early studies on perceived risk even arose from the observation that experts and people often disagreed about the risks of various technologies and natural hazards (Starr 1969). In this regard, several theories have been proposed to understand why different people make different estimations of the characteristics and severity of any one risk. While early approaches assumed that individuals always behave rationally, weighing information before making a decision, and that misjudgments of risks were caused by inadequate or incorrect information (e.g., Douglas 1985), several studies have rejected the belief that additional information can shift perceptions (e.g., Freudenburg 1993). Furthermore, previous studies have demonstrated that even people with the same information regarding a risk are likely to have different risk perceptions (e.g., Sjöberg 1998). Psychological research later revealed that numerous social and cognitive factors in risk information processing substantially predict a person's risk perceptions. In this context, especially the use of cognitive heuristics – such as representativeness heuristic, availability heuristic, and anchoring heuristic – in sorting and simplifying information was found to lead to biases in comprehension and risk perception (Tversky and Kahneman 1973). Later works identified various additional factors responsible for influencing a person's risk perception; these include dread, susceptibility, newness, stigma, and other factors (e.g., Lerner and Keltner 2000). Furthermore, numerous cognitive biases are likely to distort an individual's risk assessment. For example, since people tend to attribute to themselves various desirable characteristics that they do not necessarily possess, and interpret ambiguous information or unknown situations in self-favoring ways, they are likely to perceive themselves as having more control (i.e., illusion of control bias) and to be less vulnerable than others (i.e., unrealistic optimism; see Subsection 3.1.5) (e.g., Thompson 1999; Weinstein 1980). Errors in people's risk perceptions are likely to inevitably reduce their motivation to take necessary precautionary actions (Weinstein 1989).

In psychological research, a rich stream of literature showed that the risk perception largely predicts people's protection behavior (e.g., Rogers 1975; Weinstein 1993; Witte 1992). In particular, it has been conclusively shown that people's protection behavior usually results from a rational weighing up of the expected costs and perceived benefits of the precautionary actions (see also protection motivation theory and models in Subsection 3.1.2). In this context, psychological studies have revealed that people's beliefs about the benefits of protection behavior are predominantly predicted by their assessment of their personal threat situation, or their vulnerability to a threat (e.g., Milne et al. 2000; Weinstein et al. 1998; Witte and Allen 2000). Therefore, decision-oriented theories assume that peoples' perception of their susceptibility to threats and the perceived severity of the threats increase their perceived benefits of protection behavior (Milne et al. 2000). Accordingly, people who perceive themselves to be particularly at risk are in general more likely to assess protection behaviors as beneficial, and subsequently to take precautionary actions, such as having medical checkups, eating low-fat food, or using condoms, than other people (Breakwell 2000; Goodman et al. 1995; Weinstein and Nicolich 1993).

In economic research, perceived risk is commonly understood as the feeling of uncertainty regarding the possible negative consequences of adopting a product or service (e.g., the expectation of less associated with the purchase of a product) (Cunningham 1967). In particular, previous studies frequently demonstrated that perceived risks are an important inhibitor of purchase behavior in various contexts, ranging from automobile to food purchases (e.g., Hammitt 1990; Peter and Ryan 1976; Srinivasan and Ratchford 1991). In particular, many studies have demonstrated that the perceptions of risks are especially relevant for purchasing decisions when the decision-making is associated with uncertainty, discomfort, and/or fear, or creates conflicts with other people (e.g., Peter and Ryan 1976). Therefore, it has been revealed by various studies at the individual level that the perception of risks strongly determines the formation of adoption intentions and downstream beliefs (Ajzen and Fishbein 1980; Mitchell 1999; Murray and Schlacter 1990). At the organizational level (March and Shapira 1987), previous studies similarly revealed that the behavior of organizations is strongly influenced by its decision makers' perception of the risks related to the behavior, such as decisions to outsource business processes or to use banking services (e.g., Gewald and Dibbern 2009; Rotchanakitumnuai and Speece 2003).

In our discipline, drawing on economic and psychological literature, previous research demonstrated that people's perception of IT security risks strongly inhibits their intention to adopt technologies, such as the Internet, e-banking, or e-commerce systems (e.g., Lee 2009; Liebermann and Stashevsky 2002). Moreover, a growing stream of IS research investigates the effects of users' perception of privacy risks, which are closely related to IT security risks, on their usage behavior of different technologies, such as ubiquitous computing or online social networks (Smith et al. 2011). In this regard, people's privacy concerns were repeatedly found to considerable reduce their intention to use IT systems or disclose specific information (e.g., Dinev and Hart 2006; Krasnova et al. 2009). Based on psychological protection motivation research (see protection motivation and technology threat avoidance theory in Subsection 3.1.2), other IS studies demonstrated that the perception of ITSR strongly facilitates people's IT security behavior, like users' intention to implement certain safeguarding measures or employees' motivation to comply with corporate IT security policies (e.g., Liang and Xue 2010; Vance et al. 2012). In contrary, drawing on fear appeals research, other studies found that the perception of ITSR concurrently arouse fear on parts of the users, which in many cases reduces their intention to adopt safeguards and emotionally downplay the risk (e.g., Johnston and Warkentin 2010; Liang and Xue 2009). However, in contrast to economic research, previous IS studies regarding the perception of ITSR are predominantly focused on the individual user level and largely neglected the organizational level. Moreover, despite their theoretical importance, no IS research has been devoted to understand how the two different perspectives of perceived risks (i.e., absolute and comparative ITSR perception) affect IT security-related behaviors of people (the two different measures of risk perception in the IT security context are introduced in Subsection 3.1.4).

2.2.2   Perceived IT Security Risks in the Context of the Cloud

A considerable amount of literature has been published concerning the risks related to ITO (Ackermann 2013). Earl (1996) analyzed the risks in the context of traditional ITO, such as the possibility of hidden costs, business uncertainty, outdated technology skills, loss of innovative capacity, and technology indivisibility. Dibbern et al. (2004) and Willcocks et al. (2007) present a literature review of ITO risks. Lacity et al. (2009) published a review of risks in the context of application service provision (ASP). They revealed that the major risks are contract, security, or privacy breaches by the provider, poor capability of the service, lack of trust in the providers, and vendor lock-in effects due to high switching costs. Ackermann et al. (2011) provides a comprehensive literature review and presents a list of 70 technological risks of ITO, such as theft of intellectual property, unsatisfactory software quality, and network issues.

Previous IS studies also examined different factors of perceived risk in the context of e-services, and studied its effects on users' adoption intention. Featherman and Pavlou (2003) were the first to operationalize perceived risks in the context of e-services based on the general risk perception theory. The authors conceptualize the overall perceived risk of e-services as a multi-dimensional constructs, consisting of performance, financial, time, psychological/social, technological, and privacy risk factors. Additionally, they have proposed and empirically tested an e-service adoption model, which explicates the effects of perceived risk on the use of e-services. The results of their study thereby reveal that the development of e-services has shifted the focus of the considered risk dimensions. While for traditional IT services, mainly strategic and financial risks were relevant to decision makers, the emergence of e-services substantially increased the importance of technology-related risks (Featherman and Pavlou 2003). Benlian and Hess (2011) have studied the opportunities and risks of Cloud adoption, perceived by IS executives at adopter and non-adopter firms. In the context of the Cloud, they were able to demonstrate that the ITSR is the most important factor predicting user adoption intentions.

Ackermann et al. (2012) defined perceived ITSR in the context of CC as decision-makers' perceived risk related to the IT security of a company's systems and data if the Cloud is utilized as a delivery model. The authors proposed a framework with a set of 31 risk items, which cover the identified ITSRs of the Cloud mutual exclusively and exhaustively (see Table 2-1). The risk items are grouped into six distinct risk dimensions (see also   ): confidentiality, integrity, availability, performance, accountability, and maintainability. The risk dimension availability means that users are able to access a service and the data whenever they wish. Confidentiality means that data can be read only by authorized users. Integrity relates to risks concerning data modification by unauthorized persons. Performance denotes that service and data usage speeds meets customers' requirements. Maintainability remains intact when it is possible to adapt a service to individual requirements and when the provider ensures maintenance and support. Accountability risks arise if authentication mechanisms can be eluded and if actions cannot be attributed clearly to one user (Ackermann et al. 2012).

Table 2-1: Perceived IT Security Risks in the Context of the Cloud

Risk dimension	Brief risk description: Risk of ...
Confidentiality	... eavesdropping communications
	... supplier looking at sensitive data
	... disclosure of data by the provider
	... disclosure of internal system data
Integrity	... manipulation of transferred data
	... data manipulation at provider side
	... accidental modification of transferred data
	... accidental data modification at provider side
	... data modification in internal systems
Availability	... discontinuity of the service
	... unintentional downtime
	... attacks against availability
	... loss of data access
	... data loss at provider side
	... insufficient availability of internal systems
Performance	... network performance problems
	... limited scalability
	... deliberate underperformance
	... performance issues of internal systems
Accountability	... identity theft
	... insufficient user separation
	... insufficient logging of actions
	... access without authorization
	... missing logging of actions in internal systems
Maintainability	... limited customization possibilities
	... incompatible business processes
	... incompatible with new technologies
	... limited data import
	... proprietary technologies
	... insufficient maintenance
	... unfavorably timed updates

Although the literature on perceptions of IT security risks is predominately focused on the end-user perspective, the example of the Cloud shows that especially organizational decision makers' ITSR perceptions may be associated with major implications, such as determining the outcome of the providers' IT security risk management, which affect the security of the technology as a whole. In this thesis, we build on Ackermann et al. (2012)'s framework to analyze the ITSR perceptions of Cloud providers and their (potential) customers.

2.3   Organizational IT Security Risk Management

Established approaches in the literature of planning and managing an organization's IT security commonly use structured assessment practices and mathematically orientated evaluations
and formulas. These approaches can be subdivided into four main groups (e.g., Siponen
2005); those utilizing audit or checklist methods (e.g., Baskerville 1993; Forcht 1994), those
concentrating on risk analysis methodologies (e.g., Birch and McEvoy 1992; Kailay and
Jarratt 1995), approaches centered on accounting and cost justification (e.g., Ekenberg et al.
1995; Wolfe 1995), and finally high level conceptual management models (e.g., Cavusoglu et
al. forthcoming; McFadzean et al. 2007; Straub and Welke 1998). The different approaches in
the literature are not mutually exclusive and many frameworks, methodologies, and models
are hybrids of others. Moreover, approaches in the first three groups are typically focused on
certain processes and do not exhaustively explain the organizational IT security risk management (Dhillon and Backhouse 2001).

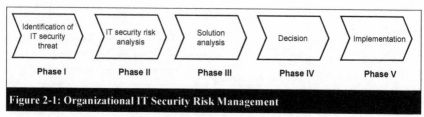

Figure 2-1: Organizational IT Security Risk Management

With great consistency, conceptual management models in the last group describe the risk
management as a process model, that consists of five phases, as shown in Figure 2-1 (e.g.,
Cavusoglu et al. forthcoming; McFadzean et al. 2007; Straub and Welke 1998). It is widely
accepted that IT security risk management frameworks play an important role in managing
and certifying information security in organizations (e.g., like ISO27001, BS7799, and their
derivatives). In particular, the established standards have adopted the process model, described above, and typically recommend an equivalent structure of the phases of the IT security risk management (e.g., Siponen and Willison 2009; Von Solms 1999). Other approaches
explaining the entire IT security risk management processes of organizations are predominately also based on these key phases as described above but suggest additional subdivisions of
the phases (e.g., Hong et al. 2003; Kwok and Longley 1999). An overview and comparison of
nine different IT security risk management models is provided by Schlaak et al. (2008). In this
thesis, we focus on the five established key phases of the IT security risk management (e.g.,
Straub and Welke 1998), which are described in more detail in the following subsections.

2.3.1 Phase I: Identification of IT Security Threat

The organizational IT security risk management usually starts with the identification of IT security threats for the organization. The results of the risk identification phase are the definition and categorization of IT security threats, which could potentially endanger the organization's goals. Therefore, the decision makers first need to obtain knowledge of existing IT security threats in the industry. Then, they need to identify possible vulnerabilities of their organization's IT systems to these IT security threats. In this regard, only those threats, which can potentially exploit existing weak points of the IT systems, are relevant for the further IT security risk management phases of the organization (Straub and Welke 1998).

There are various methods for the identification of IT security threats available to organizations' decision makers, which can be categorized into collection methods, creativity methods, and analytical search methods. Collection methods are based on the collection of data concerning IT security threats, such as expert interviews or checklists. Methods in this category predominately enable decision makers to gain knowledge of those IT security threats, which are already known in the industry. In contrast, creativity methods are based on divergent thinking, thus allowing for an anticipation of currently unknown risks. Examples for these methods are brainstorming or the Delphi method. Analytical search methods, such as attack trees and penetration tests, are focused on the organization's IT infrastructure and analyze its characteristics in terms of vulnerabilities and weak points (Ackermann 2013; Straub and Welke 1998).

Due to the fast technological progress inherent in the IT sector, the previous experience of decision makers usually has only limited utility for the identification of new IT security threats. Hence, the incorporation of external risk information sources in the risk identification phase is typically indispensable, in particular, in the context of new technological development, such as the Cloud. Therefore, security-related organizations publish current reports concerning the IT security risks related to the Cloud. These reports can, for example, be used as checklists by the providers to discover previously unknown IT security threats and vulnerabilities of the own organizations' Cloud services. For example, guidelines and practical recommendations for decision makers to ensure the security, stability, and privacy of their Cloud services are provided by the Cloud Security Alliance (CSA) (Cloud Security Alliance 2011). Furthermore, the CSA publishes whitepapers, which describe the current top threats in the context of the Cloud (Cloud Security Alliance 2013). Likewise, the Federal Office for Information Security published recommendations for providers to warrant a certain IT level of their Cloud services (Federal Office for Information Security 2011). The report describes the major ITSRs of Cloud services and presents suitable technical measures that should be implemented in the providers' services to effectively mitigate these risks. Beyond that, the European Network and Information Security Agency (ENISA) issued recommendations for (potential) users concerning the ITSRs when the Cloud is used as a delivery model (European Network and Information Security Agency 2009). The whitepaper provides guidelines for the assessment of the ITSR involved in the use of Cloud services as well as frameworks for risk mitigation. These guidelines concurrently enable the providers to get a different perspective on the ITSRs of their organizations' services, and thus to identify previously neglected risk factors. Besides, previous IT security research developed a framework that conceptualizes the perceived ITSR in the context of the Cloud (Ackermann et al. 2012), which can also be used by the providers' decision makers to support the ITSR identification processes and the IT security risk management (see also Subsection 2.2.2).

As each of the risk identification methods is able identify potential IT security threats that would not have been identified with the other methods, the extant literature typically recommends a combination of these methods in the organizational IT security risk management in order to effectively define and categorize the IT security threats of the organization (Cavusoglu et al. forthcoming). However, the risk identification is an ex-ante analysis and there is generally an inherit risk that not all relevant vulnerabilities and threats are completely captured. Since the results of the risk identification phase have strong influences on the following phases of the organizational IT security risk management, a deficient and incomplete risk analysis can cause additional, unexpected losses for the organizations (Ackermann 2013).

2.3.2   Phase II: IT Security Risk Analysis

The IT security risk analysis phase is typically placed as a bridge between the identification of IT security threats for the organization's IT systems and the search for appropriate solutions to mitigate these risks. The result of the risk analysis phase is the assessment and prioritization of the ITSRs, which is based on the quantification to what extent the previously identified IT security threats can endanger the achievements of the organizational goals. In general, the ITSR is determined by the occurrence probability of the IT security incident and the amount of potential damage associated with the IT security incident. At the organizational level, the potential damage is typically quantified by the financial loss for the organization that would be caused by an IT security incident (Cavusoglu et al. forthcoming).

An important aspect of the IT security risk analysis phase is that the decision makers have to evaluate hypothetical or future events (Cavusoglu et al. forthcoming). Accordingly, the risk analysis phase generally deals with incomplete and possibly inaccurate information about the characteristics of the two risk-related parameters. In general, risk analyses are often based on historical data concerning the likelihood and damage of potential failures in technologies, such as incidents in nuclear power plants (e.g., Paté-Cornell 1996; Reason 1997). However, due to the rapid technological development inherent in the IT sector, there is typically a lack of historical data concerning IT security incidents that would allow extrapolating the organization's actual ITSR exposure.

Therefore, previous IT security risk management research has developed multiple methods, which can be used to estimate the susceptibility of IT systems and the severity of IT security incidents, including scorecard-based reports, expert-interviews, self-assessments, and stochastic methods. Besides, there is a growing stream of literature related to risk quantification measures in form of economic IT security metrics (Ackermann 2013). For example, Patterson (2002) proposed a formula to calculate the average cost of server downtime per hour. Dubendorfer et al. (2004) presented metrics for large scale IT security attacks, including costs related to downtime, disaster recovery costs, and liability costs due to contractual penalties. Pang and Whitt (2009) analyzed the impact of service interruptions in large-scale service systems and suggested metrics to quantify these interruptions with increasing scale of the systems. An overview and comparison of the different metrics and risk measures for IT security is given by Ackermann et al. (2013).

Nevertheless, the accuracy of the results of these methods strongly depends on the quality, quantity, and actuality of the used data and information (Ackermann et al. 2013; Faisst and Prokein 2005). In particular, the necessary data to accurately quantify the risks is typically unavailable in the context of rather new technological developments, such as the Cloud. Accordingly, the results of the IT security risk analysis phase are in many cases largely predicted by the decision makers' feeling of the risks to which the organization's IT systems are exposed. In this context, previous IT security risk management research argues that the subjective ITSR perception of the decision makers is largely explained by the satisfactoriness of the implemented safeguarding measures in their organizations' IT systems, which in turn is determined by their assessments of the ITSR characteristics, the environment of the IT system, and their individual characteristics (Goodhue and Straub 1991). In particular, the subjective perception of the ITSR characteristics is predominately based on the decision makers' assessments of the industry susceptibility to the ITSR, which is strongly influenced by other organizations in the environment (e.g., security recommendations of industry associations or known previous IT security incidents in IT systems of competitors). The decision makers' assessments of the security of the environment of the IT system primarily depend on their knowing of the safeguarding measures, which are already implemented in the organizations' IT systems. Their IT security risk awareness along with their knowledge of the organizations' IT systems are also important individual characteristics of the decision makers, influencing their subjective perceptions of the ITSRs (Straub and Welke 1998).

2.3.3   Phase III: Solution Analysis

Based on the results of the IT security risk analysis phase, the solution analysis phase is aimed at the identification and evaluation of available safeguards to mitigate these risks. The result of this phase is the assessment of the appropriateness of the available safeguards against the ITSRs relevant to the organization's IT systems. In general, appropriate risk treatment approaches can range from risk reduction using technical countermeasures to the transfer of risks using insurances by third parties. Previous risk management literature subdivides the risk treatment approaches in risk reduction, risk avoidance (i.e., complete reduction of the risk, for example, by changing behaviors), and risk transfer (e.g., to insurance companies) strategies. IT security research is typically focused on the implementation of technical countermeasures against the ITSRs (e.g., Ackermann et al. 2013; Cavusoglu et al. forthcoming). Drawing on deterrence theory, existing IT security risk management literature often suggests that safeguards adopted to reduce the ITSRs can be further differentiated according to their effects into four distinct categories: deterrence, prevention, detection, and recovery measures (Nance and Straub 1988). In particular, certain safeguarding measures, such as IT security policies and guidelines, can deter system users from committing acts that implicitly or explicitly compromise the IT security of organizations' IT systems. As deterrent safeguards have no inherent provision for enforcement, they tend to be passive and depend on the willingness of system users to comply. In contrast, preventive safeguards are active countermeasures with inherent capabilities to enforce the IT security of the organizations' IT systems, such as firewalls or multi-factor authentication. Other safeguards are aimed at proactively detecting IT security incidents in the IT systems of organizations, such as the use of anti-malware software or security information and event management (SIEM) tools to identify suspicious activities. Finally, there are safeguards to remedy the harmful effects of IT security incidents on the organizations' IT systems. Backup strategies to recover lost or damaged data is an example of remedy safeguards (Nance and Straub 1988; Straub and Welke 1998).

In order to decide which safeguarding measures should be implemented in the organizations' IT systems, the decision makers need to evaluate their essential characteristics. Organizational IT security risk management guidelines recommend assessing the safeguarding measures in terms of their effectiveness against the targeted ITSRs, the feasibility of the organization to use them (e.g., compatibility with the organization's IT infrastructure or acceptance of the safeguards by the employees), and the costs associated with their use. In this regard, it is in many cases difficult for the decision makers to economically evaluate the effects of a safeguard against an ITSR as this requires the assessment of the reduction of the likelihood and the damage of future negative events due to the implementation of this safeguard (Ackermann 2013; Faisst and Prokein 2005). Therefore, the decision makers typically have to incorporate external information concerning the characteristics of the safeguarding measures, such as publications of security-related organizations or IT security experts. In this context, for example, the Federal Office for Information Security provides a discussion of minimum security requirements for Cloud providers that can support the identification and assessment of available safeguarding measures by their decision makers (Federal Office for Information Security 2011). Moreover, the CSA provides a more technical, operational security guideline for Cloud providers, including a description of safeguarding measures related to virtualization, data center operations, encryption, and key management (Cloud Security Alliance 2011).

However, the importance of implementing safeguarding measures is typically also determined by the results of the IT security risk analysis phase. Existing IT security risk management literature suggests to evaluate the safeguards through a qualitative analysis of all risks, for example, by using a risk exposure matrix, where all ITSR are placed based on the susceptibility of the organization's IT system to the risk and the severity of the risk for the organization. The organizations should not only treat those ITSRs with the highest ratings first but also grapple more intensively with the accurate evaluation of the safeguards available against these risk in order to ensure the best possible protection (e.g., by conducting simulation studies and penetration tests) (Ackermann 2013; Wheeler 2011).

2.3.4   Phase IV: Decision

Drawing on the results of the IT security risk analysis phase and the solution analysis phase, the decision phase is aimed at making decisions about which safeguarding measures should be implemented in the organization's IT systems (Straub and Welke 1998). Since it is in general impossible to reach 100% security, decision makers need to balance the increased IT security level against the costs associated with the safeguards. Moreover, the implementation of additional safeguarding measures may also introduce new complexities to the IT systems (Ackermann 2013; Wheeler 2011). Therefore, organizational IT security risk management literature postulates that the decisions are typically based on a rational weighing up of the implementation costs and the expected benefits of a safeguard (Faisst and Prokein 2005). In this context, decision makers are in many cases confronted with the problem to economically evaluate all possible safeguards as this requires the comparison of all measures' impacts (i.e., their contribution to the mitigation of the ITSRs) and the costs associated with the implementation of the measures (Ackermann 2013). In particular, the assumptions underlying the decision making are frequently based on more or less inaccurate data and information (see also non-availability of quantified data concerning the ITSR in Subsection 2.3.2). Besides, the vast amount of safeguarding measures that is theoretically available to mitigate the ITSRs make it difficult for the decision makers to get an overview of the existing measures and to identify those safeguards, which are best suited for the organizations' IT systems (Faisst and Prokein 2005; Stoneburner et al. 2002).

Existing IT security risk management literature suggests several approaches that support IT security-related investment decisions. Straub and Welke (1998) recommend the use of the countermeasure matrix model, which is derived from management science and calculates a security impact level for each safeguarding measure based on a qualitative analysis of its addressed ITSRs. Decisions to implement a safeguard are made based on a predefined minimum security impact level, which has to be exceeded by all implemented safeguards (e.g., Baker et al. 2007). Gordon and Loeb (2002) propose an economic model, which, based on the vulnerability of a given IT system to the ITSRs and the potential financial losses resulting from an IT security incident, estimates an optimal IT security investment level to protect this IT system. Huang et al. (2006) present another economic model which incorporates the effects of multiple simultaneous attacks. Sonnenreich et al. (2006) suggest the return on security investment (ROSI), which measures the effects of the implementation of a certain safeguard in relation to its costs. It is based on the classical return on investment (ROI) that captures the financial gain of a project in relation to its total costs. A game theory-based model which can be used to identify the most cost-effective configuration of safeguarding measures based on the probabilities of IT security incidents and the costs associated with the manual monitoring of possible incidents is presented by Cavusoglu et al. (2004b). Other game theoretic approaches to estimate the optimal IT security investment level are presented by Grossklags et al. (2008) and Cremonini and Nizovtsev (2009). Cavusoglu et al. (2008) propose a game theory for determining IT security investment levels, and compare game theory and decision theory approaches on several dimensions such as the investment levels, susceptibility, and payoff from IT security investments. A dynamic model of the relationship between technical and behavioral security factors is developed by Dutta and Roy (2008). The authors investigate changes in the value of an organization's IT system over time to quantify the impact of safeguarding measures. Herath and Herath (2008) develop a model, which can be used for the assessment of the economic value of the protection against the ITSRs, and for the evaluation of the corresponding safeguarding measure based on real options. The concept of Value-at-Risk to measure the stochastic behavior of financial losses due to IT security incidents has been introduced by Wang et al. (2008a). A comprehensive literature review of approaches to support IT security investment decisions is provided by Ackermann (2013).

In the context of the Cloud, Ackermann et al. (2013) present a model that supports IT security investment decisions in service-based IT systems. The model supports decision makers in analyzing the cost-benefit trade-off related to safeguards by proposing an approach to efficiently estimate the probability functions of potential losses for a service-based IT system, such as the Cloud. In particular, the approach enables decision makers to choose the optimal IT security investment level (i.e., the most economically reasonable combination of security measures) based on individual security metrics.

2.3.5   Phase V: Implementation

The IT security risk management process is concluded by the implementation of the selected safeguarding measures in the organization's IT systems (Straub and Welke 1998). The activities in this phase can, for example, range from the installation of technical measures in the organization's IT systems to the issuance of IT security policies for the organization's employees.

Beyond that, extant IT security risk management literature recommends continuously reviewing and evaluating the effectiveness of the implemented safeguarding measures (Cavusoglu et al. forthcoming). As such, the previous IT security risk management phases (i.e., the identification of the IT security threats, the IT security risk analysis, the solution analysis, and the decision phase) are based on an ex-ante consideration of the ITSRs. Accordingly, the assumptions and decisions in the previous IT security risk management phases should also be critically evaluated by ex-post analyses (e.g., analyses of the actual financial losses caused by the ITSRs and the real effectiveness of the implemented safeguards) (Ackermann 2013). Moreover, the characteristics of the ITSRs as well as the available safeguards constantly evolve, because of the fast technological development in the IT sector. Therefore, an effective IT security risk management is generally a continuous process in the organizations (e.g., Cavusoglu et al. forthcoming; Faisst and Prokein 2005).

3 Part I: The Inhibiting Role of Unrealistic Optimism in Providers' IT Security Risk Management

In this chapter, we present our empirical analysis of the role of the decision makers' subjective ITSR perceptions in the Cloud providers' IT security risk management. In particular, we demonstrate the inhibiting effects of unrealistic optimism (UO) in the ITSR perceptions of Cloud providers' decision makers on the outcome of the providers' IT security risk management. Therefore, we first show the theoretical background and the hypotheses development of this part (Section 3.1). In this section, we also show the development of the proposed theoretical model of Cloud providers' IT security risk management. Afterwards, we show the research methodology of the empirical study (Section 3.2), including the proposed approaches to measure UO in the ITSR perceptions of providers' decision makers. Then, we present the analyses of the collected data along with the results (Section 3.3). The findings of this part are summarized and discussed (Section 3.4).

3.1 Theoretical Background and Hypotheses Development

In this section, we describe the theoretical backgrounds and the development of the comprehensive framework of Cloud providers' IT security risk management processes, which is based on an infusion of four distinct but related streams of literature and explicates the effects of the subjective risk and coping perceptions of the providers' decision makers. First, we draw on organizational IT security risk management research (Subsection 3.1.1) and technology threat avoidance theory (Subsection 3.1.2) to theorize in which ways, and to what degree, the outcome of the providers' IT security risk management processes are predicted by subjective perceptions of their decision makers. Second, based on institutional theory (Subsection 3.1.3), we hypothesize how the actions and demands of the providers' stakeholders influence the IT security risk management decisions of the providers' decision makers. Third, drawing on psychological risk perception research (Subsection 3.1.4), we postulate that there are two important perspectives on decision makers' ITSR perceptions (i.e., absolute and comparative ITSR perceptions), which eventually determine the outcome of the organizational IT security risk management processes. Fourth, based on psychological literature, we introduce the phenomenon of unrealistic optimism (UO) (Subsection 3.1.5) and derive our main hypothesis regarding the existence and consequences of systematic errors in the decision makers' ITSR assessments (see interlocking of theoretical underpinnings of the proposed theoretical model of Cloud providers' IT security risk management in Figure 3-1).

3.1.1   Organizational IT Security Risk Management

In order to be able to relate to all processes of the providers' IT security risk management and how they are determined by the decision makers' perceptions, we built on Straub and Welke (1998)'s well-established model, that explicates the entire organizational IT security risk management process (see also IT security risk management in Subsection 2.3).

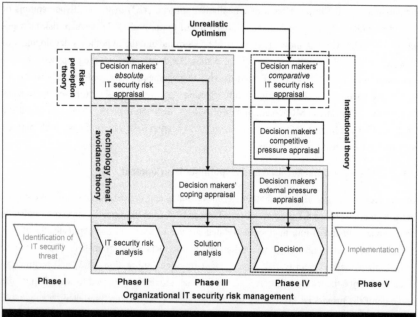

Figure 3-1: Theoretical Foundations of the IT Security Risk Management Model

As shown in Figure 2-1, the normative model suggested by the authors, which is grounded in previous management science research and derives its structure from Simon (1960)'s model of decision-making, separates the organization IT security risk management process into five distinct stages and their outcomes: the identification of IT security threats, the ITSR analysis, the solution analysis, the decision, and the implementation phase. The IT security risk management process generally starts with the identification and formulation of threats concerning the risk of IT security breaches by the providers' decision makers (e.g., a security loophole in the providers' authentication systems was discovered). The central risk analysis phase is situated as a bridge between identified IT security threats and the assessment of available solutions, and preceding the decision phase. The analysis of the ITSR is inherent in the identified threat areas and includes the threat identification and prioritization of the risks resulting from the IT security threats. The preceding solution analysis phase includes the assessment of the available safeguards with regard to the protection needs, as specified during the risk analysis phase. Based on the matching of the prioritized ITSRs with appropriate safeguards, the decision phase contains the selection and prioritization of the organization's IT security projects. The final implementation phase embraces the realizing of the projects by implementing the safeguards into the organization's IT systems (e.g., the Cloud service) (Straub and Welke 1998).

3.1.2   Technology Threat Avoidance Theory

Drawing on previous research, we argue that the results of the organizational IT security risk management phases are predominately predicted by the decision makers' perceptions, which are determined by coping processes – similar to the individual level. Coping theory postulates that people cope with disruptive situations through two key processes that influence each other: primary appraisal (i.e., the assessment of the expected consequences of a situation) and secondary (coping) appraisal (i.e., the assessment of the options to control the situation). The theory has been widely applied to health-related domains, like coping with death, sexually transmitted diseases, cancer, and pain (Lazarus 1993). Based on coping theory (Folkman 2013), previous psychological research proposed the protection motivation theory (Rogers 1975) and the health belief model (Janz and Becker 1984) to explicate people's decisions to take precautionary actions and protect themselves against detrimental situations. At the core of these theories is the argument that, confronted with a disruptive (or potentially risky) situation, people's risk appraisals trigger their coping appraisals and subsequently, their coping behaviors (Folkman 2013). Therefore, it is generally assumed that coping behaviors result from a rational weighing up of the (potential) costs (e.g., costs of periodic health evaluation) and (possible) benefits (e.g., better chances to cure a disease due to its early detection) of the behavior (e.g., Janz and Becker 1984; Rosenstock 1966).

Based on these theories, prior IT security research investigated, for example, employees' motivation to comply with the IT security policies (Vance et al. 2012), users' motivation to practice safe computing (Anderson and Agarwal 2010; Aytes and Connolly 2004; Workman et al. 2008), users' intention to adopt antivirus software (Johnston and Warkentin 2010; Ng et al. 2009), and users' intention to implement security features on their wireless-networks (Woon et al. 2005). Technology threat avoidance theory (TTAT), which is mainly derived from coping and protection motivation theory, proposes a theoretical model to clarify IT security protection behaviors (Liang and Xue 2009). Based on a slightly modified version of the theory, the authors later empirically investigated users' protection behaviors against being attacked by malware (Liang and Xue 2010).

TTAT submits that when people perceive an IT security threat to be a serious risk for themselves, they are motivated to actively avoid the risk by implementing a safeguarding measure if they perceive the risk to be (reasonably) avoidable by this safeguarding measure. If people, however, believe that the ITSR is not avoidable by any safeguarding measure available to them, TTAT proposes that they will passively avoid the risk by performing so-called emotion-focused coping (Liang and Xue 2009). Emotion-focused coping strategies aim to mitigate people's negative emotions and discomforts related to risks (e.g., fear and stress). Most of the strategies only require cognitive efforts and are oriented towards the self (Liang and Xue 2009). As such, emotion-focused coping processes refer to individuals' cognitive and behavioral efforts to regulate emotional distress associated with a risk, without changing the objective reality (Lazarus 1966). Besides, even if emotions were demonstrated to affect organizational decision-making processes by previous management research, the effects are typically different from those at the individual level and more subtle, like a more careful reflection of prior decisions (e.g., Gaudine and Thorne 2001; Maitlis and Ozcelik 2004; Singh 1986). However, since we aim to analyze the relationship between the decision makers' perceptions and the IT security of the organizations, we focus on problem-focused coping and the implementation of safeguards in this study.

At the organizational level, it can be assumed, consistent with coping theory, that the decisions to implement certain IT security safeguards primarily result from a rational weighing up of its costs and benefits in terms of preventable damages to the organization, as perceived by the decision makers (e.g., Cavusoglu et al. 2004b).

In this context, IT security risk management literature recommends various analytical tools that can assist decision makers in selecting an appropriate set of safeguards (see also Subsection 2.3.4), like, the countermeasure matrix model (e.g., Straub and Welke 1998). Derived from management science, the countermeasure matrix model is frequently recommended by IT security guidelines and suggests calculating a score for each available safeguard, which is based on the assessment of the measure's appropriateness, in relation to the assessment of its addressed risks. Decisions to implement a security measure are then made based on a predefined minimum security impact level, which has to be exceeded by all implemented safeguards (Baker et al. 2007; Fenz and Ekelhart 2011). Besides, previous research found IT security risk management decisions in many cases to be additionally driven by heuristic approaches (e.g., Von Solms and Von Solms 2004).

However, regardless of whether analytical tools or heuristics are utilized, the decisions are triggered by weighting the ITSRs and the reasonableness of avoiding these risks. As such, consistent with the structure of TTAT and coping theory, organizational IT security risk management models also describe the decisions to implement a safeguarding measure as determined by the outcomes of the preceding risk and solution analysis phases. Moreover, some

authors even argue that the structure of the organizational IT security risk management processes was originally determined by the behavior of the decision makers and are subsequently
grounded in coping processes, as submitted by coping theories (Straub and Welke 1998).
However, due to the congruence of organizational IT security and coping processes, we regard TTAT as a valid theoretical lens to analyze the decision-making and upstream perceptions in the organizational IT security risk management processes. In particular, we expect
that the implementation of safeguards in the organization's service against an ITSR is determined by decision makers' intention to increase the IT security level,[1] which, in turn, is predominately affected by their risk assessment.

In general, ITSR can cause painful privacy and financial losses. As demonstrated by various
studies in the IT security context at the individual level, the higher people's perception of the
ITSR, the higher their motivation to avoid these risks (e.g., Liang and Xue 2010; Vance et al.
2012). TTAT defines the avoidance motivation as the degree to which people are motivated to
implement safeguarding measures in order to avoid the ITSRs (Liang and Xue 2009).

At the organizational level, the quantification of the impact of ITSRs is typically measured by
their financial impacts on the organization (e.g., Garg et al. 2003; Sonnenreich et al. 2006). In
line with previous IT security risk management literature (see also Section 2.3), we regard a
provider's ITSR as the organization's overall financial loss resulting from a potential compromise of its service's IT security (e.g., due to damage to reputation, contractual penalties,
costs to recover the service). In this context, the service's IT security is defined according to
Ackermann et al. (2012)'s conceptualization as the protection of the customers' systems and
data against availability, accountability, confidentiality, integrity, maintainability, and performance risks when the Cloud service is used as a delivery model (see a detailed description
of the ITSR in the context of the Cloud, in Subsection 2.2.2).

However, the financial damage, and particularly the likelihood of the damage caused by an
ITSR, has to be assessed by the decision makers. In this context, prior IT security risk management research argues that the assessment of the ITSR is predominately a function of the
decision makers' beliefs about the industry risk (e.g., the likelihood and damage of an identity
theft in the Cloud), the actions already taken by their own organization to effectively secure
the systems (e.g., implementation of two-factor authentication), and the decision makers' individual characteristics, like awareness of previous systems breaches (e.g., the knowledge that
their own organization's service was attacked three times last month, one account successfully

---

[1] As a hardly comprehensible and understandable range of IT security measures is theoretically
available to protect IT services at the organizational level in general and Cloud services in particular (e.g., Federal Office for Information Security 2011), we regard the providers' coping behavior
with ITSRs as an increase of the organization's IT security level in this study (see also Subsection
2.3.3). In this context, monetary values are typically utilized to measure the IT security level at the
organizational level.

penetrated, causing the theft of several confidential documents and a damage suit brought by the respective customer), and background in security work (e.g., high IT security awareness of the responsible decision makers) (Goodhue and Straub 1991). Accordingly, the results of the risk analysis phase are not only determined by the decision makers' general assessments of the risks but also by their basic understanding of the range of technical and managerial controls that are already implemented in the systems to cope with the ITSRs (e.g., the effectiveness of two-factor authentication against identity theft in the Cloud). In sum, the results of the ITSR analysis phase strongly depend on the decision makers' knowledge and perceptions (e.g., Choi et al. 2008; McFadzean et al. 2007; Straub and Welke 1998).

In line with TTAT, we hypothesize that the motivation of a provider's decision maker to increase the IT security level of his or her organization's Cloud service by implementing additional safeguards is determined by their assessments of the service's exposure to the ITSR:

H1.1:   The higher the perception of a provider's decision maker of the exposure of his/her organization's Cloud service to the IT security risks, the higher his/her intention to increase the IT security level of his/her organization's Cloud service.

However, the perceived risk alone cannot determine what coping measure will be taken. Instead, it leads to a sense of urgency that motivates people to engage in coping behavior (Folkman 2013). Drawing on coping theory, TTAT postulates that the ITSR perception, resulting from the risk appraisal process, concurrently provides the initial motivation for people to start the coping appraisal process and seek appropriate safeguarding measures to pursue active ITSR avoidance. An important judgment that people need to make in this context is to determine the avoidability of an ITSR. In this regard, perceived avoidability is defined as the person's assessment of the likelihood s/he will be able to avoid the ITSR if they implement a specific safeguarding measure (Liang and Xue 2009). Based on expectancy theory (Vroom 1964) and protection motivation theory, TTAT particularly proposes that people are generally motivated to take those safeguards, which could bring them the most valued outcome. Thus, their intention to adopt a certain safeguard is also determined by the degree to which the safeguard makes the ITSR avoidable (Liang and Xue 2009).

At the organization level, the IT security risk management model places the solution analysis phase between the risk analysis and the decision phase. The solution analysis includes the identification and evaluation of safeguards to meet the organizational needs, as specified during the risk analysis phase. Altogether, we expect, in line with TTAT, that decisions to cope with the ITSR also depend on the assessment of their avoidability:

H1.2:   The higher a provider's decision maker's perception of the IT security risk avoidability, the higher his/her intention to increase the IT security level of his/her organization's Cloud service.

Based on preceding research on health protective behavior (Janz and Becker 1984; Rogers 1975) and self-efficacy (Bandura 2001; Compeau and Higgins 1995), TTAT postulates that people evaluate a safeguard by assessing how effectively it addresses the ITSR, what costs are associated with it, and how confident they feel about using it. In other words, people assess how avoidable an ITSR is if the safeguard is implemented by considering the three factors: effectiveness, cost, and self-efficacy (Liang and Xue 2009).

Previous studies identified the effectiveness of the safeguarding measure and its expected costs as the central considerations of the solutions analysis phase, at the organizational level (e.g., Sonnenreich et al. 2006; Straub and Welke 1998). Beside cost-effectiveness analysis, prior IT security research also revealed the analysis of the organization's feasibility to be a crucial factor in considerations to implement certain safeguarding measures (e.g., Baskerville 1991; Kankanhalli et al. 2003; Sun et al. 2006). Moreover, for example, IT security research frequently recommends the use of the countermeasure matrix model for solution analysis. As one of the Six-Sigma key risk management methods, the countermeasure matrix model suggests calculating a score for each safeguarding measure by multiplying the assessment of the costs, the effectiveness, and the feasibility of the safeguard by the assessment of the susceptibility and severity of its addressed risks (e.g., Stoneburner et al. 2002). Altogether, we assume that the costs, the effectiveness, and the feasibility of a safeguarding measure are likewise the determining factors of the solution analysis phase in the IT security domain.

Perceived safeguard effectiveness in TTAT is defined as the assessment of how effectively a safeguard can be applied to avoid the ITSR (Liang and Xue 2010). It reflects people's perception of the objective outcomes produced by using the safeguarding measure, which is similar to the concept of outcome expectancy (Bandura 1982). Thus, perceived effectiveness is related to perceived usefulness, a major determinant of users' attitude or behavioral intention in TAM (Davis 1989; Davis et al. 1989). As such, perceived effectiveness could be viewed as the usefulness of the safeguard, in terms of its ability to objectively avoid an ITSR. Nevertheless, there are theoretical differences between the two constructs: perceived usefulness is typically conceptualized with the assumption that users have a certain goal, like to improve their job performance, whereas perceived effectiveness does not have an assumed goal.

At the organizational level, previous IT security studies argue that safeguarding measures can generally help to avoid ITSRs by deterring, preventing, detecting, and/or remedying IT security breaches (e.g., Lee et al. 2004; Straub and Nance 1990). Accordingly, frameworks recommend to rate the effectiveness of safeguarding measures for organizations based on the four factors: deterrence, prevention, detection and remedies, regarding each prioritized ITSR (e.g., Kankanhalli et al. 2003; Straub and Welke 1998). Consistent with TTAT and the organizational IT security risk management literature, we expect that a decision maker's perceived effectiveness of a safeguarding measure is increased when s/he assesses the safeguard to be useful to reduce the ITSR exposure of their organization's Cloud service, with regard to any of the four effect dimensions. Accordingly, we hypothesize that:

H1.2a: A providers' decision maker's assessment of the effectiveness of an increased IT security level of his/her organization's Cloud service positively affects his/her perception of the IT security risk avoidability.

Feasibility is defined as a person's confidence in their capabilities to take the safeguarding measure (Liang and Xue 2009). The construct is closely related to self-efficacy, which refers to a person's subjective judgment on his or her personal skills, knowledge, or competency about conducting a behavior, like taking a certain precautionary action (Bandura 1982). Self-efficacy has been frequently demonstrated by psychological research to have a major effect on people's protection behavior. In particular, it is arguedBandura (1982) that behavior is best predicted by considering both self-efficacy and outcome beliefs (Bandura 1982). In this regard, previous studies have demonstrated that people are more motivated to perform IT security behaviors, like adopting anti-malware software and using network encryption when the level of their self-efficacy increases (e.g., Johnston and Warkentin 2010; Woon et al. 2005). TTAT postulates that the higher a person's perceived self-efficacy regarding a safeguard, the higher his or her motivation to avoid the ITSR by using this safeguarding measure (Liang and Xue 2009).

In the organizational context, previous studies also found employees' self-efficacy to have considerable effect on their intention to comply with companies' IT security policies (Vance et al. 2012). Previous IT security risk management research submits that the organization's feasibility to implement a certain security measure (e.g., fulfillment of technical requirements, employee acceptance, available resources) is an important factor and should be evaluated carefully during the solution analysis phase (e.g., Fenz and Ekelhart 2011; Stoneburner et al. 2002). At the organizational level, the perceived feasibility is also clear-cut from the estimated costs (see below), because budget limits usually restrict the decision makers' possibilities to (unlimitedly) increase their organization's feasibility (e.g., an organization's IT security budget does not allow for the implementation of a certain safeguarding measure) (e.g., Cavusoglu et al. 2008). As such, the feasibility of the organization is the basic requirement to effectively implement and operate a safeguarding measure in the Cloud service in order to avoid a certain ITSR. Hence, we expect that:

H1.2b: A provider's decision maker's assessment of his/her organization's feasibility to increase the IT security level of his/her organization's Cloud service positively affects his/her perception of the IT security risk avoidability.

In addition, previous research found that the perceived costs of the protection behavior play a significant role by reducing people's behavioral motivations (e.g., Rosenstock 1966). The costs refer to the physical and cognitive efforts needed – such as time, money, inconvenience, and comprehension – to adopt the protection behavior (Rosenstock et al. 1994). Protection motivation research conclusively demonstrated that people usually compare the benefits and costs of a certain protection behavior before they decide to engage in it, and if the costs are too high, they are unlikely to take the precautionary action (e.g., Janz and Becker 1984; Rogers 1975). Previous IT security research revealed that the costs, for example, associated with network security and anti-malware software adoption, significantly reduce people's motivation to use the safeguarding measures (e.g., Liang and Xue 2010; Woon et al. 2005).

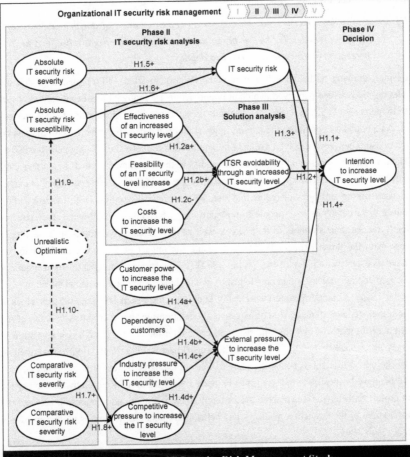

Figure 3-2: Research Model of the IT Security Risk Management Study

In the organizational context, the safeguard costs are typically viewed as the overall financial effort related to the implementation and operation of the safeguarding measure in the organization's IT systems, including costs of software licenses, redundant hardware, employee training, reduced ease of system use (e.g., Sonnenreich et al. 2006). Since providers are typically profit-oriented organizations and the decision-making largely depends on critical cost-benefit analyses, we thus assume that these efforts are likely to reduce the decision makers' perception of the reasonableness of avoiding the ITSR and subsequently create considerable barriers to implementing a safeguarding measure. In line with TTAT and previous IT security research at the individual level, we hypothesize that:

H1.2c: A provider's decision maker's assessment of the cost associated with an increase of the IT security level of his/her organization's Cloud service negatively affects his/her perception of the IT security risk avoidability.

Besides, drawing on health behavior research (Weinstein 2000), TTAT postulates that the relationship between perceived avoidability and avoidance motivation is negatively moderated by perceived ITSR. Precisely, the relationship is weaker when the perceived ITSR increases. As a boundary condition, the authors suggest that if the perceived risk is zero, there is no relationship between perceived avoidability and avoidance motivation (Liang and Xue 2009). The proposition is based on psychological studies in the health arena, which found that individuals facing health risks typically experience psychological stress and adopt emotion-focused coping strategies to reduce the state of emotional discomfort (e.g., Lazarus 1966). While these behaviors help people to maintain their psychological well-being, they concurrently reduce their alertness to the risks as well as their reliance on protection behaviors to cope with the threat (Rogers 1975). As a result, the impact of the protection behavior on avoidance motivation diminishes (Witte 1992). For example, a frequently used emotion-focused coping strategy is that people just try not to think about the detrimental situation (e.g., Witte 1994). Although people theoretically know that the risk is still present, they block it from their rational thinking. In consequence, the relationships between the assessment of the behavior, in terms of avoiding the risk, and behavioral motivation at high risk levels are in many cases weaker than those at low risk levels (Lazarus 1993; Witte 1992). Nevertheless, psychological research conclusively showed that some degree of fear arousal, resulting from the perceived exposure to the risk, must be present in order to induce a motivation to engage in protection behavior (see above). Accordingly, there is usually no relationship between the assessment of the protection measures and behavioral intentions, if there is no perceived risk (e.g., Janis 1964).

In the IS context, previous research argues that an IT security breach has serious consequences for a user, ranging from tremendous financial losses over theft of sensitive documents to disclosure of compromising information and is thus similar in character to health risks, which directly impair the well-being of all persons concerned. Hence, the authors assume that the ITSRs similarly arouse fear on the part of the users (e.g., Johnston and Warkentin 2010). Drawing on health protection behavior research, the studies revealed downstream effects of the fear appeal treatment on the relationship between users' ITSR perception and perceived effectiveness (both studies propose that avoidance motivation is predominately determined by the perceived effectiveness of the safeguarding measure, which is not mediated by perceived avoidability) of an anti-malware adoption (e.g., Johnston and Warkentin 2010; Liang and Xue 2010).

However, at the organizational level, we suspect that the ITSRs do not arouse the same extent of fear in the decision makers' perceptions so that fear appeal does generally not affect the IT security risk management. In comparison with, for example, health threats (e.g., serious illness and death caused by a disease), ITSR breaches in the organization's IT systems are likely to have much less invasive and more indirect negative consequences for the responsible decision makers, such as reduced job satisfaction, loss of reputation, or sanctions by the employers (e.g., Van Niekerk and Von Solms 2010). Even more importantly, prior IT security research submits that the decision-making in organizational IT security risk management is typically supported by tools, which aim to ensure the rational weighing up of costs and benefits of the safeguarding measures, like the countermeasure matrix approach (e.g., Straub and Welke 1998).

In contrast to TTAT, we thus expect that even a high ITSR perception does not induce fear in the perceptions of the decision makers and particularly does not affect the rationality of organizational IT security risk management decisions. Based on IT security risk management research, we suspect that ITSRs, which are perceived to be critical by the decision makers, are in general, subject to more careful and detailed analyses in terms of their avoidability. In this regard, previous IT security risk management literature proposes that the ITSRs are prioritized based on the decision makers' beliefs about their potential impact on the organization's IT systems and only the risks classified as relevant are subject to further analyses (Straub and Welke 1998). Accordingly, the boundary condition is that if the decision makers' perception of an ITSR is zero, the risk is not included in the solution analysis processes and subsequently, neither the ITSR nor its avoidability encourages the intention to implement safeguarding measures. However, the appropriateness of available solution analysis techniques (e.g., checklists, independent security experts, case studies, simulation-based analysis) generally depends on the complexity and importance of the targeted ITSR (e.g., Stoneburner et al. 2002). As a more comprehensive analysis of the available solution reduces the uncertainty of the resulting decisions, we expect that an increased ITSR perception intensifies the organization's solution analysis phase, which, in turn, strengthens the relationship between the results of this phase and the decision makers' intentions to implement the safeguarding measure. In sum, and contrary to the propositions of TTAT, we hypothesize that:

H1.3:   A provider's decision maker's perception of the IT security risk of his/her organization's Cloud service increases the relationship between his/her assessment of the IT security risk avoidability and his/her intention to increase the Cloud service's IT security level.

3.1.3   Institutional Theory

In addition to the rational weighing up of potential costs and benefits, previous psychological research demonstrated that social norms can have considerable effects on people's intention to adopt protection behaviors (e.g., Bandura 2004; Tanner et al. 1991). In these studies, social norms are usually measured by perceived social pressures. In particular, the authors propose, in the health context, that human health is a social matter, not just an individual one (e.g., Bandura 2004). In this regard, other researchers oftentimes argued that the social contexts of cognitions have no direct influence or have to be viewed as a logical refinement of the benefits of protection behavior, so that social norms are not included in many of the established protection behavior models, like the protection motivation theory (e.g., Janz and Becker 1984; Rogers 1975). In the IT security arena, only one of the previous studies investigated the social context of protection behaviors and revealed that the subjective norm significantly affects users' intentions to adopt anti-malware software (Johnston and Warkentin 2010). As TTAT is primarily derived from coping and protection motivation theory, it does not take social contexts into account to explain people's IT security behavior (Liang and Xue 2009).

However, drawing on previous results of IS research at the organizational level, we expect the external pressure to have strong effects on organizations' decisions to implement safeguards. In particular, we assume that the external pressure can induce decision makers' intentions to implement a certain safeguarding measure, even if they assess the ITSR not to be critical or difficult to avoid (e.g., important customers press for permanent encryption of their stored data without any possibilities for the provider to decrypt and access their data). Prior IT security research noted that environmental factors, like actions taken by competitors to secure the IT systems and demands of customers, have in many cases considerably influenced an organization's IT security risk management decisions (e.g., Anderson 2001; Cavusoglu et al. 2004a; Gordon and Loeb 2001). We draw on institutional theory to conceptualize and frame the effects of external pressure on the organizational IT security risk management. The institutional approach submits that organizations respond to an environment that consists of other organizations. Therefore, the other organizations also respond to their environment, which consists of organizations responding to an environment of organizations' responses (Schelling 2006). Thus, organizations are subject to pressures, which are isomorphic with their environment and incorporate both interconnectedness and structural equivalence. The interconnectedness refers to relations between organizations, which are characterized by the existence of transactions, binding organizations to one another. Structural equivalence refers to the holding of a similar position in a network of organizations (Burt 1987). Institutional approaches differentiate between three types of isomorphic pressures put on organizations: coercive and normative pressure generally acts through interconnectedness, while mimetic pressure operates through structural equivalence (Powell and DiMaggio 2012).

Previous research argued that institutional theory can be viewed as an extension of system theory, which is generic in its nature and has been widely applied to IT security in the past – from the functioning of a computer system, via humans and their actions, to international entities (Bjorck 2004; Dacin et al. 2002). Nevertheless, institutional theory is more specific and only applicable if the unit-of-analysis exhibits some form of social behavior. Drawing on institutional theory, previous IS research investigated, for example, the use of EDI software, the adoption of e-commerce, adjustment of IT functions, and social media assimilation in organizations (e.g., Bharati et al. 2014; Chatterjee et al. 2002; Swanson and Ramiller 2004; Teo et al. 2003). In the IT security context, prior research argued that institutional theory offers promising possibilities to better understand the organizational IT security risk management by identifying institutional forces and their effects on decisions to implement safeguarding measures (e.g., Bjorck 2004). Based on the theoretical underpinnings, as presented above and the results of previous IT security research, we suggest that:

H1.4:   *A provider's decision maker's perception of the external pressure to increase the IT security level of his/her organization's Cloud service positively affects his/her intention to increase the IT security level of his/her organization's Cloud service.*

Previous IS research typically found the competitors, customers, and industry associations to be the most relevant stakeholders of organizations (e.g., Chwelos et al. 2001). In particular, the actions of these stakeholder groups induce different types of isomorphic pressures. Coercive pressure is defined as formal or informal pressures exerted on organizations by other organizations, upon which they are dependent (Powell and DiMaggio 2012). Empirical evidences suggest that the coercive pressure primarily stems from resource-dominant organizations and is built into exchange relationships. In particular, a dominant actor that controls important resources may demand that organizations, which are dependent on it, adopt structures or behaviors that serve its interests. The dependent organizations may comply with the demands to secure their own survival (Pfeffer and Salancik 2003). In general, the success, and hence the survival of organizations, directly depends on the adoption of its products or services by its customers. In the context of EDI adoption, previous studies found that important customers exert pressure on organizations to adopt EDI solutions in order to reduce their administrative disbursement costs and enhance systems' efficiencies (Teo et al. 2003). Similarly, based on previous IT security research results (e.g., Ackermann et al. 2012), we expect that providers are often put under pressure by key customers that want to ensure the security of their systems and data when the service is used as a delivery model. However, even if the organization strongly depends on those customers, there is no pressure exerted on the organizations if there are no demands made by the customers. Accordingly, the overall perceived coercive pressure is typically conceptualized by previous studies as a function of the degree of dependency on the customer organizations and the strength of the customer demands (e.g., Chwelos et al. 2001). In these studies, both dimensions were found to significantly increase the perceived external pressure and, ultimately, the behavioral intentions of the decision makers (Teo et al. 2003). Drawing on these results, we hypothesize that the perceived dependency on the customers and the enacted customer power to implement safeguarding measures put pressure on the providers and subsequently increase their intentions to implement the safeguards:

H1.4a: The higher a provider's decision maker's perception of his/her organization's dependency on existing customer relationships, the higher his/her perception of the external pressure exerted on his/her organization to increase the IT security level of the Cloud service.

H1.4b: The higher a provider's decision maker's perception of the enacted customer power to increase the level of IT security of his/her organization's service, the higher his/her perception of the external pressure exerted on his/her organization to increase the IT security level of the Cloud service.

Normative pressure refers to gaining knowledge of the benefits and costs associated with a certain structure or behavior through direct or indirect connections to other organizations, persuading the organization to act similarly (Powell and DiMaggio 2012). Empirical results suggest that normative pressure manifests itself through dyadic inter-organizational channels of professional, trade, business, and other key organizations in the environment. The norms are typically shared through relational channels among the organizations in the environment, which, in turn, increases the strength of these norms and their potential influence on organizational behavior (Burt 1987; Powell and DiMaggio 2012). Prior IS research found that the normative pressures faced by an organization predominately stem from an increased prevalence of systems by suppliers as well as the organization's participation in professional, trade, or business organizations, that encourage the system adoption (e.g., Chatterjee et al. 2002; Chwelos et al. 2001; Teo et al. 2003). In the organizational IT security context, professional, trade, or business organizations typically offer IT security incident reports, ITSR analysis, and IT security risk management recommendations, like checklists of necessary safeguarding measures for organizations (e.g., Stoneburner et al. 2002). As there is typically a lack of quantitative data, which would allow for an objective assessment of the ITSRs and subsequently, the available safeguards, these organizations' reports are usually important indicators for organizations to estimate the benefits and costs associated with the implementation of certain safeguarding measures (e.g., Choi et al. 2008). Besides, the IT security recommendations for providers concurrently constitute central reference points for potential customers to evaluate the security of the providers (e.g., Ackermann et al. 2012). As such, we expect that the normative pressure exerted on the providers principally stems from the industry organizations and significantly influences the decisions to implement safeguards in their service. Accordingly, we hypothesize that:

H1.4c: *The higher a provider's decision maker's perception of the industry pressure to increase the level of IT security of his/her organization's Cloud service, the higher his/her perception of the external pressure exerted on his/her organization to increase the IT security level of the Cloud service.*

Mimetic pressure causes organizations to change over time to become more like other organizations in their environments (Powell and DiMaggio 2012). Previous studies found mimetic pressure to be manifested in two ways: the prevalence of a structure or behavior in the organization's environment, and the perceived success of those organizations in the environment that have adopted the structure or behavior. Regardless of the technical value of the structure or behavior, an organization will imitate the actions of other (structurally equivalent) organizations because those organizations have a similar position in the environment and thus follow similar goals, create similar products, target similar customers, and experience similar constraints (Burt 1987). Especially in uncertain situations, decision makers tend to succumb to mimetic pressures from the environment to economize search costs, to minimize experimentation costs, or to avoid risks of early adopters (e.g., Burt 1987; Cyert and March 1963; Teo et al. 2003).

Previous IS research revealed that the behavior of competitors exert considerable pressure on organizations, leading to mimetic adjustments of the organizations. For example, earlier studies demonstrated that the adoption of inter-organizational linkages by competitors induced mimetic pressure on organizations as soon as their decision makers perceived the adoption to be a competitive advantage for the competitors (e.g., Chwelos et al. 2001; Teo et al. 2003). In these studies, the mimetic pressure is typically directly conceptualized as competitive pressure. Since previous IT security studies found that the perceived ITSRs of the Cloud considerably inhibit organizational users' adoption decisions (e.g., Ackermann et al. 2012; Benlian and Hess 2011), an increased IT security level is generally a competitive edge for those providers. Hence, we expect that resulting competitive pressure significantly increases the perceived external pressure to increase the IT security of the service and ultimately, the decision makers' intention to implement the safeguards. In line with previous IS research, we thus hypothesize that:

H1.4d: The higher a provider's decision maker's perception of the competitive pressure to increase the level of IT security of his/her organization's Cloud service, the higher his/her perception of the external pressure exerted on his/her organization to increase the IT security level of the Cloud service.

3.1.4   Decision Makers' IT Security Risk Perceptions

Empirical evidence suggests that the perceived ITSRs significantly motivate people to adopt safeguarding measures (e.g., Liang and Xue 2010; Vance et al. 2012). In this study, we expect the decision makers' ITSR perceptions to considerably influence the results of the providers' IT security risk management. In general, risk perceptions were revealed to be important factors in many protection behavior models, like the health belief model (Janz and Becker 1984), protection motivation theory (Rogers 1975), and the precaution adoption process model (Weinstein and Sandman 1992). In this context, recent psychological research has conclusively demonstrated that the two established risk measures – absolute (e.g., "What is the risk that you will get a serious disease?") and comparative (e.g., "How does your risk of getting a serious disease compare with that of someone similar to you?") – are independently associated with affect, cognition and behavior. In this regard, previous studies have demonstrated that absolute risk perceptions and comparative risk perceptions explain different aspects of people's anxiety, worry and behavioral intentions. Furthermore, the results of these studies suggest that people are nearly equally responsive to comparative and absolute risk perceptions (e.g., Lipkus et al. 2000; Rose and Nagel 2013). Specifically, the measures are assumed to represent different domains of the overall construct of risk perception (e.g., Dillard et al. 2012; Zajac et al. 2006). As such, absolute risk assessments were typically demonstrated to have more direct effects on people's protection behaviors, whereas comparative risk assessments were found to influence the perceptions of situational factors and attitudes, such as their sensitivity to risk information, and attention to prevalent protection behaviors and general recommendations (e.g., Gold 2007; Klein 2003). Nevertheless, as comparative risk perceptions frequently strongly elevate worries and fears, the total effects on people's behavioral intentions were revealed in many cases to even exceed those of absolute risk perceptions (e.g., Dillard et al. 2012; Radcliffe and Klein 2002). Moreover, prior studies revealed that people even engage in protection behavior strategies to protect their favorable comparative statuses (e.g., Klein and Weinstein 1997). Previous psychological research argued that comparative risk assessments are frequently even more accurate than absolute estimates, because people's understanding of objective risk is limited and subject to various biases, like people's tendency to underestimate large risks and overestimate small risks (e.g., Rothman et al. 1996). As a result, people can in many cases more easily judge how their own risk compares with that of other people, regardless of the absolute risk level (Radcliffe and Klein 2002).

However, most of the early protection behavior theories only use absolute risk measures (e.g., Janz and Becker 1984; Rogers 1975). As studies in the IT security context and TTAT were built on these theories, the proposed theoretical model incorporates people's risk perception by merely utilizing absolute scales. According to recent findings in psychological research (e.g., Dillard et al. 2012; Klein 2003), these studies are thus likely to only partially capture people's risk perceptions and subsequently, only explain a part of people's intentions to implement safeguarding measures (e.g., Liang and Xue 2010; Woon et al. 2005).

Drawing on psychological risk perception research, we expect that the absolute and the comparative risk perception of the decision makers independently determine different aspects of the decisions to implement safeguards. First, we follow TTAT and expect that the absolute ITSR perceptions of the decision makers have direct effects on the outcome of the organizational IT security risk management. TTAT assumes that the absolute ITSR perception is shaped by the perceived susceptibility to the ITSR and its perceived severity. The perceived susceptibility is defined as a person's subjective assessment of the probability that an ITSR will negatively affect him or her, and the perceived severity is defined as the extent to which a person estimates that the negative consequences associated with the ITSR will be serious (Liang and Xue 2009). This definition matches that given by Cunningham (1967), who defined risk exposure as the probability of a negative outcome times the expected loss if the outcome is negative (see also Subsection 2.2.1). Strong empirical support for the importance of considering both the perceived susceptibility and the perceived severity of a risk when investigating protection behaviors comes from previous psychological research, which has demonstrated that people's perception of the susceptibility and their perception of the severity of a risk largely determine people's motivation to take precautionary actions. In particular, protection behavior models, like the health belief model (Janz and Becker 1984), protection motivation theory (Rogers 1975), analogously postulate that people's motivation to take precautions depends on the perceived probability that a negative situation will occur if no action is taken and the perceived severity of the situation.

In the IT security context, prior studies of the effects of the perceived susceptibility and the perceived severity on the people's protection motivation have obtained inconsistent results. The empirical studies conducted by Liang and Xue (2010) and Workman et al. (2008) demonstrated that both the perceived susceptibility and the perceived severity of the ITSRs have significant effects on users' IT security behavior. However, Johnston and Warkentin (2010) and Woon et al. (2005) also found that the perceived susceptibility to the ITSRs significantly influences people's intention to adopt safeguarding measures but found the perceived severity of the ITSR to have no significant effects. In contrast, Ng et al. (2009) only found the perceived severity of the ITSRs to determine users' IT security behavior.

Despite conflicting findings by previous IS research, we expect, in line with TTAT and risk perception theory, that the absolute perceptions of the organization's susceptibility to the ITSRs and the severity of the ITSRs for the organizations by its decision makers significantly affect the overall ITSR perception and ultimately, their decisions to implement safeguarding measures. At the organizational level, we suggest that the decision makers' perceived ITSR susceptibility is determined by the estimated likelihood that the organization's IT systems will be compromised by the ITSRs. Furthermore, we assume that the decision makers' perceived severity of an ITSR is determined by the estimation of the organization's overall financial loss, resulting from a potential compromise of its IT security. In this regard, previous IT security research revealed that monetary values are usually utilized to control the organizational IT security risk management. As such, the expected financial damage of an ITSR is frequently an important index (e.g., Sonnenreich et al. 2006). Altogether, based on the theoretical underpinnings presented above, we hypothesize that:

H1.5:   The higher a provider's decision maker's perception of the susceptibility of his/her organization's Cloud service to the IT security risks, the higher his/her perception of the overall IT security risk of his/her organization's Cloud service.

H1.6:   A provider's decision maker's perception of the severity of the IT security risks for his/her organization's Cloud service, the higher his/her perception of the overall IT security risk of his/her organization's Cloud service.

Second, drawing on risk perception theory, we additionally expect the decision makers' assessment of their own organization's IT security in comparison to that of the average competitor significantly affects their intention to implement safeguarding measures. However, we assume that the comparative ITSR perceptions have more indirect effects on the organizational IT security risk management, other than directly increasing the overall ITSR assessments and the intentions to implement safeguarding measures.

According to institutional theory research results, the mimetic pressure faced by organizations is a function of the decision makers' assessment of the extent of other similar organizations, which have already adopted a certain structure or behavior and the perceived success of these organizations due to the structure or behavior (Powell and DiMaggio 2012). In the organizational IT security context, as described above, we particularly expect that the mimetic pressure exerted by the organizations is largely equivalent to the competitive pressure. In line with findings of psychological risk perception research, we argue that the comparative risk rating represents the underlying perceptions of this function and subsequently explains downstream competitive pressure assessments made by the decision makers. In general, the comparative risk is measured by a person's assessment of his or her risk in relation to the risk of a comparison or referent group, typically a group of the same age, gender, location, or other attributes (e.g., Klein 2003). There are two types of comparative risk measures – direct comparative and indirect comparative – which differ in the way people are engaged in the comparison process. Both measures have been frequently utilized by previous psychological research (e.g., Harris and Smith 2005; Weinstein and Klein 1995). Direct comparative risk measures request a person to consider his or her own risk and the average others' risk, at the same time. Indirect comparative risk measures require separate assessments of one's own absolute risk and also others' absolute risk. Indirect comparative risk is then computed as a difference score (see detailed description of the comparative risk measures in Subsection 3.2.1.2). Regardless of whether direct or indirect measurement types are employed, the comparative risk can be interpreted as a difference between the perception of a person's own risk and the assessment of the risk of the referent group (own risk - average others' risk) (Ranby et al. 2010).

However, when assessing the average others' risk, people typically average over their assessments of each person's risk in the comparison group, who come to their minds (Aucote and Gold 2005). In general, the average is obtained by dividing the sum of a set of quantities by the number of quantities in the set. For example, as shown in Figure 3-3, when a decision maker has estimated the ITSR of all known competitors, the arithmetic mean represents the average competitor's ITSR exposure. Specifically, the arithmetic mean splits the comparison group into a number of competitors with higher ITSR, and with lower ITSR, than average. When a decision maker in the example perceive his or her organization to be at lower ITSR than the average competitor, he or she thinks of a certain number of competitors which are at higher ITSR than his or her organization (i.e., white area in Figure 3-3) but at the same time he or she thinks of a certain number of competitors which are at lower ITSR than the own organization (grey shaded area in Figure 3-3). Therefore, the lower the decision maker's comparative risk assessment (e.g., the decision maker may perceive his or her organization to be at average risk or worse), the higher the known number of competitors which are at lower ITSR than their own organization (i.e., black dotted line in Figure 3-3 moved to the left and the grey shaded area is enlarged).

As such, the comparative risk perception by the decision makers encompasses the knowledge about the number of competitors, which are at higher and at lower ITSR than their own organization. Therefore, the number of competitors which are at lower ITSR exposure than their own organization is logically equal to the extent of competitors which have a higher IT security level and thus, more (effective) safeguarding measures implemented than their own organization. As stated above, the competitive pressure on the organization exerted by the decision makers predominately stems from the extent of other similar organizations, which have already adopted a certain structure or behavior. Hence, the higher the perceived number of competitors with higher IT security levels, the higher the perceived competitive pressure to increase the organization's IT security level.

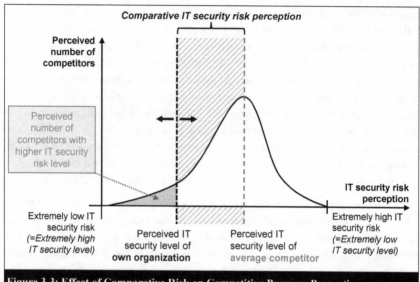

Figure 3-3: Effect of Comparative Risk on Competitive Pressure Perceptions

Altogether, according to the theoretical underpinnings as presented above, we expect that the decision makers' comparative risk perceptions induce competitive pressure, which, in turn, increases the decision makers' intentions to implement safeguard measures. Even if the preceding psychological studies are mainly focused on the effects of comparative risk susceptibility (e.g., Dillard et al. 2012), we assume that – similar to the absolute risk perceptions and as described above – the decision makers' assessments of their organization's susceptibility to the ITSRs in comparison to that of the average competitor as well as their evaluation of the severity of the ITSR for their own organization in comparison to the average competitor predict the overall comparative risk perception. Accordingly, following the same logic, we expect that both facets of the comparative ITSR assessment induce competitive pressure and propose that:

H1.7:   *The higher a provider's decision maker's perception of the susceptibility of his/her organization's Cloud service to IT security risks in comparison to the competitors, the higher his/her perceived competitive pressure to increase the level of IT security of his/her organization's Cloud service.*

H1.8:   *The higher a provider's decision maker's perception of the severity of the IT security risks for his/her organization's Cloud service in comparison to the competitors, the higher his/her perceived competitive pressure to increase the level of IT security of his/her organization's Cloud service.*

3.1.5   Unrealistic Optimism in Decision Makers' IT Security Risk Perceptions

In many cases, people tend to systematically underestimate their vulnerability to risks (Weinstein and Klein 1996). The underestimation of risks may stem from both motivational sources, like the desire to deny their own vulnerability to harm, or to present a favorable image, and from cognitive processes, like the overestimation of personal control, egocentric thinking, or misuse of the representativeness heuristic (Chambers and Windschitl 2004; Shepperd et al. 2002). Previous psychological studies labeled this phenomenon as unrealistic optimism (UO) and demonstrated it in a wide variety of negative events, ranging from natural disasters to project completion times (e.g., Buehler et al. 1994; Burger and Palmer 1992; Waters et al. 2011). As such, UO constitutes a serious threat, for example, by undermining preventive actions, interfering with precautionary behavior, and aggravating risk-seeking tendencies (e.g., Helweg-Larsen and Shepperd 2001; Weinstein and Klein 1996).

In general, UO can be viewed as the difference between the risk estimate a person makes for himself or herself and the risk estimate suggested by a relevant, objective standard, like epidemiological, base-rate data. Moreover, UO includes a person's overly favorable estimate of his or her risk, in comparison with others. As risk perceptions normally encompass two distinct perspectives (i.e., absolute and comparative risk), the bias may manifest itself in an underestimation of the absolute risk exposure as well as the comparison with others. The psychological literature typically distinguishes between two general and largely independent types of UO: absolute UO and comparative UO (Shepperd et al. 2013).

Absolute UO refers to the erroneous perception that personal negative outcomes, assessed on some form of absolute risk scale, are less risky than would be objectively expected. However, finding an objective standard to determine the accuracy of individual risk perception is typically the biggest challenge of this approach (Weinstein 1980). In this regard, as shown in Table 3-1, absolute UO has two forms. At the individual level, absolute UO occurs when a person's perception of his or her risk is lower than some personal objective standard. Previous psychological studies used personal outcomes that actually occurred at a later time (e.g., a person did have a heart attack some years later) or personal risk, as calculated from an empirically validated individualized risk-assessment algorithm (e.g., a risk calculator) as objective standards (e.g., a heart attack risk calculator that is based on the measurement of a person's known health risk factors) (e.g., Sharot et al. 2011; Strecher et al. 1995). As such, a person is asserted to display absolute UO if his or her perception is lower than the objective outcome prediction made by the risk algorithm, or other actuarial approaches, like models which are based on group data (Shepperd et al. 2013). Beside health-related risks such as cancer and heart attacks, previous psychological studies demonstrated individual absolute UO in very different situations, like the economy predictions of financial analysts or the estimation of task completion times by employees (e.g., Buehler et al. 1994; Calderon 1993).

Table 3-1: The Faces of Unrealistic Optimism

	Organization	Industry
Absolute	**Absolute Unrealistic Optimism – Organization** A decision maker assesses their own organization's ITSR to be lower than indicated by an objective standard for the organization (e.g., a decision maker estimates that the ITSR is 20% but a risk calculator scores it at 30%).	**Absolute Unrealistic Optimism – Industry** Decision makers provide ITSR assessments for their own organization. The average of these assessments is lower than the absolute ITSR of an industry-level objective standard (e.g., the average of the decision makers' ITSR assessments is 20% but the industry risk is 30%).
Source of Bias	Inaccuracies in own organization's ITSR assessments	
Comparative	**Comparative Unrealistic Optimism – Organization** A decision maker provides a comparative ITSR assessment that is lower than indicated by an individual-level comparative standard (e.g., a decision maker assesses that their own organization's ITSR is below average but a risk calculator says that it is above average).	**Comparative Unrealistic Optimism – Industry** Decision makers provide ITSR assessments that compare their organization's risk with that of their competitors. The average of these assessments is lower than the industry (e.g., on average, the decision makers assess that their own organization's ITSR is lower than that of the industry).
Source of Bias	Inaccuracies in own organization's ITSR assessments, comparative ITSR estimates, or both	

In contrast, at the group level, it is usually impossible to decide whether any given person's risk perception is subject to absolute UO or not (Weinstein and Klein 1996). However, objective group-level standards could oftentimes be found in cases where individual-level standards are undeterminable (Shepperd et al. 2013). A group of people is regarded as unrealistic when the average of their risk estimates is lower than a group-level objective standard, such as the base rate for an event in this group (e.g., the base rate for divorces in the U.S.) (Helweg-Larsen et al. 2011). At the group-level, researchers found strong evidence of absolute UO, for example, divorce, chlamydia, unwanted pregnancy, and human papillomavirus (e.g., Rothman et al. 1996; Weinstein and Lyon 1999).

Likewise, two forms of comparative UO can be distinguished. At the individual level, a person displays comparative UO when he or she underestimates his or her risk in comparison to other people. For example, a person may incorrectly judge that his/her risk of having a heart attack is below that of the average person of the same sex and age, even though data from an empirically validated individualized risk-assessment algorithm indicates his/her risk is actually above average. In this regard, for example, prior psychological research frequently utilizes the health risk appraisal (HRA) approach as a risk calculator, which uses epidemiological data, in conjunction with participant data, to calculate a person's 10-year mortality risk. By comparing an individual's HRA-calculated risks with the population average for that person's age and sex, these studies determined a person's objective comparative risk for a specific health problem (e.g., Radcliffe and Klein 2002). Using an objective standard to evaluate comparative risk assessments, previous psychological studies showed that people are unrealistically optimistic in various contexts, like experiencing serious drinking problems, or developing breast cancer (e.g., Dillard et al. 2009; Lipkus et al. 2005).

At the group-level, comparative UO refers to situations in which the average of all persons in a sample assess that they are less likely to experience a negative outcome than the average of their peers. Therefore, if all people perceive their risks are less than average, they are clearly making a systematic error, thus demonstrating comparative UO (Weinstein 1980). Since no objective is necessary to identify COU at the group-level, a large number of psychological studies were able to demonstrate people's comparative UO for a wide variety of negative events, such as drug addiction, asthma, food poisoning, and sunstroke (e.g., Weinstein 1987). Based on this approach, it is generally impossible to decide whether a given person displays comparative UO or not. However, the average difference between the assessments of the own risks and the assessments of the comparison target's risks allows for an analysis of the average underestimation of the comparative risk in a given sample (Weinstein and Klein 1996).

As the individual- and group-level approaches measure a bias in the risk assessments, relative to some objective standards or comparison targets, the psychological literature suspects the two forms are tapping the same underlying construct (Shepperd et al. 2013). In this regard, preceding psychological studies found individual- and group-level measures of absolute UO and comparative UO to be highly correlated and thus interchangeable (e.g., Lipkus et al. 2000). Differences between the two forms can be generally affiliated to measurement issues (Shepperd et al. 2013). In contrast, as the underlying risk estimates are generally independent (see Section 3.1.4), absolute and comparative UO are expected, by psychological literature, to largely reflect different constructs (Shepperd et al. 2013). Prior studies repeatedly demonstrated that people can be accurate in comparative estimates, irrespective of the accuracy of their absolute estimates, and vice versa. For example, studies showing that women overestimate their breast cancer risk independently revealed both absolute UO and comparative UO (e.g., Lipkus et al. 2005; Waters et al. 2011). However, absolute UO and comparative UO were demonstrated, by various studies, to have different consequences for people's protection behavior. As people are generally less likely to take precautionary actions if they perceive their absolute risk is low, absolute UO was repeatedly found to directly undermine preventive behaviors, like lower intentions to quit smoking or inadequate allocation of time to complete tasks (e.g., Buehler et al. 1994; Dillard et al. 2006). By contrast, previous psychological studies found comparative UO to be associated with more indirect and subtle consequences. For example, one study reported people with strong degrees of comparative UO about their risk of a heart attack to be less able to retain new information about the risk factors for heart disease, less sensitive for professional health recommendations, and less worried about having a heart attack (Radcliffe and Klein 2002). Furthermore, another study demonstrated that even people who had objective statistical data about the absolute risk of being involved in an automobile accident, had significantly lower intentions to utilize seat belts, to drive more slowly, and to use public transportation, when they were led to believe that their risk is lower than average (Klein 1997).

In the IT security context, prior research has revealed optimistic tendencies regarding the risks of Internet usage, the perception of IT-related risks among IS executives, and the assessment of ITSRs by Cloud providers' decision makers (Campbell et al. 2007; Loske et al. 2013; Rhee et al. 2012). However, these studies merely demonstrated the existence of comparative UO in the perception of ITSRs and did not explicitly examine its consequences. Moreover, none of these studies analyzed the existence of absolute UO and its effects on the adoption of safeguarding measures.

Drawing on UO literature, as shown in Table 3-1, we expect that both the comparative and the absolute ITSR perception of the providers' decision makers are subject to UO. In particular, as with all new technology developments, there is a lack of historical data regarding the impact and probability of ITSRs that would allow an objective quantification of the actual risk of the Cloud services with traditional risk analysis tools (e.g., Ackermann et al. 2012; Hopkin 2012). Additionally, IT security incidents in the Cloud often go undetected, unreported, or systematically undocumented, so that there is, typically, no quantitative data of the ITSRs available (Kankanhalli et al. 2003). In light of the unavailability of reliable quantified data about the ITSRs, the decision makers have to use other, less objective, sources to determine the exposure of their organization's service to certain ITSRs, like industry reports, security experts, and comparison of their own service to those of the average competitor (Straub and Welke 1998). For instance, if a certain safeguard is a de facto industry standard to prevent identity thefts, an accumulation of corresponding IT security incidents in the competitors' Cloud services would also indicate that their own organization's service is at high risk, as long as no improved safeguarding measures were implemented.

In particular, the less that quantified data exists, the more that the ITSR analysis phase depends on the subjective perceptions of the decision makers. Additionally, it is becoming increasingly difficult to verify the results of the ITSR analyses when less quantitative data is available. As such, for example, similar to causes of UO at the individual level (Shepperd et al. 2002), a decision maker's perception that their own service is better protected than average would not only increase his or her satisfaction regarding professional success but also help to present a more favorable image of their own service. Furthermore, previous studies have already demonstrated that decision accuracy is in many cases negatively influenced by IS managers' overconfidence (Vetter et al. 2011). In this context, previous IT security research found that an overestimation of their own organization's control over ITSRs by the decision makers is likely to cause a denial of risks (Loske et al. 2013). According to the theoretical underpinnings, as presented above, we expect that the comparative, as well as the absolute, ITSR perceptions of the decisions-makers are influenced by systematic errors, in terms of UO.

However, in contrast to the individual-level, organizational IT security risk management is typically described as a strategic decision process in the literature, so that it can be assumed that in many cases more than one person is involved in the decision-making (e.g., Cavusoglu et al. forthcoming; Straub and Welke 1998). Dependent on the rationality of all decision makers, previous research on strategic decision processes commonly found negotiated decisions to be affected by cognitive biases, like individual decisions (Schwenk 1985). In particular, prior studies revealed that the presence of multiple decision makers does not increase the likelihood that the group will recognize the lack of rationality in decisions. Moreover, group polarization and escalation of commitment were found to oftentimes increase the negative effects of cognitive biases on the rationality of decisions (e.g., Neale and Bazerman 1985). For example, previous management research found that organizational outcomes, like strategic choices and performance levels, are largely predicted by the characteristics and (biased) beliefs of all managers (e.g., Hambrick and Mason 1984). As such, we hypothesize that:

H1.9:   *Providers' decision makers' absolute perceptions of the IT security risks of their organizations' Cloud services are subject to Unrealistic Optimism.*

H1.10:   *Providers' decision makers' comparative perceptions of the IT security risks of their organizations' Cloud services are subject to Unrealistic Optimism.*

3.2   Research Methodology

The research methodology is presented in this section. We first show the measurement model of this study (Subsection 3.2.1). Then, the administration of the large-scale empirical study (Subsection 3.2.2) and the characteristics of the obtained sample are shown (Subsection 3.2.3). Finally, we present the techniques utilized to analyze the collected data in this study (Subsection 3.2.4).

3.2.1   Measurement Model

We examined our hypotheses by drawing on data from an empirical study of the ITSR perceptions of providers' decision makers and their beliefs, related to the organization's IT security risk management. Therefore, a questionnaire was developed and pretested by cognitive interviews (Bolton 1993) with five IS researchers and four IS professionals.

The first part of the questionnaire contained socio-demographics. In particular, since provider firms typically offer more than one service, we first asked the respondents to describe their organization's service that has created the most revenue last year (defined as the provider's primary service in the questionnaire) and to answer all following questions, with respect to this service. In this regard, the questionnaire contained a salient hint on the top of every page in order to remind the respondents to answer all questions regarding the organization's prima-ry service. As different application types are generally exposed to different ITSRs and thus require different protection levels, we afterwards asked the respondents for the application types of the primary service. Additionally, we asked for the organization of the IT security risk management of the primary service and its degree of formalization, ranging from event-triggered approaches to certified IT security risk management systems. Furthermore, we asked the respondents to state the IT security budget of the primary service, as a percentage of its overall IT budget, both for this year and the next year, the so-called IT security investment level (all socio-demographics are shown in Table A-1).

Then, the main part of the questionnaire contained the indicators, which are necessary to ana-lyze the ITSR perception of the decision makers, in terms of UO (see measurement approach-es below) followed by the indicators to estimate the proposed theoretical model regarding the effects of decision makers' ITSR perception on the IT security risk management of the pro-viders (all indicators shown in Table A-1). In particular, we developed an approach, which based on a comparison of all providers' IT security investments in relation to their decision makers' ITSR assessments in a representative sample, enabled us to classify whether the ab-solute ITSR perceptions of a decision maker are subject to UO or not (Subsection 3.2.1.1). Additionally, drawing on psychological literature, we present an established approach to measure the average degree of UO in the comparative risk assessments of Cloud providers' decision makers (Subsection 3.2.1.2).

Content validity was established by adopting validated measurement items from previous re-search studies, with minor changes in wording. Most of the indicators were measured using a seven-point Likert scale, with 1 referring to the lowest score (e.g., complete disagreement) and 7 to the highest score (e.g., complete agreement). To measure the comparative risk as-sessments, the participants were asked to complete sentences by choosing where their position lies on a 7-point scale between two bipolar adjectives. The IT security investment levels were measured in percentage values (all scales are shown in Table A-1).

3.2.1.1 Measurement of Absolute Unrealistic Optimism

Absolute UO refers to the erroneous perception that the exposure of their own organization's service to the ITSRs is lower than is objectively warranted. Since the actual ITSR of a service is generally unknown, finding an objective standard to determine the accuracy of people's absolute risk perceptions is, typically, very difficult (e.g., Weinstein 1980). In particular, for a standard to be useful, the objective indicator must apply to the specific respondents being studied, so that quantitative data about the overall risk – like the average likelihood of a certain IT security incident in the industry – is usually not sufficient (e.g., Shepperd et al. 2013). As there is no quantified data about the ITSR exposure of a given provider, we followed an approach of previous psychological research and utilized the results of an empirically validated individualized risk-assessment algorithm, instead of an objective standard, to evaluate the accuracy of the decision makers' ITSR perceptions (e.g., Kreuter and Strecher 1995; Radcliffe and Klein 2002).

Therefore, we developed a classifier, which, based on a given provider's financial efforts to protect its service in comparison to those of the other providers, enabled us to decide whether the ITSR perceptions of a given decision maker can be viewed as accurate or not. As such, the provider's current IT security investments, in relation to those of other providers, function as a proxy for the service's actual protection against the ITSRs, in relation to that of other providers, which, in turn, can be used to estimate a given provider's relative actual exposure to the ITSRs. In particular, we categorize a provider's decision maker's perception as unrealistic if s/he estimates his or her own organization's service to be significantly better protected than other providers' decision makers assess their service, even though the other providers' IT security investments, and thus their actual protections against the ITSRs, are considerably higher.

To measure the provider's IT security investments, we utilized the so-called IT security investment level, which is defined as the provider's IT security investment concerning the protection of its service, in relation to its service's overall IT investments (e.g., Cavusoglu et al. 2004b). The IT security investment level is well-established in organizational IT security risk management research and is also a frequently used index in practice (e.g., Cavusoglu et al. 2008; Karofsky 2001). Accordingly, it is very likely to be known by the providers' decision maker, who is responsible for the organization service's IT security, and thus is especially not perceived by the decision makers. Additionally, previous research revealed retrospective reports of strategic level managers having in general, a significantly higher accuracy when numeric values are stated, in comparison with psychosocial and behavioral outcome variables (e.g., Huber and Power 1985). In this context, a psychological state of discomfort typically arises when wrong statements regarding theoretically verifiable values are reported (e.g., Bernard et al. 1984). Besides, online survey technologies provide more privacy in the self-reporting process, which, typically, enhance the accuracy of self-reports, particularly regarding sensitive information (Fan et al. 2006). Since the respondents in this study were informed that all data was anonymously collected and processed and it is impossible to draw inferences from the answers about the participating organization, there was no particular motivation for the decision makers to deliberately state wrong values. Altogether, we expect that the IT security investment level is unlikely to be significantly influenced by decision makers' motivated or unmotivated cognitive biases, such as UO.

In line with findings of previous research in the field of IT security, we expect the IT security investment level to be an adequate proxy for the providers' actual protection level (Cavusoglu et al. 2008; Sonnenreich et al. 2006). However, it had to be assumed that different application types of Cloud services principally require different protection levels (Jansen and Grance 2011) and accordingly, dissimilar IT security investment levels. For example, due to the criticality of the assets and legal regulations, financial and accounting applications may generally require considerably more safeguarding measures than office applications in the Cloud. Accordingly, the proposed classifier only compares the IT security investment levels, in relation to the decision makers' absolute ITSR assessments of those organizations, which provide services of the same application type. Nonetheless, the validity of the IT security investment level, as an objective indicator of the Cloud providers' actual ITSR exposure, is based on three additional assumptions.[2]

First, it had to be assumed that a higher IT security investment level, on average, results in a lower probability of an IT security incident. Due to the non-availability of quantified data in the context of the Cloud, the exact level of protection against the ITSRs that can be reached with a certain IT security investment level is unknown. Nevertheless, it can be generally expected that IT security investments exhibit a diminishing marginal return in reducing the vulnerability to the ITSRs (Cavusoglu et al. 2008). As the proposed classifier is based on comparisons of IT security investment levels, it does not impose any additional assumptions regarding the type of correlation of the IT security investment level and the resulting protection level.

However, to allow for a comparison of the IT security investment levels, the approach requires that the same IT security investment level equals the same level of protection among all providers. In this regard, the service characteristics (e.g., different number of customers) influence the IT security investment that is required to ensure the protection of a service (Cavusoglu et al. 2008). For example, in comparison with a large and widely-used service, a relatively new service with a few customers will, on average, require significantly less IT infrastructure, which has to be protected against, for example, fire, overheating, damage due to water, overvoltage and power failure. Thus, a smaller service is, on average, equally protected against the ITSRs with a lower IT security investment than a large service. This relationship applies to most of the IT security recommendations put forward for Cloud providers (e.g.,

---

[2] Please note: The validity of the assumptions is tested together with the analysis of the results regarding the existence of absolute UO in the ITSR perceptions of the decision makers in Subsection 3.3.2.1.

Federal Office for Information Security 2011). Accordingly, the necessary effort for Cloud providers to implement IT security measures directly depends on the size of the services. As the (overall) IT investment of a service, which is the denominator of the IT security invest-ment level, also varies in relation to the service's characteristics, we follow the line of reason-ing of previous IT security research (e.g., Cavusoglu et al. 2008) and assume that the IT secu-rity investment level will remain constant and subsequently, compensate differences in the sizes of the analyzed services.

Second, we assume that continuous IT security investments by the providers are necessary to ensure enduring protection of the services. In particular, due to the fast development of both the services and the ITSRs, a constant adjustment of the organization's IT security risk man-agement is generally needed, for example, the replacement of outdated or obsolete IT security controls or the implementation of additional IT security controls against newly discovered IT security threats. Accordingly, we assume that providers will have to continuously invest in the IT security in order to ensure the protection of its service, which is also supported by findings of previous IT security research (e.g., Gordon and Loeb 2002). Specifically, a very high IT security investment level in the past, without corresponding follow-up IT security invest-ments, does not result in a sustainable high protection level against the risks in the highly dy-namic IT security context.

Third, we expect that a given provider is generally not able to invest its IT security budget more effectively than any other provider. Otherwise, a provider with a lower IT security in-vestment level could actually attain a higher level of protection against the ITSR than a pro-vider with a higher investment level. Accordingly, this provider's decision maker's assess-ment that the organization's service is at low ITSR would wrongly be classified as inaccurate. This assumption is also commonly used in IT security studies (e.g., in mathematical optimiza-tion models for the optimal IT security level) (e.g., Ackermann et al. 2013; Cavusoglu et al. 2008; Sonnenreich et al. 2006).

In the following, we present an example of the classifier's method of operation. As shown in Figure 3-4, a given provider i's decision maker perceives his or her organization's service to be at higher protection than 70% of the other decision makers' assessment of their organiza-tion's service (Perceived Protection Ranking). In line with previous IT security research (e.g., Goodhue and Straub 1991), the perceived protection was measured in terms of decision mak-ers' perceived ITSR so that the example provider i's decision maker also perceives his or her organization's service to be at lower ITSR than 70% of the other decision makers would as-sess the ITSR of their own organizations' services. Accordingly, provider i should also have a higher IT security level than 70% of the other providers (Calculated Protection Ranking). Since it had to be assumed that every provider generally utilized a compound of different IT security measures to protect its service, the same IT security investment level might create slightly different protection levels. Hence, the proposed classifier includes a threshold of error regarding the difference between the perceived and the calculated protection level of a provider, in order to compensate for the fact that one provider might have slightly superior safeguarding measures implemented. The presented example is based on a threshold of 10%.

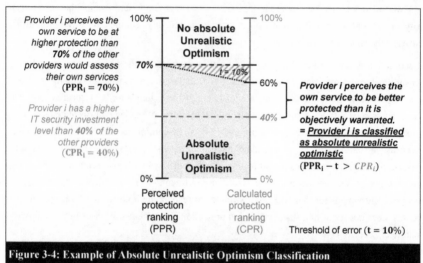

Figure 3-4: Example of Absolute Unrealistic Optimism Classification

Due to the threshold, the perception of the service protection by the decision maker would thus not be classified as unrealistic optimistic if provider i's IT security investment level is higher than that of at least 60% of the other providers. In this context, even if the ITSR perceptions of all decision makers are universally biased in terms of UO, the proposed classifier would nevertheless identify the decision makers' perceptions with a significantly higher degree of UO than the other decision makers. In particular, since the utilized approach is based on the relative ranking of the ITSR perception instead of absolute values, its manner of functioning cannot be affected by universal biases. However, in the presented example, provider i has an IT security investment level, which is only higher than that of 40% of the other providers. Hence, the calculated protection level of provider i falls considerably short of the perceived protection level by the decision maker. As a result, the assessment of provider i's decision maker is classified as unrealistic optimistic.

In the following, we present the mathematical implementation of the classifier as used in the study (see also Table 3-2). It categorizes a provider i as unrealistic optimistic if the decision maker's Perceived Protection Ranking (PPR_i) minus the threshold of error (t) is greater than the Calculated Protection Ranking (CPR_i) of this provider (1).

(1) $UO_i = \begin{cases} 1, & PPR_i - t > CPR_i \\ 0, & otherwise \end{cases}$

PPR_i was defined as the absolute number of the set of providers with the same application type as i whose decision makers perceive their service to be at higher ITSR than the decision maker of i in relation to the absolute number of the result of function $A(i)$ (set of providers with the same application type as i) (2).

(2) $PPR_i = \dfrac{|\{j|R_j > R_i; \forall j \in A(i)\}|}{|A(i)|}$

Similarly, CPR_i was defined as the absolute number of the set of providers with the same application type as i that have a lower IT security investment level than i in relation to the absolute number of the result of function $A(i)$ (3).

(3) $CPR_i = \dfrac{|\{j|B_j < B_i; \forall j \in A(i)\}|}{|A(i)|}$

$A(i)$ is a function that returns the set of providers with the same application type as i (4).

(4) $A(i) = A_l$ with $i \in A_l$ and $l \in \{1 \dots k\}$

Table 3-2: Variables of the Classifier for Absolute Unrealistic Optimism	
Variable	**Description**
$0 \leq t \in \mathbb{R} \leq 1$	Threshold of UO-Classifier
A	Set of all providers
$i, j \in A$	Provider
$k \in \mathbb{N}$	Number of application types
$l \in \{1 \dots k\}$	Application type
$A_l \subseteq A$	Set of providers with application type l
$R_i \in \mathbb{R}$	Average IT security perception of provider i
$B_i \in \mathbb{R}$	Relative IT security budget of provider i
$A(i): A \rightarrow A$	Set of providers with the same application type as provider i
$0 \leq CPR_i \in \mathbb{R} \leq 1$	Percentage of providers with same application type and lower IT security investment level than provider i (high = higher IT security investment level)
$0 \leq PPR_i \in \mathbb{R} \leq 1$	Percentage of providers with same application type and lower perceived protection against the IT security risks than provider i (high = higher perceived protection)
$AUO_i \in \{0,1\}$	absolute UO classification of provider i

3.2.1.2 Measurement of Comparative Unrealistic Optimism

In general, there are two ways to measure a person's perceived risk in comparison to that of a peer: the direct method and the indirect measurement method (Chambers and Windschitl 2004; Helweg-Larsen and Shepperd 2001). The direct method involves a single question, in which a respondent directly compares his or her risk with that of a specified peer. The indirect method involves two separate absolute questions about their own risk and a specified peer's risk. The difference between their absolute own risk perception and the assessment of the comparison target represents a person's perceived comparative risk standing. Since the direct and indirect measurement methods were found to have certain advantages and disadvantages (Rose 2010), we followed recommendations of psychological research approaches (e.g., Shepperd et al. 2002) and utilized both methods in this study. In particular, the direct method was revealed by prior studies to be a better predictor of people's beliefs and intentions, induced by the comparative risk assessments (e.g., Aucote and Gold 2005). In particular, the calculation of differences between their own risk perception and the assessment of the comparison target's risk is associated with theoretical uncertainties that may, in some cases, reduce the predictive utility of indirect measures (Rose 2010). Accordingly, we utilized the direct method to analyze the effects of the decision makers' comparative ITSR assessments on the providers' IT security risk management. Nevertheless, due to the determination of differentiated values for self-perception as well as peer assessment, the indirect method enables researchers to conduct further analyses of the underlying cognitive processes (Weinstein 1982). As such, in order to strengthen validity and reliability of the results, we used both methods to investigate the existence of comparative UO in the decision makers' ITSR perceptions.

Since the social distance may significantly influence the extent of CO and comparability of the results, a clear definition of the peer is generally crucial for the survey design (Shepperd et al. 2002). In this study, the average competitor was chosen as their own organization's peer. The average competitor was defined as a provider with similar application types and specifications, in the same market segment. In this way, the social distance can be fixed and the risk evaluation can be related to equivalent objects of comparison. Thus, even distinct offerings can be compared in absolute terms (Karakayali 2009).

We followed Weinstein (1980)'s approach to studying the decision makers' comparative UO at the group level and asked participants to estimate exposure of their own service to ITSRs in comparison to their average competitors who offer the same applications and use the same delivery models. The approach of comparing a group's own risk perceptions with their perceptions of a peer group – the average persons exposed to the same risk, such as the average smokers of the same sex and age – allows us to analyze whether or not there is UO in the risk perceptions of a group. For example, if the risk perceptions of a representative smoker group are unbiased, the smokers should, on average, perceive to be at the same risk as the average smoker, because, on average, smokers cannot be at lower risk than the average smoker. In other words, if all people perceive their risk of experiencing a negative event to be less than average, they are clearly making a systematic error, thus demonstrating UO (Weinstein 1980). Accordingly, if the decision makers' ITSR perception is unaffected by UO, the mean differences of the assessment of their own organization's service and that of their average competitor's service should be close to zero. If not, it indicates that the ITSR perceptions of providers' decision makers are subject to a systematic bias, because, on average, not all providers can be at lower ITSR than all other providers.

3.2.2   Survey Administration

We identified 3104 SaaS providers based in North America in the ISVW global software industry database. To support the external validity of our study, we did not constrain the sample to specific application types or to providers of a specific organizational size. Decision makers in charge of the IT security of the providers' service were identified via an online social business network and an online search. As far as information was available, we directly contacted the responsible IT security manager or CIO. The invitation was sent via mail and e-mail, including a short study description. Participation was further encouraged by offering a results' report, including an overview of competitors' risk assessments, and a raffle for a tablet device. For some small providers, only the CEO could be identified. As the case may be that the CEO is not directly responsible for the IT security of the organization's service, we additionally asked, in these cases, that our request be forwarded to the person in charge. The questionnaire was distributed through an online survey system.

The data collection of the study took place between February 16 and March 25, 2014. After completion of the first half of the data collection period, all known contacts were reminded of the study via e-mail. One week before the end of the data collection period, another e-mail was sent to the contacts. At the end of the study timeframe, we had received 191 completed data sets (response rate: 6.15%). This response rate is satisfactory considering the difficulties in obtaining survey responses from IS executives and corporate-level managers (e.g., Poppo and Zenger 2002). Due to missing data and low data quality, we had to exclude 14 responses from the sample. In particular, we only used data sets without missing values for calculations so that all questionnaires which were not fully completed by participants were excluded.

3.2.3   Sample Characteristics

Thus, the results presented in this article are based on a final sample size of 177 valid responses. More than 50% of all respondents were CIOs, IT security managers, or IT security specialists. Another 36% of the respondents were CEOs or other IT managers with authority to decide. A total of 89% of the respondents answered that they were directly responsible for the IT security of their organization's primary service (see sample characteristics in Table 3-3). The distribution of organization sizes and offered application types was similar to the average of the Cloud market (Velten and Janata 2011), which points to a good representative status of the obtained sample.

As shown in Table 3-3, the organization of the service's IT security risk management was revealed to have, on average, a rather low degree of formalization. In particular, most of the providers predominately followed an event-triggered (23.9%) or best-practice (28.9%) approach to control their IT security risk management. This is especially important, because the implementation of safeguarding measures in these cases directly depends on the experience, knowledge, and ITSR assessments of the providers' decision makers. Thus, potential systematic errors are likely to have more impact on the effectivity of those providers' IT security risk management. However, in comparison, only a small proportion of the providers operated uncertified (9.9%) or completely certified (8.8%) information security management systems (ISMS), which mitigate the influence of decision makers' subjective assessments. Besides, a considerable amount of providers used standardized procedures, which are internally defined within the organization to control the service's IT security risk management (24.4%).

Although the comparison of the respondents' characteristics with those of the original target sample did not show major differences, we conducted further analysis for possible nonresponse bias. We followed Armstrong and Overton (1977)'s approach and compared the first 25% with the last 25% of the received answers in order to examine if the participants' interest in the topic had any effects. We could not identify significant differences among the responses in the considered variables, utilizing t-tests. We also performed a series of chi-square comparisons, which also showed no significant differences between early and late responses. Besides, we received 134 e-mails of contact persons who were not allowed to, or did not want to, take part in the study. In particular, the most important reasons for nonparticipation were that organizational policies generally forbid taking part in surveys for security reasons, or the contacted decision maker was too busy to participate.

Given the single method used to collect the data, we conducted a series of common method bias (CMB) tests. We performed Harman's single factor test with principal axis factoring and a restriction of the extracted factors to one. The results showed that a single factor accounted for only 28% of the total variance, which is well below the critical value of 50% (Podsakoff et al. 2003). Additionally, we used a CMB marker variable approach and included two marker items in each questionnaire, which are unrelated to our research model but are subject to the same measurement effects (e.g., "my needs and desires are taken into account in planning the company's benefit program"). The CMB markers had the smallest correlation with all other manifest measures in our data set (Rönkkö and Ylitalo 2011). Accordingly, all tests suggest that CMB is unlikely to have significant effects on our analyses and results.

Table 3-3: Sample Characteristics of the IT Security Risk Management Study

Category	%	Category	%
Size of organization (employees)	%	Participant position	%
Small (< 50)	28.3%	CEO	23.7%
Medium (50 - 249)	45.7%	CIO	13.0%
Corporation (> 249)	26.0%	IT security manager	20.3%
Organization revenue (U.S. Dollars)	%	IT security specialist	16.9%
< 1.000.000	14.7%	IT manager	13.0%
1.000.001 - 5.000.000	15.8%	Business manager / COO	8.5%
5.000.001 - 10.000.000	10.7%	Other manager	4.5%
10.000.001 - 25.000.000	16.4%	IT security investment level	%
25.000.001 - 50.000.000	24.9%	Communication and collaboration	20.4%
> 50.000.000	17.5%	Customer relationship management	18.7%
Service application type (SaaS)	%	Business process management	22.4%
Communication and collaboration	16.9%	Financial / Accounting solutions	34.0%
Customer relationship management	8.5%	Web / E-commerce solutions	13.8%
Business process management	6.2%	Supply chain management	25.8%
Financial / Accounting solutions	9.0%	Project / Knowledge management	26.2%
Web / E-commerce solutions	8.5%	Human resource management	26.9%
Supply chain management	10.2%	Content / Document management	20.3%
Project / Knowledge management	6.8%	Office solutions	9.1%
Human resource management	7.3%	Enterprise resource planning	27.1%
Content / Document management	8.5%	IT security risk management form	%
Office solutions	10.7%	Event triggered	23.9%
Enterprise resource planning	7.3%	Best practice	28.9%
Participant experience	%	Corporate procedures	24.4%
1 year or less	9.6%	Uncertified ISMS	9.9%
2 - 5 years	37.3%	Certified ISMS	8.8%
6 - 10 years	18.1%	Other security management system	4.0%
11 years or more	35.0%		

Please note: n=177.

3.2.4   Data Analyses

All hypotheses regarding the effects of decision makers' subjective ITSR perceptions on the providers' IT security risk management (H1.1 – H1.8) were tested collectively using a partial least squares (PLS) analysis approach, which simultaneously assesses the reliability and validity of the measures of theoretical constructs and estimates the relationships among these constructs (Ringle et al. 2005).

PLS is a variance-based approach that maximizes the explained variance of the constructs by estimating partial model relationships in an iterative series of ordinary least squares regressions. In general, PLS is recommended in an early stage of theoretical development in order to test and validate exploratory models. Furthermore, the PLS technique is best suited for prediction-oriented research with the focus on the explanation of endogenous constructs (Hair et al. 2012). Besides, PLS has modest requirements regarding sample size, in comparison with covariance-based structural equation modelling (CB-SEMs) approaches (Reinartz et al. 2009). For this study, the PLS technique is appropriate and well-suited because of its prediction-oriented character and the obtained sample size. In particular, this survey is the first large-scale test of the proposed theoretical model that explicates the role of decision makers' subjective perceptions in the providers' IT security risk management. Hence, the research model is not based on "strong theory", as required by covariance-based approaches, like LISREL (Goodhue et al. 2006). Additionally, some of the constructs in the model are multidimensional – formative first-order, reflective second-order constructs – which cannot be adequately modeled using covariance structure analysis due to the assumptions it imposes (Polites et al. 2012). With its component-based approach, PLS can estimate these kinds of hierarchical construct models (Wetzels et al. 2009).

Moreover, with n=177, the sample size of this study is substantially above the rule of thumb for robust PLS estimations that requires a minimum sample size of ten times the maximum number of paths pointing at any variable (Barclay et al. 1995; Hair et al. 2012). Since this rule of thumb is generally controversially discussed and the suggested sample size was in many cases found to be too small to obtain a sufficient statistical power (e.g., Goodhue et al. 2012), we followed recommendations of established SEM guidelines and used Cohen (1992)'s statistical power approach to determine the minimum necessary sample size. According to this approach, to attain statistical power with a medium population effect size of $\beta > 0.15$, a minimum significance criterion of $\alpha = 0.05$, and 10 independent variables, a minimum sample size of n=118 would be sufficient in this study.

Although PLS, in contrast to covariance-based approaches, does not impose any assumptions regarding the distribution of the sample and previous research has shown its robustness in cases of non-normal data (Reinartz et al. 2009), guidelines for PLS use nevertheless suggest firstly checking data distribution for extreme values of non-normality (Hair et al. 2012; Ringle et al. 2012). West et al. (1995) recommends that absolute skew values of >2 and kurtosis values >7 are an indicator for substantial deviation from normality. In the obtained sample, we found only a small deviation from normality distribution (up to skew 1.6 and kurtosis 5.9), which is unlikely to cause problems in the data analysis.

The hypothesis regarding the existence of absolute UO (H1.9) was tested with descriptive analyses of the differences in the perceptions between those providers' decision makers whose absolute ITSR perceptions were classified as unrealistic and those whose absolute ITSR estimates were classified as not unrealistic. The hypothesis that the decision makers' ITSR perceptions are subject to comparative UO (H1.10) was tested with descriptive analyses of the scores of the ITSR assessments in the obtained sample.

3.3   Results

In this section, the results of the data analyses are presented. We first analyzed the effects of providers' decision makers' ITSR perceptions on the IT security risk management (Subsection 3.3.1). Afterwards, we investigated the existence of UO in the decision makers' ITSR perceptions (Subsection 3.3.2). The combination of these results enabled us to draw conclusions regarding the inhibiting effects of UO in the decision makers' ITSR perception on the outcome of the organizational IT security risk management (see next section).

3.3.1   Impacts of Decision Makers' IT Security Risk Perceptions on Providers' IT Security Risk Management

In this subsection, we assess the validity of the measurement model (Subsection 3.3.1.1). Then, we show the results of the empirical testing of the theoretical model concerning the role of decision makers' ITSR perceptions in the providers' IT security risk management (Subsection 3.3.1.2).

3.3.1.1   Assessment of Measurement Validation

According to established guidelines for PLS use (Ringle et al. 2012), we first tested the reliability and validity of the reflective multi-item measures. As shown in Table 3-4, with the exception of the competitive pressure to increase IT security level, Cronbach's alpha (CA) of all constructs was between 0.84 (Enacted customer power to increase level of IT security) and 0.98 (Overall IT security risk), which clearly exceeded the suggested minimum of 0.7 (Nunnally 1978). The CA of competitive pressure was 0.67, which is slightly below the proposed threshold. However, especially in cases of rather small sample sizes (i.e. <200) and strong theory (competitive pressure is based on the well-established institutional theory and was measured based on Chwelos et al. (2001)), CA values above 0.6 are generally regarded as acceptable, in terms of internal consistency (e.g., Hair et al. 2006; Moss et al. 1998; Nagpal et al. 2010).

The Composite Reliability (CR) values of all constructs ranged from 0.60 (Competitive pressure to increase IT security level) to 0.94 (Overall IT security risk), which is above the recommended cut-off value of 0.6 (Bagozzi and Yi 1988). These results point to strong internal consistency and reliability of our measures.

Furthermore, the convergent validity of the constructs was evaluated by calculating the average variance extracted (AVE) value. All constructs have an AVE between 0.77 (Competitive pressure to increase IT security level) and 0.97 (Overall IT security risk), which met the suggested threshold value of greater than 0.5 (Fornell and Larcker 1981). Additionally, the validity of the individual indicators was assessed by examining the relationships between each indicator and its assumed latent construct. All completely standardized factor loadings were found to be greater than 0.6 and statistically significant at the p<0.001 level (Chin 1998). Overall, these results suggest convergent validity of the used constructs.

Table 3-4: Assessment of the IT Security Risk Management Measurement Model

Construct	Factor Loadings	Cronbach's alpha	Composite reliability	Square roots of average variance extracted
AVOID_COST	0.87-0.94	0.93	0.81	0.90
AVOID_EFF	0.88-0.96	0.94	0.84	0.91
AVOID_FEA	0.90-0.97	0.95	0.85	0.92
CITSR_SEV	0.83-0.94	0.89	0.74	0.86
CITSR_SUS	0.91-0.95	0.94	0.83	0.91
EP_CDEP	0.79-0.89	0.87	0.70	0.84
EP_COMP	0.56-0.86	0.67	0.80	0.77
EP_CPWR	0.80-0.86	0.84	0.64	0.80
EP_IND	0.88-0.93	0.90	0.82	0.91
IIITSL	0.89-0.96	0.91	0.76	0.87
ITSR	0.96-0.98	0.98	0.94	0.97
ITSR_SEV	0.92-0.96	0.96	0.89	0.95
ITSR_SUS	0.91-0.95	0.95	0.85	0.92

Please note: n=177. Constructs: AVOID_COST = Costs to increase IT security level, AVOID_EFF = Effectiveness of increased IT security level, AVOID_FEA = Feasibility to increase IT security level, CITSR_SEV = Comparative IT security risk severity, CITSR_SUS = Comparative IT security risk susceptibility, EP_CDEP = Dependency on existing customer relationships, EP_COMP = Competitive pressure to increase IT security level, EP_CPWR = Enacted customer power to increase IT security level, EP_IND = Industry pressure to increase IT security level, IIITSL = Intention to increase IT security level, ITSR = IT security risk, ITSR_SEV = IT security risk severity, ITSR_SUS = IT security risk susceptibility.

We followed a bootstrapping approach for assessing discriminant validity in variance-based structural equation modeling by calculating confidence intervals for the heterotrait-monotrait (HTMT) ratios of the correlations between all possible combinations of constructs and 5,000 resamples. The approach was found to identify a lack of discriminant validity at high sensitivity rates (Henseler et al. 2014). As none of the 45 estimated HTMT intervals contained the value 1, the true correlation between all constructs is most likely different from one, indicating that they are different constructs. Moreover, all estimated absolute HTMT values were significantly below the recommended conservative threshold of 0.85, pointing to the latent variables' excellent divergent validity (Henseler et al. 2014). Additionally, the factor loadings (loadings in Table 3-4) of our reflective indicators were higher, with regard to their conceptually corresponding constructs, than with regard to any other construct, thereby further supporting our constructs' discriminant validity (MacKenzie et al. 2011). As the square roots of AVE (see Table 3-4) of the indicators within a construct were always higher than their correlation with any other construct (see Table A-2), all constructs additionally fulfilled Fornell and Larcker (1981)'s criterion of discriminant validity.

Additionally, we followed O'Brien (2007)'s approach to test if our results suffer from any multicollinearity problems. Utilizing a series of ordinary least squares (OLS) regression analyses, and calculated the variance inflation factors (VIFs) for every possible combination of constructs as dependent and independent variables. Since all VIFs ranged between 1.01 and 1.71, which is well below the recommended threshold value of 2, we found no indication of multicollinearity.

3.3.1.2 Results of the Structural Model Testing

We tested our hypotheses by examining the path significance of each hypothesized association in the research model (see Figure 3-2), together with the explained variance (R^2 value) of each construct (Ringle et al. 2012). Therefore, a PLS bootstrapping technique with no sign changes and 5,000 resamples, consisting of the same number of cases as in the original sample, was utilized to determine the statistical significance of the path estimates (Hair et al. 2012).

As presented in Figure 3-5, the decision makers' perceptions of their own organizations' service's ITSR were revealed to strongly influence their intentions to increase their service's IT security levels ($\beta=0.329$; $p<0.001$), thereby supporting Hypothesis H1.1.

The providers' decision makers' assessments of the avoidability of the ITSRs, by using additional safeguards, was found to considerably influence their decisions to increase the IT security levels of their organization's service ($\beta=0.319$; $p<0.01$).[3] Hence, Hypothesis H1.2 is supported. Specifically, the costs associated with an increase of the IT security level were re-

---

[3] Please note: The decision makers' perceived avoidability of the ITSR by an increased IT security level is theoretically a broad construct, encompassing many different assessments. According to the theoretical underpinnings, as presented above, it can be completely captured by its three sub-dimensions: perceived effectiveness of the increased IT security level; perceived feasibility to increase the IT security level; and estimated costs of an increased IT security level. In the proposed theoretical model, the perceived avoidability of the ITSR was operationalized as a reflective first-order, formative second-order construct. In this form of multidimensional construct, the dimensions are algebraically aggregated to form a construct, while the indicators of each dimension are different manifestations of their respective dimensions (Polites et al. 2012). In other words, the construct is a theoretical abstraction that related the three sub-dimensions to each other and thus provides a holistic representation of the decision makers' perceived avoidability of the ITSRs.

vealed to play a significant role in the formation of the decision makers' assessments of the avoidability of the ITSRs (β=-0.654; p<0.001). Additionally, the decision makers' perceptions of the effectiveness of an increased IT security level were found to strongly influence their assessments of the ITSR avoidability (β=0.661; p<0.001). In comparison, the assessments of the organization's feasibility to increase the IT security levels were found to have limited influence on the formation of the providers' decision makers' perceptions of the avoidability of the ITSRs by increasing the IT security levels (β=0.397; p<0.05). Accordingly, Hypotheses H1.2a - H1.2c were found to be supported.

Altogether, these results thus confirmed the central role of decision makers' ITSR perceptions, along with their coping assessments, in the providers' IT security risk management processes. In this context, results of previous IT security risk management research submit that the risk analysis is typically placed as a bridge between the IT security threat identification and the analysis of available safeguarding measures (e.g., Straub and Welke 1998). In support of Hypothesis H1.3, further analyses thus showed that the decision makers' perceptions of the ITSRs are an important moderator of the relationship between their assessments of the avoidability of the ITSRs and their decisions to increase the IT security levels of their organization's service. More precisely, when the decision makers perceive their organization's service to be at higher ITSR, the relationship between their assessments of the ITSR avoidability and their intentions to increase the IT security levels of their organization's service was found to be largely increased (β_M=0.161; p<0.01).

Beyond that, the perceived external pressure to increase the IT security level was revealed to significantly elevate the providers' decision makers' intentions to increase the IT security levels and subsequently, to have strong influence on the outcomes of the IT security risk management (β=0.245; p<0.01), [4] confirming Hypothesis H1.4. Specifically, the enacted customer powers to urge the providers to increase their service's IT security levels were found to be a strong driver and significantly influence the formation of decision makers' perceptions of the external pressure (β=0.397; p<0.001). The providers' assessment of their organization's dependencies on the existing customer relationships was also confirmed to be a significant aspect of the decision makers' assessments of the external pressure faced by their organization

---

[4]   According to institutional theory, the perceived external pressure is generally formed by mimetic, coercive, and normative pressure appraisals. Therefore, each dimension represents one clearly defined aspect of the overall external pressure. Accordingly, the higher the perceived pressure in each of the dimensions, the higher the overall pressure faced by the decision makers to adopt certain behaviors or structures (e.g., Teo et al. 2003). In order to holistically capture the nature of external pressure, previous IS research typically operationalized it as a reflective first-order, formative second-order construct, which algebraically combines all pressure dimensions to an overall abstraction (e.g., Chwelos et al. 2001). In this study, we follow this approach to operationalize the external pressure exerted by the providers' decision makers as a multidimensional construct with the pressure dimensions as manifest indicators.

(β=0.214; p<0.001). Additionally, the IT security standards and recommendations published by industry organizations were found to have a significant impact on external pressure to increase the IT security levels of their organization's service, as perceived by the providers' decision makers (β=0.317; p<0.001). Furthermore, the IT security behavior of the direct competitors was revealed to be the most important factor exerting external pressure on the providers' decision makers to increase their organization service's IT security levels (β=0.437; p<0.001). Accordingly, all external factors were confirmed to apply significant pressure on the decision makers to increase their service's IT security levels and subsequently, to have considerable effects on the providers' IT security risk management. Thus, Hypotheses H1.4a - H1.4d are supported.

Overall, the decision makers' ITSR perceptions, together with their assessments of the avoidability of the ITSR by an increased IT security level, and their perceptions of the external pressures were found to explain a large part of the decision makers' intentions to increase the IT security levels of their organization's service (R^2=0.402).

Recent findings of prior psychological research showed that people's protection behaviors can be independently influenced by both absolute risk perceptions and comparative risk estimates (e.g., Dillard et al. 2012; Gold 2007; Mason et al. 2008). As hypothesized, we found the overall ITSR perceptions of the decision makers to be strongly determined by their absolute ITSR perceptions. Specifically, the perceived severity of the ITSRs for their organizations (β=0.474; p<0.001) as well as the perceptions of the susceptibility of their service to the ITSRs (β=0.515; p<0.001) were found to largely predict their overall ITSR assessments.

Moreover, the ITSR susceptibility and severity perceptions together explained a large portion of the variance in the decision makers' overall ITSR perceptions (R^2=0.619), pointing to the importance of these antecedents. As such, Hypotheses H1.5 and H1.6 were confirmed.

Beyond that, the decision makers' perceptions of the susceptibility of their organization's service to the ITSRs in comparison to the average competitor were revealed to significantly increase their perceptions of the competitive pressures put on their organizations to increase the service's IT security levels (β=0.402; p<0.001). The decision makers' assessments of the severity of the ITSRs for their own organization in comparison to the average competitor were also revealed to have significant effects on the perceived competitive pressures to implement safeguarding measures (β=0.145; p<0.05). The comparative risk assessments thereby account for 21.2% of the variance of the decision makers' competitive pressure assessments (R^2=0.212), supporting the hypothesis that the comparison of their own service with those of their direct competitors is an important factor in the formation of the perceived competitive pressure to increase the IT security level of the service. Accordingly, Hypotheses H1.7 and H1.8 are supported.

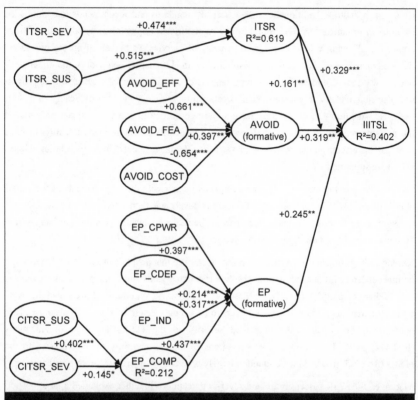

Figure 3-5: Empirical Testing of IT Security Risk Management Model

Please note: n=177. Measurement model not shown for purposes of clarity. Path significance: ***p<0.001; **p<0.01; *p<0.05. Constructs: AVOID = IT security risk avoidability through an increased IT security level, AVOID_COST = Costs to increase IT security level, AVOID_EFF = Effectiveness of increased IT security level, AVOID_FEA = Feasibility to increase IT security level, CITSR_SEV = Comparative IT security risk severity, CITSR_SUS = Comparative IT security risk susceptibility, EP = External pressure to increase IT security level, EP_CDEP = Dependency on existing customer relationships, EP_COMP = Competitive pressure to increase IT security level, EP_CPWR = Enacted customer power to increase IT security level, EP_IND = Industry pressure to increase IT security level, IIITSL = Intention to increase IT security level, ITSR = IT security risk, ITSR_SEV = IT security risk severity, ITSR_SUS = IT security risk susceptibility.

As the way that comparative risk perceptions influence protection behavior is controversially discussed in the psychological literature (e.g., Craciun et al. (2010) and Rose and Nagel (2013), arguing that the comparative risk assessments directly affect the formation of worry as an antecedent of the overall risk perceptions), we tested alternative structural models. Specifically, we examined the effects of the absolute and the comparative ITSR estimates together on the formation of overall IT security risk perceptions (alt_1) as well as the sole effects of the comparative ITSR perceptions on the formation of overall IT security risk perceptions (alt_2). Besides, we examined the influence of absolute risk estimates on the decision makers' perceptions of the competitive pressure exerted on their organizations (alt_3).

We found that the decision makers' assessments of their own service's susceptibility to the ITSRs in comparison to those of the average competitor to have significant influence on the overall ITSR perceptions (β_{alt_1}=0.279; p<0.01). In contrast, the perceptions of the severity of the ITSRs for their own organizations in comparison to the average competitor were not revealed to have any effects on the formation of the overall ITSR perceptions (β_{alt_1}=0.050; p≥0.05). Whereas the effect of the absolute ITSR severity assessments on the overall ITSR perceptions was not significantly changed (β_{alt_1}=0.504; p<0.001), the relationship between the absolute susceptibility perceptions of the services to the ITSRs and the overall ITSR perceptions was found to be considerably weakened (β_{alt_1}=0.396; p<0.01). Besides, the addition of the decision makers' comparative ITSR assessments did not significantly increase the explained variance of the overall ITSR perceptions ($R^2{}_{alt\_1}$=0.676). As such, it can be concluded that the decision makers' comparative ITSR susceptibility perceptions account for the same variance of the overall ITSR perceptions as their absolute ITSR susceptibility perceptions. As the absolute risk perceptions are typically also the comparison standard for comparative risk assessments, absolute and comparative risk perceptions are generally not mutually exclusive (e.g., a person has to assess his or her own standing on a risk factor in order to decide whether the comparison target is exposed to a higher or lower risk than himself or herself).

In this regard, the comparative ITSRs perceptions alone only explain 32.2% of the variance of the overall risk perceptions ($R^2{}_{alt\_2}$=0.322). Furthermore, the relationship between the decision makers' estimations of their own organization service's susceptibility to the ITSR (β_{alt_2}=0.394; p<0.001) as well as the severity of the ITSRs (β_{alt_2}=0.280; p<0.01), in comparison to those of the average competitors were found to be considerably weaker. Moreover, the influence of the decision makers' comparative ITSR assessments was found to be completely mediated by the effects of the perceptions of the competitive pressures on their intentions to increase the IT security levels (β_{alt_2}=0.034; p≥0.05) (Zhao et al. 2010). Altogether, the analyses of the alternative structural models confirmed that the overall ITSR risk perceptions of the decision makers are predominantly determined by their absolute ITSR assessments, supporting the validity of the proposed theoretical model in this study.

Similarly, the absolute ITSR perceptions were found to have negligible effects on the decision makers' perceptions of the competitive pressures to increase their service's IT security levels. In particular, the decision makers' absolute assessments of the susceptibility of their own organization's service to the ITSRs were revealed to have no significant effects on the perceptions of the competitive pressures (β_{alt_3}=0.089; p≥0.05). Likewise, the assessments of the absolute severity of the ITSR did not significantly apply competitive pressures on providers' decision makers to increase their service's IT security levels (β_{alt_3}=0.141; p≥0.05). Accordingly, the absolute risk perceptions were not found to explain additional parts of the variance of the perceived competitive pressures exerted on the providers ($R^2_{alt\_3}$=0.214). In sum, the perceived competitive pressure was confirmed to be primarily induced by the decision maker's comparative ITSR estimate, thereby supporting the proposed theoretical model.

Moreover, the results of the calculation model revealed that both the decision makers' absolute and their comparative ITSR perceptions have effects on the formation of their intentions to increase the IT security level and thus the providers' IT security risk management. In particular, the decision makers' assessments of the own service's susceptibilities to the ITSRs have a strong indirect effect (ind) on their intentions to increase the IT security levels (β_{ind}=0.181). Likewise, the assessments of the severities of the ITSRs for their own organizations significantly drive the decision makers' intentions to increase the IT security levels (β_{ind}=0.167). Furthermore, the decision makers' perception of their own organization service's susceptibilities to the ITSRs in comparison to the average competitors was also found to have a considerable indirect effect on their intentions to increase the IT security levels of their service (β_{ind}=0.056). In contrast, since, as described above, the decision makers' assessments of the severities of the ITSRs for the own organizations in comparison to those for the average competitors were not found to significantly induce competitive pressures, the comparative ITSR severity could not have any indirect effects on downstream beliefs and intentions. However, as the sampling distribution is not known, we used Preacher and Hayes (2008)'s bootstrapping based approach to test the joint statistical significance of the indirect effects. In this context, models with more than one mediator are straightforward extensions of the single-mediator cases and the joint statistical significance can thus be generally examined with the same tests (MacKinnon et al. 2007). Utilizing a bootstrapping procedure with no sign changes, we first calculated 5,000 resamples with replacement from the data set of our study, consisting of the same number of cases as in the original sample. Afterwards, the product of the coefficients that constitute the mediated path were tabulated across these samples in order to provide an empirical sampling distribution that can be used to derive a value for the standard error of the mediation. On a 95% confidence level, we estimated bias-corrected bootstrap confidence (BC) intervals between 0.091 and 0.268 for the indirect effects of the decision makers' absolute ITSR susceptibility estimations on their intentions to increase IT security levels and a BC between 0.112 and 0.234 for the effects of the absolute ITSR severity assessments on their intentions. Analogously, we calculated a BC between 0.011 and 0.098 for the indirect effects of the decision makers' assessments of their own service's susceptibility to the ITSR in comparison to the average competitors on their decisions to increase the IT security levels. As none of these BCs include zero, the null hypothesis that one of the mediated paths equals zero can be rejected and it can thus be concluded that the indirect effects of the absolute and comparative ITSR perceptions on the decision makers' intentions to increase the IT security levels are statistically significant at the $p<0.05$ level. In this context, bootstrapped BCs do not require that the coefficients which constitute the mediated path have a normal distribution (MacKinnon et al. 2007; Preacher and Hayes 2008). However, a normal theory test revealed z-ratios of $z=3.046$ for the indirect effects of the absolute ITSR susceptibility estimates, and $z=2.985$ for the indirect effects of the absolute ITSR severity assessments on the decision makers' intentions to increase the IT security levels of their organization's service. Moreover, we calculated a z-ratio of $z=2.155$ for the indirect effect of the comparative ITSR susceptibility assessments of the decision makers on their decisions to increase the IT security levels. Z-values greater than 1.96 point to the statistical significance of the mediated paths at the $p<0.05$ level (MacKinnon et al. 2007).

Additionally, we tested the influences of the control variables (revenue of organization, employees of organization, experience of decision maker, responsibility of decision maker, involvement of decision maker, and IT security risk management formalization) on all latent constructs of the proposed theoretical model. None of the control variables were found to have significant effects on other variables.

In sum, based on the results of the theoretical model testing, we were able to demonstrate that both the absolute and the comparative ITSR assessments of the decision makers have statistically significant effects on their intentions to increase the IT security levels and ultimately, on the resulting IT security risk management of the providers.

3.3.2   Existence of Unrealistic Optimism in the IT Security Risk Perceptions of Providers' Decision Makers

In the following, we first present results of our analysis regarding the existence of UO in the absolute ITSR perceptions of the providers' decision makers (Subsection 3.3.2.1). Then, the results of analyses of the decision makers' comparative ITSR perceptions, in terms of UO, are described (Subsection 3.3.2.2).

3.3.2.1   Analysis of Absolute Unrealistic Optimism

As the protection requirements of Cloud services, and thus the necessary IT security investment levels, differ in relation to the provided application types,[5] we first grouped the provid-

---

[5]   For example, in the obtained sample, 9.11% of the overall IT budget of office solutions (n=19) was on average invested in the IT security of the services, whereas 34.02% of the overall IT investment was averagely invested in the IT security of financial and accounting solutions (n=16) (see also sample characteristics in Table 3-3).

ers by the application type of their primary Cloud services. The proposed classifier (see description of the classifier in Subsection 3.2.1.1) enabled us to decide, which of the decision makers' ITSR perceptions are accurate in this group of providers. Since the results of the classifier generally do not allow for an analysis of the absolute degree of UO in the decision makers' ITSR assessments, we afterwards consolidated the results of all groups and searched for differences in the average assessments of those decision makers whose absolute ITSR assessments were classified as inaccurate, and those decision makers whose estimates were classified as accurate. Therefore, we utilized two-sided t-tests to analyze if those differences are statistically significant. In this context, as the Cronbach's alpha values of all constructs of the proposed theoretical framework were well above 0.85 (see Table 3-4), pointing to their excellent internal consistency (MacKenzie et al. 2011), we averaged the scores of all indicators to calculate the differences in the providers' decision makers' assessments.

Prior to this analysis, we tested the first two assumptions of the proposed classifier in order to ensure that we correctly identify those decision makers whose absolute ITSR perceptions are subject to UO (see assumptions of classifier in Subsection 3.2.1.1).

First, we analyzed the relationship between the size of the provided service and their IT security investment level in the obtained sample (n=117[6]). Therefore, by using an OLS regression approach, we revealed no significant correlation between the service size and the IT security investment level (β=0.048, p=0.574, R^2=0.002). Hence, the IT security investment level was found to control differences in the size of the service, warranting the comparability of IT security investment among the providers in the sample. Accordingly, the same IT security investment level corresponds to the same level of protection against the ITSR for all providers in a group with services of the same application type (see above). Together with the theoretical underpinnings, as presented in Subsection 3.2.1.1, this analysis strongly supports the first assumption.

Second, we analyzed the relationship between the providers' current IT security investment level and the planned level in the next year in order to identify possible irregularities and their effects on the protection levels. In particular, if a provider had a very high IT security investment level in the last year followed by a low investment in the next year, the actual protection of his service could still be higher than that of a provider with constant but rather low IT security investment levels. By utilizing an OLS regression approach, we revealed that the IT security investment level of the current year is highly correlated and largely explains that of the next year (β=0.908; p<0.001 R^2=0.824). Since the planned IT security investment level was found to be largely predicted by the previous investments, the results indicated that the providers have in general mostly constant IT security investments. Hence, irregularities are un-

---

[6]   Please note: Service size statement was optional.

likely to influence the results of the proposed classifier and the second assumption is supported.

We used the proposed classifier with a 10% threshold of error in order to identify decision-
makers whose absolute ITSR perceptions are inaccurate, with a high level of confidence. Although the 10% margin of error is consistent with the approaches used by psychological studies (e.g., Kreuter and Strecher 1995; Radcliffe and Klein 2002), we also tested different
thresholds. As shown in Table A-3, we revealed no significant difference to the reported results when we redefined UO based on a 0% to 5% and then a 15% to 20% threshold of error.
In particular, the number of the decision makers classified as unrealistic optimistic and the
mean scores of their assessments was only slightly decreased when the threshold of error was
increased. However, there were no changes in the significance levels of the differences in the
observed variables. Altogether, the reported results were not found to be strongly influenced
by the selected threshold of error.

As shown in Table 3-5, we found significant difference in the assessments of those decision
makers who displayed absolute UO in their ITSR assessments (n=75) and those who did not
(n=102). Since the results of the classifier are completely independent of the absolute ITSR
perception levels, we were also able to analyze the impact of the absolute UO on the decision
makers' absolute assessments of their organization service's ITSRs. In particular, we found a
significantly lower perception of their own organization service's susceptibility to the ITSRs
(1) when their decision makers' perceptions were classified as inaccurate (Δ=-0.94; p<0.001).
In other words, the decision makers' absolute UO was revealed to mislead the decision makers to significantly underestimate their own organization service's susceptibility to the ITSR
by an average score of -0.94 in the obtained sample. Moreover, the decision makers whose
absolute ITSR perceptions were classified as inaccurate assessed their own organization's
service to be at rather low susceptibility to the ITSR (average score: 3.16). In contrast, the
decision makers whose ITSR assessments were not classified as inaccurate perceived the susceptibility of their organization's service to the ITSR to be medium (average score: 4.11).
Accordingly, Hypothesis H1.9 is strongly supported.

Regarding the ITSR severity for their own organization (2), we found no significant difference between the assessments of the two groups (Δ=-0.24; p≥0.05). This is consistent with
findings of previous psychological research, that usually only their own vulnerability to negative events is subject to systematical underestimations and not the expected negative consequences of these events (e.g., Gold 2008; Perloff and Fetzer 1986). Both groups assessed the
potential financial damage caused by the ITSR as rather severe (average score of decision
makers who were classified as absolute UO: 4.93; average score of other decision makers:
5.17).

Since the overall ITSR assessment (3) is largely predicted by the perceptions of the absolute ITSR susceptibility (see results of structural model in Subsection 3.3.1.2), it was found to be considerably lower when the decision makers' absolute ITSR perceptions were classified as unrealistic ($\Delta=-0.84$; $p<0.001$). Specifically, those decision makers whose absolute ITSR assessments were classified as unrealistic assessed their organization's service to be at medium overall ITSR (average score: 4.11), whereas the other decision makers perceived their service to be at rather high overall ITSR (average score: 4.95).

Table 3-5: Effects of Absolute Unrealistic Optimism on IT Security Risk Management

Construct / Group	Mean		T	Difference
	absolute UO	no absolute UO		
n	75	102		
% of sample	42.37	57.63		
IT security risk management model				
IT security risk susceptibility (1)	3.16	4.11	-4.925	-0.94***
IT security risk severity (2)	4.93	5.17	-1.075	-0.24[ns]
IT security risk (3)	4.11	4.95	-3.718	-0.84***
Comparative IT security risk susceptibility (4)	2.64	2.85	-0.876	-0.21[ns]
Comparative IT security risk severity (5)	4.03	4.05	-0.197	-0.03[ns]
Effectiveness of increased IT security level (6)	4.51	4.34	1.539	0.16[ns]
Feasibility to increase IT security level (7)	4.14	3.78	2.718	0.36**
Cost to increase IT security level (8)	3.75	3.63	0.658	0.12[ns]
Competitive pressure to increase IT security level (9)	5.22	5.32	-0.456	-0.10[ns]
Dependency on existing customer relationships (10)	3.04	3.25	-1.441	-0.20[ns]
Enacted customer power to increase IT security level (11)	3.67	3.85	-1.301	-0.19[ns]
Industry pressure to increase level of IT security (12)	3.85	3.80	0.083	0.05[ns]
Intentions to increase IT security level (13)	4.76	5.10	-2.052	-0.33*
IT security investment level (next year) (14)	16.47	30.39	-6.504	-13.92***
Control				
Revenue of organization (15)	465.4	489.7	-0.174	-24.39[ns]
Employees of organization (16)	41.1	39.0	0.073	2.16[ns]
Experience of decision maker (17)	5.7	5.8	-0.355	-0.07[ns]
Responsibility of decision maker (18)	5.9	5.9	-0.005	0.00[ns]
Involvement of decision maker (19)	5.6	5.6	-0.030	-0.01[ns]
IT security risk management formalization degree (20)	3.53	4.16	-2.397	-0.62**

Please note: n=177. Classification based on risk-calculator with a 10% threshold of error. Significance values with two-sided t-tests: ***p<0.001; **p<0.01; *p<0.05; [ns]p≥0.05.

Moreover, no significant differences between the comparative ITSR susceptibility (4) and severity (5) assessments of the two groups were found in the obtained sample, suggesting that the decision makers' ITSR perceptions in comparison to the average competitors and subsequently, a potential comparative optimism of the decision makers, are not influenced by the UO in the absolute ITSR perception. These results confirm findings of recent psychological research, which suggest that people's risk perception can be independently subject to absolute UO, comparative UO, or both (Shepperd et al. 2013). Specifically, both groups perceived their organization's service to be less susceptible to the ITSR than the average competitor (average score of decision makers whose absolute ITSR perceptions were classified as unrealistic: 2.64; average score of the other decision makers: 2.85). Moreover, all decision makers, on average, assessed the ITSR to be as severe for their own organization as for the average competitor (average score of decision makers whose absolute ITSR perceptions were classified as unrealistic: 4.03; average score of the other decision makers: 4.05).

With the exception of the estimated feasibility of their own organization (7) to increase the IT security level ($\Delta=0.36$; $p<0.01$), none of the constructs forming the perceived avoidability of the ITSRs (6, 8) were found to be significantly different when the decision maker's absolute ITSR assessment was categorized as unrealistic optimistic. In this regard, previous psychological studies repeatedly demonstrated that the overestimation of their own feasibility, in terms of illusion of control, is an important factor facilitating people's UO (e.g., McKenna 1993). In particular, in the IT security context, a recent study (Loske et al. 2013) demonstrated that the overestimation of their organization's control over the ITSR is a major cause for an underestimation of its exposure to the ITSRs. As such, it can be assumed that the slightly higher perceptions of the organization's feasibilities to increase the IT security level by those decision makers whose ITSR perceptions were classified as unrealistic optimistic may be one of the causes for their underestimation of the ITSR. However, we are not able to analyze the causality of the effects of the decision makers' overestimation of their organization's feasibilities to increase the IT security level, based on the obtained data. Since the perceived feasibility to increase the ITSR was revealed to be the weakest factor in determining the avoidability of the ITSR, it can be concluded that the decision makers' absolute UO has comparably little effect on the decision makers' intentions to increase the IT security level of their organization's service through the overestimation of their feasibilities. In particular, based on the results of the structural model testing as presented in Subsection 3.3.1.2, we found an indirect effect of $\beta_{ind}=0.127$ of the feasibility assessment on the decisions to increase the IT security level. Following Preacher and Hayes (2008)'s bootstrapping approach with 5,000 resamples (see description in Subsection 3.3.1.2), we revealed that the indirect effect of the perceived feasibility to increase the IT security level on the decision makers' intentions is not significant at the $p<0.05$ level. Accordingly, a potential overestimation of their organization's feasibility due to absolute UO would be unlikely to have other effects, such as elevating the decision makers' intentions to increase the IT security level.

Besides, as shown in Table 3-5, our analyses revealed no significant differences in the assessment of the external pressure factors (9 - 12) by the decision makers whose absolute ITSR perceptions were classified as inaccurate in comparison to those of the other decision makers whose ITSR perceptions were not classified as inaccurate. In other words, the decision makers' absolute UO was not found to affect their sensitivity to external influences in the obtained sample.

As expected, based on the results of the structural model testing, the reduced perceptions of their own organization's absolute exposure to the ITSRs were found to significantly inhibit decisions to increase the IT security level (13) (Δ=-0.33; p<0.05) of those decision makers whose absolute ITSR perceptions were classified as unrealistic. Subsequently, when the decision makers' absolute ITSR were classified as unrealistic, the providers' IT security investment level of the next year (14) was revealed to be substantially lower than that of other organizations (Δ=-13.92; p<0.001). In particular, the decision makers, whose absolute ITSR assessments were classified as being subject to UO, on average, stated that their organization will invest 16.47% of their IT budget in IT security in the next year. In contrast, the other decision makers, whose absolute ITSR assessment were not classified as unrealistic, stated that their organization will, on average, spend 30.39% of the service's IT budget on IT security. As such, these results not only demonstrated the negative effects of the decision makers' absolute UO on the providers' IT security risk management but also strongly supported the validity of the proposed theoretical model regarding the influence of the decision makers' absolute ITSR perceptions.

Moreover, none of the control variables in the obtained sample differed between the decision makers who demonstrated absolute UO in their absolute ITSR perceptions and those who did not. In particular, we found no empirical evidence that decision makers of smaller or larger organizations are more likely to display UO in their absolute ITSR perceptions (15, 16). Beyond that, we revealed no significant differences concerning the decision-makers' experience (experienced and self-reported), involvement, and responsibility (17 - 19) between the groups of decision-makers, whose absolute ITSR assessments were classified as inaccurate and those whose absolute ITSR perceptions were classified as accurate (p≥0.05). In contrast, we found that the formalization of the organizational IT security risk management (20) of a provider is significantly lower when its decision maker's ITSR perception is regarded as more unrealistic (Δ=-0.62; significance level with two-sided t-tests: p<0.001) than that of other providers (e.g., event-triggered IT security risk management). Conversely, the IT security risk management of providers whose decision-makers' perceptions were not classified as unrealistic optimistic was considerably more formalized and mature (e.g., by the implementation of a completely certified IT security risk management system (ISMS)). Based on the obtained results, it is not possible to decide if the lower IT security risk management formalization is caused by lower

IT security investments due to decision makers' absolute UO regarding the ITSR exposure, or if the decision makers' underestimation of the ITSR is facilitated by a lack of formalized risk management procedures. However, a less formalized IT security risk management (e.g., a best-practice approach) is generally more dependent on the subjective assessments of the decision makers and thus, more prone to the negative effects of UO than a more formalized approach (e.g., a certified IT security risk management system). Even more importantly, the results indicated that the IT security risk management of the providers in the UO group is unlikely to be more effective than that of other providers. In particular, it is extremely unlikely that the providers can reach a higher level of protection against the ITSR with a lower level of IT security investment, which concurrently supports the third assumption of the proposed classifier.

Overall, as none of the decision makers' beliefs and assessments, which were not hypothesized as being downstream of the decision makers' absolute ITSR perceptions, were found to be significantly affected by the systematical errors in the absolute ITSR perceptions, the validity of the proposed theoretical model that explicates the role of decision makers' ITSR perception in the providers' IT security risk management is strongly supported. Moreover, all revealed effects are in line with UO literature and the findings of previous psychological research, confirming the validity of the utilized classifier. In this context, we separately tested the structural model with different subsamples. First, we estimated the model with the responses of all decision makers in the sample (see results in Subsection 3.3.1.2). Additionally, we tested the structural model with a subsample that only contained the data of those decision makers whose absolute ITSR perceptions were classified as inaccurate as well as with another subsample that only included the responses of those decision makers who were classified as accurate. By using a multi-group analysis technique, we revealed no significant differences in the hypothesized relationships (see Table A-4), which indicates that the impact of the decision makers' absolute UO, regarding the ITSRs on the outcome of the providers' IT security risk management, is not compensated by considerably weaker (indirect) effect sizes of the absolute ITSR assessments.

Altogether, the analyses showed that the absolute ITSR perceptions of the providers' decision makers are in many cases subject to UO, which negatively affects their IT security risk management decisions.

3.3.2.2 Analysis of Comparative Unrealistic Optimism

We used two-sided t-tests to analyze whether the decision makers' assessments of their own service's exposure to the ITSRs, on average, significantly deviate from their assessments of the vulnerability of the average competitor's service to the ITSRs. Therefore, we conducted several tests to confirm that the indicators measure the underlying ITSR perception constructs (see Table 3-4). In particular, Cronbach's alpha values of all scales, in the context of decision makers' ITSR perceptions, were above 0.85, pointing to the constructs' excellent internal consistency (MacKenzie et al. 2011). Accordingly, we utilized mean scores of all indicators representing a construct in order to conduct all analyses in this part (see also Table A-1).

The comparison of the ITSR perceptions of their own service with that of the average competitor (indirect method) revealed highly significant (at the $p < 0.001$ level) differences in the assessments of the service's susceptibility to the ITSRs, with an average score of -1.57. Since we deducted the perceptions of the average competitor's service from the perception of their own service, a significant negative difference generally shows a systematic underestimation of their own service's vulnerability to ITSRs by the providers' decision makers, in terms of comparative UO. In this context, the size of the negative difference represents the average degree of comparative UO in the ITSR perceptions (Weinstein and Klein 1996). Accordingly, Hypothesis H1.10 is strongly supported. However, comparing the decision makers' average assessments of the ITSR severity for their own organization's service and for that of the average competitor revealed a slightly positive but not significant difference ($p \geq 0.05$), with an average score of 0.24. Thus, the decision makers do not underestimate, on average, the severity of the ITSRs for their own service in comparison to that of the average competitors. However, according to prior psychological research (see Subsection 3.1.5), the cognitive mechanisms that cause people to believe that they are less likely to experience a negative event than others are generally not known to affect beliefs about the negative consequences of this event at the same time (Weinstein 1984). As such, significant differences in the severity perceptions could have pointed to the influence of other cognitive factors on the ITSR perception of decision makers.

Table 3-6: Existence of Comparative Unrealistic Optimism

Comparative risk measure	Construct	Mean		SD	T	Difference
		Own organization	Average competitor			
Indirect	IT security risk susceptibility	3.70	5.28	1.88	-10.035	-1.57***
	IT security risk severity	5.02	4.78	1.42	1.953	0.24[ns]
Direct	Comparative IT security risk susceptibility	2.76		1.26	-13.045	-1.24***
	Comparative IT security risk severity	4.04		0.65	0.843	0.04[ns]

Please note: n=177. Difference of comparative IT security risk (direct measurement method according to Weinstein (1980)) is mean difference from 4 (= same as average competitor). SD = standard deviation, T = t-value. Significance levels: ***p=<0.001, [ns]p≥0.05.

The use of the indirect measurement method allows for a detailed analysis (Rose 2010) and revealed that the decision makers averagely consider the susceptibility of their own organization's service to the ITSRs as rather low, with a mean score of 3.70. Concurrently, the decision makers assess the susceptibility of the average provider's service to the ITSRs as fairly high, with an average score of 5.28. As such, the results indicate that the decision makers are generally aware of the theoretical vulnerability of their service to the ITSRs. The potential financial loss caused by a compromise of the service's IT security is mostly considered as rather high by the providers' decisions; the mean scores are 5.02 for their own service and 4.78 for the average competitor's service.

Very similar results were found with the direct measure of the providers' comparative status. If all decision makers claim their organization's service is at lower ITSRs than average, at least some of them are clearly making a systematic error, thus showing comparative UO. In this study, a score significantly different from 4 (=same as average) thus indicates a systematic bias in the ITSR perceptions by the providers' decision makers on the group level. Two-sided t-tests confirmed the results of the indirect measurement method and also demonstrated that the decision makers, on average, significantly (at the $p<0.001$ level) underestimate the likelihood that their own organization's service will be compromised by the ITSRs, with a mean score of 2.76 (average difference from 4 equals -1.24). In general, due to differences between the used scales, the direct measure typically shows lower comparative perceptions (e.g., Rose 2010). Analogous to the indirect method, the result revealed no systematic errors in the decision makers' assessments of potential financial damage to their own organization that may be caused by the ITSRs. We revealed a non-significant ($p{\geq}0.05$) difference from 4 of, on average, 0.04 (mean score 4.04). Even if the indirect and the direct comparisons were not perfectly correlated, the substantial correlations support the validity of our results regarding the existence of UO in the ITSR perceptions of the providers' decision makers; the average Pearson correlation of the direct and indirect measures was 0.76 regarding the ITSR susceptibility and 0.71 regarding ITSR severity (both $p<0.001$). In particular, the results show that both methods generally capture the same cognitive factors and errors in the ITSR perceptions of the decision makers (Aucote and Gold 2005).

Furthermore, we tested the correlation between the decision makers' comparative status concerning the service's susceptibility to ITSRs and the decision makers' perception of the ITSR severity. Unlike some other studies (e.g., Hoorens and Buunk 1993; Weinstein 1982), we found no relationship between the perceived severity of ITSRs and the decision makers' average comparative optimism on their organization's exposure to the ITSRs. The mean Pearson correlation was 0.14 with the indirect method and 0.06 with the direct method (all $p{\geq}0.05$). In this regard, cognitive mechanisms, which can be influenced by the severity of the ITSRs and are causes of comparative UO, such as the underestimation of other's control over the risks, might play a minor role in the decision makers' comparative ITSR perceptions.

In sum, our results provide strong empirical evidence that the providers' decision makers, on average, underestimated the ITSR of their own service in comparison to those of their average competitors. Accordingly, Hypothesis 1.10 is supported.

3.4   Discussion of Study Findings

The results of the study described in this part revealed that the decision makers' subjective perceptions of the ITSR play a central role in the providers' IT security risk management. Moreover, we demonstrated that the decision makers in many cases significantly underestimate the exposure of their own organization's service to the ITSRs, which undermines an effective IT security risk management, thus putting the IT security of the service in jeopardy.

In line with psychological risk perception literature, we revealed that the decision makers' ITSR perception generally encompasses both the absolute assessment of the ITSRs of their own organization's service and the estimation of their own organization service's ITSRs in comparison to those of the average competitors. Moreover, we showed that the decision makers' absolute and comparative ITSR perceptions affect the outcome of the providers' IT security risk management in different ways and to different degrees. The decision makers' ITSR assessment in comparison to the average competitors was demonstrated to predominately elevate their perceptions of the competitive pressure exerted, which, in turn, facilitates an increase in the IT security level. Accordingly, the effects of the comparative ITSR perceptions on the providers' IT security risk management were found to be slightly weaker but still highly significant.

Moreover, the decision makers' absolute ITSR perceptions were revealed to be the strongest driver of decisions to increase their own organization service's IT security level. In contrast to findings of previous IT security research at the individual level, the absolute ITSR perceptions were found to moderate the relationship between the decision makers' perceived avoidability of the ITSR and their intentions to increase the IT security level. Thus, the results indicate that the absolute ITSR assessments of the decision makers not only facilitate decisions to increase the service's IT security level but also trigger further processes to analyze in depth the avoidability of the ITSR by an increased IT security level. In this regard, the decision makers' assessments of the effectiveness of the increased IT security level to mitigate the ITSR and the costs associated with an increase of the IT security level were revealed to be the most important factors in the formation of decision makers' avoidability assessments. In contrast, the decision makers were found to put less weight on the assessments of the organization's feasibility to increase the IT security level when determining the avoidability of the ITSRs. At the organizational level, the feasibility of the organization to increase the IT security level is related to the costs associated with an increase in the service's IT security level. For example, organizations are generally able to increase the knowledge and competency availability by taking on additional staff, which, in turn, is associated with additional costs. Nevertheless, not all aspects of the organizational feasibility to increase the IT security level can be improved with additional financial investments in the short term (e.g., in the next year). For example, the IT strategy requires employees to focus on different activities in the next period, or a given IT security budget does not allow for taking on additional staff in the short run. In these cases, it is not feasible for the organization to increase the IT security level in the next year, even if the associated costs are relatively low. However, monetary values are typically utilized to control the organizational IT security risk management and are thus more likely to be present in the decision makers' minds, increasing their weight in the formation of downstream beliefs (Cavusoglu et al. 2004b).

Besides, the results of our analyses indicated that the external pressure perceived by the decision makers has substantial effects on the IT security risk management at the organizational level. Specifically, all dimensions of external pressure, as postulated by institutional theory, were found to significantly contribute to the formation of external pressure and subsequently affect the decisions to increase the IT security level of the organization's service. In particular, competitive pressure was revealed to be the most important factor in exerting external pressure on providers to increase IT security levels. The IT security behavior of direct competitors was found to put even more pressure on the decisions to implement additional safeguarding measures than the directly enacted power of the providers' customers to increase the IT security level, together with the providers' dependency on the existing customer relationships. In this regard, especially due to its high degree of standardization and rapid elasticity without the need of dedicated IT infrastructure, customer companies are oftentimes enabled to change between different Cloud service providers with minimal management efforts (see essential characteristics of the Cloud in Subsection 2.1.1). As a result, in comparison with traditional concepts of IT outsourcing, the dependency of the customers on a Cloud provider is, typically, considerably lower. At the same time, it becomes significantly easier for the providers to attract new customers by convincing them to change the service because of the superior features of their own organization's service (e.g., a higher IT security level than the direct competitors). Accordingly, customer connectivity is, typically, much lower in the context of the Cloud, reducing the exerted pressure on the providers by the demands of their customers. Concurrently, the actions taken by the direct competitors and their success with these actions become increasingly important for the Cloud providers to remain competitive (e.g., when the direct competitors have implemented additional safeguarding measures against a given ITSR).

In this context, the comparative ITSR assessments of the decision makers were revealed not to influence the overall ITSR perceptions but to significantly elevate the decision makers' perceptions of the competitive pressure on their organizations to increase their service's IT security level, which, in turn, influences the providers' IT security risk management. Specifically, as a high IT security level is generally regarded as a competitive advantage, the decision makers are more likely to increase the IT security level, when they assess that their organization's service is less well protected than those of their competitors. As such, in line with results of previous psychological risk perception research (Dillard et al. 2012), the comparative ITSR perceptions of the decision makers were found to have more indirect effects on their decisions to increase the IT security levels of their organization's service than the absolute ITSR perceptions.

Based on a comparison of all decision makers' ITSR perceptions, in combination with their organization's IT security investment level in the obtained sample, we were able to identify those decision makers whose absolute perceptions of their service's ITSR exposure are contradictory to their organization's IT security behavior. Following this approach, we revealed a significant underestimation of the susceptibility of their own organization's service to the ITSRs by the providers' decision makers in many cases. We found no systematic error in the decision makers' perception of the severity of the ITSR for their organizations. The results are in line with UO literature and, together with various other analyses, supported the validity of the utilized approach. Moreover, we were able to show that the decision makers' absolute UO regarding their service's ITSR exposure considerably reduced their overall ITSR assessment, which, in turn, mitigates their intentions to implement additional safeguards. We revealed no dissimilarities in the comparative ITSR assessments between those decision makers whose absolute ITSR assessments were classified as unrealistic and the others. These results indicate that the UO in the decision makers' absolute ITSR perceptions is, to a large extent, independent from the comparative ITSR assessments and subsequently, systematic errors in the comparative ITSR assessments, such as comparative UO. Besides, we found neither significant differences regarding the estimations of the ITSR avoidability with an increased ITSR level nor differences regarding the assessments of the external pressure between those decision makers whose absolute ITSR assessments were classified as unrealistic and those whose ITSR assessments were classified as not being subject to UO. Furthermore, we were not able to reveal any correlation between the IT security knowledge and experience of the decision makers and their degree of UO. Likewise, there was no significant relationship between the sizes of the providers and the degree of UO in the ITSR perception of their decision makers. In this regard, findings of previous psychological research also suggest that people can generally display UO, regardless of their knowledge in the risk domain or prior experience with the risk (Shepperd et al. 2013). Moreover, we revealed a significant relationship between the classification of the decision makers' absolute ITSR perceptions in terms of UO and the degree of formalization of the providers' IT security risk management. In particular, the providers were found to have, on average, a considerably less formal IT security risk management (e.g., more frequently event-triggered or best-practice-based approaches), when their decision makers' ITSR assessments were classified as being subject to UO. In contrast, when the decision makers' ITSR assessments of the ITSR were classified as realistic, the formalization of the providers' IT security risk management was, on average, found to be much higher (e.g., certified IT security risk management systems were more widely spread). However, based on the data obtained in our study, we were not able to further investigate the causality of this relationship. On the one hand, the lower formalization facilitates the influence of the decision makers' subjective ITSR assessments by opening up new possibilities for inaccuracies in the providers' IT security risk management processes. On the other hand, as we found the outcomes of the providers' IT security risk management to be largely predicted by the decision makers' ITSR assessments, a systematical underestimation of the ITSRs inhibits future IT security investments, like efforts to certify the organizational IT security risk management. As such, the results may point to the existence of a potential vicious circle: the higher the decision makers' underestimation of the ITSR, the lower the perceived necessity of a formalized IT security risk management. Concurrently, a lower level of IT security risk management formalization increases the impact of subjective ITSR perceptions and thus, the effects of UO. Therefore, even if a decision maker only displays a rather small degree of UO, both its magnitude and its negative effects are likely to rise, over time.

Moreover, by utilizing a well-established approach, we also revealed that the decision makers, on average, significantly underestimate the ITSR of their own organization's service in comparison to that of the average competitors. Specifically, we were able to show that the decision makers, on average, assessed the ITSR exposure of their own organization's service to be significantly lower than they assessed the ITSR of the average competitor's service. Since the ITSR exposure of the providers, on average, cannot be lower than that of the average provider, the decision makers are obviously making a systematic error, thus displaying comparative UO at the group level. Similar to the errors in the absolute ITSR perception, we found no empirical evidence for inaccuracies in the decision makers' assessments of the severity of the ITSR for their own organization in comparison to that of the average competitors. Moreover, since the systematic errors in the decision makers' absolute ITSR perceptions were found to be independent of their comparative ITSR assessments, a decision maker's ITSR perception can, generally, be subject to absolute UO, comparative UO, or both. These results are aligned with findings of previous psychological research regarding the manifestation of people's UO (Shepperd et al. 2013).

Altogether, the absolute assessment of the ITSRs as well as the perception of the ITSR exposure of their own organization's service, in comparison to those of the average competitor, were demonstrated to have a considerable impact on the decision makers' intention to increase the IT security level of their organization's service. As such, the underestimation of their own service's susceptibility to the ITSRs, both in an absolute sense and in comparison to that of the average competitor, inhibits an effective IT security risk management of the providers. In contrast to the inaccuracies in the absolute ITSR assessments, the utilized approach to analyze comparative UO is based on group-level comparisons, so that we were not able to decide whether the comparative ITSR perception of a given decision maker is unrealistic or not. Nonetheless, we were able to measure both the average degree of UO in the decision makers' absolute ITSR perceptions and the average degree of UO in the decision makers' comparative ITSR perceptions. Specifically, the decision makers were found, on average, to unreasonably assess their own organization services' absolute susceptibility to the ITSR to be 13.4% too low because of UO. Accordingly, a comparison of the decision makers whose absolute ITSR perceptions were classified as inaccurate and those whose ITSR assessments were not classified as inaccurate showed that the decision makers' intentions to increase the IT security level of their organization's service was 4.71% lower when their absolute ITSR perceptions were classified as being subject to UO. In this regard, since the decision makers' perceived absolute ITSR susceptibility of their organization's service both significantly facilitates their intentions to increase the ITSR level (indirect effect size of 0.181) and strengthens the relationship between the perceived avoidability of the ITSR (sample mean value of 4.94) and intention to increase the IT security level of their own organization's service (average moderation effect of 0.135), the proposed framework explains 78.76% of the inhibiting effects of UO on the providers' IT security risk management, pointing to its high validity and predictive power. However, beyond that, we were able to demonstrate an average inaccuracy of 18.1% in the decision makers' assessments of the susceptibility of their own organization's service to the ITSR, in comparison with that of the average competitor (comparative UO of 1.24), which was found to have significant effects on their decisions to increase the IT security level of their organization's service (indirect effect size of 0.056). Based on the estimation of our theoretical model, the decision makers' comparative UO was revealed, on average, to unjustifiably lessen their intentions to increase the IT security level of their organization's service by another 1%. In sum, the systematic errors in the decision makers' ITSR perceptions were thus demonstrated to considerably inhibit an effective IT security risk management of the providers by mitigating up to 6% of decisions to implement necessary safeguards.

4 Part II: Perceptual Incongruences regarding the IT Security Risks as a Barrier to Cloud Adoption

In the course of this chapter,[7] we present our empirical analysis of the role of providers' decision makers' ITSR perceptions in the formation of customer companies' intention to adoption the Cloud services. In particular, we demonstrate that the perceptual distance between providers and their (potential) customers regarding the ITSR has detrimental effects on the use of Cloud services by customer companies.

First, we show the specific theoretical background for this part and the development of our hypotheses (Section 4.1). Then, we present the research methodology of the dyadic empirical study with Cloud providers and their (potential) customer companies (Section 4.2), followed by the results of the analyses of the collected data (Section 4.3). We conclude with a summarization and discussion of the findings of this part (Section 4.4).

4.1 Theoretical Background and Hypotheses Development

In this section, we introduce the specific theoretical background and present the development of the hypotheses of this part. First, we draw on perceptual incongruence research (Subsection 4.1.1) and an established framework of perceived ITSR in the context of the Cloud (Subsection 4.1.2) to develop our basic hypotheses regarding the existence of a perceptual incongruence between the providers and their (potential) customer companies concerning the ITSRs of the Cloud. Second, based on cognitive dissonance theory (Subsection 4.1.3), expectation confirmation theory (Subsection 4.1.4), and technology acceptance research (Subsection 4.1.5), we propose a theoretical model that explicates the effect of the perceptual incongruence on (potential) customers' IT managers' intention to adopt Cloud services. As such, we expect that the perceptual incongruence between providers and customer companies not only increases the ITSR perceptions of the customers but also directly reduces their intentions to adopt Cloud services.

4.1.1 Perceptual Congruence

In psychology research, the degree to which there is alignment, fit, or agreement in the perceptions of the same stimulus by different persons is typically labeled as perceptual congruence (the contrary is often called perceptual distance or incongruence) (e.g., Srull and Wyer 1988; Turban and Jones 1988). In general, the perceptual process of human beings is influenced by many individual factors, including experience, personality, and cognitive complexity, which, in turn, influence interests, values, and attitudes (Allport 1955). As such, these fac-

---

[7] Compare, in the following, Loske et al. (2014).

tors predict how people perceive and interpret the world, leading them to attend to certain stimuli but filter out others. Accordingly, people may be congruent in their perceptions of certain concepts but incongruent in their perceptions of others. In this regard high perceptual congruence implies great agreement in people's perceptions of the same stimulus, whereas low perceptual congruence implies large differences in perceptions (Benlian 2013; Srull and Wyer 1988).

Drawing on perceptual congruence theory, previous IS research investigated the fit of perceptions of different stakeholders regarding the assessment of IS staff and services (e.g., Benlian 2011; Boyd et al. 2007; Chen et al. 2005; Jiang et al. 2002; Jiang et al. 2003; Tesch et al. 2005), of software development processes (e.g., Huisman and Iivari 2006; Sheetz et al. 2009) or of business and IS planning integration processes (e.g. Teo and King 1997). The majority of these studies found substantial perceptual gaps between IS professionals (e.g., IT staff or personnel of the IT service provider) and users on IS service quality factors, which were in most cases measured based on SERVQUAL framework (Parasuraman et al. 1988) by four distinct dimensions (i.e., tangibles, reliability, responsiveness, and rapport) (e.g., Benlian 2011; Watson et al. 1998). These studies consistently found that the IS professionals have typically significantly higher perceptions of their own services' performance than the IS users (e.g., Boyd et al. 2007; Jiang et al. 2002; Jiang et al. 2003; Klein and Jiang 2001). However, while the majority of these studies are focused on whether there is agreement or disagreement among the relevant stakeholders on IS service quality, little attention has been paid to the consequences of perceptual congruence or distance on important outcomes, like the behavior or attitudes of users. However, extant literature in this context revealed that a lack of agreement between IS professionals and users usually has a significant negative effect on the users' satisfaction with a service, which was predominately measured by their intention to use the product or service (Benlian 2011; Klein and Jiang 2001; Tesch et al. 2005).

Besides, previous research in the IT context investigated classical IT services, where the supplier provides the service on the premises of the customers (e.g., Benlian 2011; Klein and Jiang 2001; Tesch et al. 2005). Although these studies provide insights into the formation and consequences of perceptual incongruences between professionals and users of IT services, there is no research, which considers the special characteristics of service-based IT systems, such as the Cloud (see also Section 2.1). The concept of service-based IT systems represents a further stage of the classical delivery concept by utilizing modern communication technologies. In particular, it enables many customers to share the same service, which is provided by a single supplier firm. In general, service-based IT systems provide a variety of technical and economic advantages in comparison to classical concepts but also induce a new complexity of ITSR to ubiquitous and on-demand network access of resources. Previous research in the context of e-services and the Cloud has especially found the perceived risks to be one of the most salient factors influencing the user satisfaction with a service (e.g., Benlian and Hess 2011; Featherman and Wells 2010; Heart 2010). As a result, perceptual incongruences on the ITSR between Cloud providers and their (potential) customer companies are likely to have an important impact on the customers' satisfaction and, ultimately, their intentions to adopt Cloud services.

4.1.2 Perceptual Incongruences regarding the IT Security Risks

The specific characteristics of ITO in general and the Cloud in particular, like asymmetric information and different levels of controllability, are likely to inevitably diverge the ITSR perception of providers and customer companies (e.g., Aubert et al. 1998; Kaiser et al. 2012; Kishore et al. 2003; Shepperd et al. 2002). In particular, when a company uses Cloud services the customer's data will be stored at the provider's data center. Therefore, the customer company gives the provider direct control of their sensitive data, which is likely to be a critical asset of the company (e.g. Jurison 1995), without knowing exactly how the provider will secure their data (e.g., which backup and disaster recovery strategies are used in the Cloud service). Even if service level agreements (SLAs) may describe the maintained data security levels, there is in general no guarantee for an adequate protection of the customers' data. In this context, for example, previous studies found that the customers are in many cases unaware of the potential security risks arising from the contractual flexibility at the time when they sign the contract of a service (Hart 1988). Accordingly, the customers were frequently found to be very afraid that there are uncertainties and loopholes in the contracts, which may be exploited and result in opportunistic behavior of the providers (e.g., Ackermann et al. 2012; Willcocks et al. 1996). Furthermore, the Cloud is still a rather new development, so that the customers typically have no or very little experience with Cloud services, which is likely to increase discomfort and anxiety towards is usage (e.g., Ackermann 2013; Featherman and Wells 2010). For example, previous research in this field revealed that the (potential) customer companies are in many cases especially concerned about the risk that the supplier might look at their sensitive data when the Cloud is used as delivery model, because they got the feeling to lose control over their company's data and have to rely on the promises of the providers (Ackermann et al. 2012). At the same, the providers' decision makers are likely to perceive this risk significantly lower than the customers' IT managers, as, for example, they typically personally know and trust their organizations' employees.

Beyond that, there is typically a lack of historical data regarding the impact and the probability of ITSRs in the Cloud, that would allow an objective quantification of the actual risk with traditional risk measures – probability of incident occurrence multiplied by seriousness of consequences (Hopkin 2012). This lack of quantitative information is on the one hand based on the fact that IT is subject to a fast technology development (e.g., the development of the Cloud). On the other hand, the organizations do in many cases not detected, not reported, or not systematically documented IT security incidents in their IT systems (e.g., Kankanhalli et al. 2003). Thus, there is oftentimes no accurate and consistent risk information that would allow an anchoring and adjustment of the risk estimations of (potential) customers' IT managers (Slovic et al. 1982). Additionally, as presented in Chapter 0 of this thesis, the Cloud providers' decision makers in many cases systematically underestimate the ITSR exposure of their own organizations' services. In this context, the UO of Cloud providers' decision makers not only considerably inhibits the implementation of necessary safeguarding measures in the services but also inevitably increases the perceptual incongruence between the providers and their (potential) customer companies concerning the ITSRs. Accordingly, due to the different situations of providers and (potential) customers together with the UO in the ITSR perceptions of the providers' decision makers, we hypothesize that:

H2.1:   The customers will perceive the IT security risks associated with the Cloud services to be significantly higher than the providers.

In line with risk perception research (e.g., Benlian and Hess 2011; Featherman and Pavlou 2003), Ackermann et al. (2012) suggest perceived ITSR to be a multidimensional construct encompassing six major sub-dimensions that together form the overall ITSR perception (see also the nature of perceived ITSR in the context of the Cloud in Subsection 2.2.2). In this regard, previous research on perceptual incongruences between IT users and professionals regarding the IT service quality factors, which are typically also conceptualized as a multidimensional construct (e.g., SERVQUAL), found that when the perceptual difference in one of the sub-dimensions (i.e., tangibles, reliability, responsiveness, and rapport) was increased, the overall perceptual incongruence on the service quality was also increased (e.g., Huisman and Iivari 2006; Jiang et al. 2002; Tesch et al. 2005). Similarly, we expect that the overall perceptual incongruence on the ITSRs of the Cloud services is fueled by the disagreements between the providers and their (potential) customers on the six sub-dimensions of the perceived ITSRs (i.e., confidentiality, integrity, availability, performance, accountability, and maintainability) (Ackermann et al. 2012). Therefore, the higher the perceptual difference concerning each of the sub-dimensions of the ITSRs, the higher the overall perceptual incongruence between the providers and their (potential) customers regarding the IT security of the Cloud services. We therefore assume that:

H2.1a-f: The higher the perceptual incongruences on confidentiality risks (H2.1a), integrity risks (H2.1b), availability risks (H2.1c), performance risks (H2.1d), accountability risks (H2.1e), and maintainability risks (H2.1f), the higher the overall perceptual incongruence between a provider and its (potential) customers regarding the IT security risks of the Cloud service.

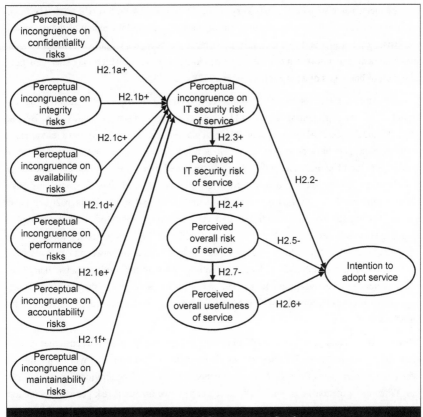

Figure 4-1: Research Model of Perceptual Incongruence Study

4.1.3   Cognitive Dissonance Theory

As shown in Figure 4-1, we draw on cognitive dissonance and technology acceptance research to develop our hypotheses on the effects of the perceptual incongruence on the adoption attitudes and beliefs of (potential) customers' IT managers towards the adoption of Cloud services and to explicate the psychological mechanisms underlying these effects. As such, this study is similar in spirit to Davis (1989)'s formulation of the technology acceptance model (TAM) in that it adapts cognitive dissonance theory (CDT) from psychology research to suggest a model of Cloud acceptance, just as TAM adapted the theory of reasoned action from the consumer behavior literature to propose a model of IT adoption. CDT postulates that when a person is confronted with two cognitive structures (i.e., beliefs, attitudes, and/or actions) that are inconsistent with each other, a psychological state of discomfort will arise. The intensity of the discomfort varies based on the importance of issue and the extent of the perceptual inconsistency (Szajna and Scamell 1993). To meet the need for cognitive consistency, this psychological discomfort induces a dissonance reduction strategy, which may change beliefs, attitudes, or behaviors of a person (Festinger 1957).

In our discipline, CDT has been used to theorize the consequences of confirmation or disconfirmation of user expectations regarding IT adoption, usage, and service quality (e.g., Benlian 2011; Bhattacherjee 2001; Brown et al. 2012; Venkatesh and Goyal 2010). Different kinds of comparison targets have been used by previous research to examine consistencies or inconsistencies in the IT context. Several researchers compared users' pre-adoption expectations on a technology, which are frequently influenced by training initiatives or social influence through third-parties, with their post-adoption beliefs or attitudes (e.g. Benlian 2011). Other studies investigated the gap between user expectations and the ability of IT service providers to understand their desires (e.g. Pitt et al. 1998). Ginzberg (1981) presented the concept of the so-called expectation gap, which suggests that a gap in expectations between IT providers and users will lead to a significantly reduced user satisfaction with the services. Later, Jiang et al. (2003) extended this concept and proposed a performance gap in which the performance perceptions of users are compared with those of IT service providers in order to determine the satisfaction of users.

However, the second part of this thesis adopts the perspective of (potential) customer companies and argues that their IT managers' satisfaction with a Cloud services will be the highest when their perceptions of ITSRs are in congruence with those of the providers' decision makers. When the (potential) customers' IT managers perceive that their risk perceptions are met and confirmed by the ITSR assessments of the Cloud providers, they will feel that there is a shared and mutual understanding of their concerns regarding the ITSRs of the Cloud (Szajna and Scamell 1993). According to CDT, this consistency in perceptions will lead to a state of psychological consonance, leading to a higher satisfaction of the (potential) customers' IT managers with the Cloud service (Allport 1955). The other way around, a state of dissonance arises if the ITSR perceptions of (potential) customers' IT managers are inconsistent with the assessments of the Cloud providers. In these cases, the (potential) customers' IT managers will experience a mental conflict caused by the disagreement on the ITSRs. Due to this psychological state of discomfort, they will use a dissonance reduction strategy, resulting in a negative effect on their attitude, such as a lower satisfaction with the evaluated Cloud service. As described above, the important of the issue generally predicts the degree of inconsistency and thus the intensity of the dissonance reduction reactions. Since previous studies found the perceived ITSRs to be the most salient factor not to use e-services or the Cloud (e.g., Ackermann et al. 2012; Benlian and Hess 2011; Featherman and Pavlou 2003), a perceptual incongruence concerning the ITSRs is likely to have considerable impacts on the (potential) customers' IT managers' satisfaction with the Cloud services. In this context, the satisfaction is an attitude, which can be measured as a positive (satisfied), indifferent, or negative (dissatisfied) feeling. Affect (i.e., attitude) has been theorized and validated in technology acceptance model (TAM) based studies as an important predictor of intention regarding the use of IT systems (Davis 1989). In particular, previous studies found the satisfaction to be positively associated with people's intention to use IT (e.g., Davis 1989; Karahanna et al. 1999; Taylor and Todd 1995). Previous research typically captured the attitude of a person in terms of their satisfaction with an IT system by their behavioral intent towards the system (e.g., Benlian 2011; Klein and Jiang 2001; Tesch et al. 2005). Altogether, we hypothesize that:

H2.2:   *The perceptual incongruence between the providers and their (potential) customers regarding the IT security risks directly reduces the customers' intention to use Cloud services.*

4.1.4   Expectation Confirmation Theory

Beyond that, we expect that the perceptual incongruence among providers and their (potential) customer companies regarding the ITSRs predicts an expectation gap that increases the customers' perception of the ITSRs associated with the use of the Cloud services. According to expectation confirmation theory (ECT), the extend of conformation is determined by the users' level of expectation and their perceived performance of the product (Oliver 1980).

We argue that the expectation of the (potential) customer companies regarding the protection of the Cloud services against the ITSRs is determined by the customers' perception of ITSRs. In this context, previous studies conclusively demonstrated that people's IT security behavior is largely predicted by their perception of the ITSRs (e.g., Johnston and Warkentin 2010; Vance et al. 2012). However, in contrast to traditional IT systems, the specific characteristics of the Cloud do not allow the customers to directly control the ITSRs to which their systems and data are exposed when a Cloud service is used as delivery model (e.g., by implementing additional safeguarding measures). Accordingly, they will expect the providers to have installed adequate safeguards against the ITSRs in their Cloud services (e.g., Pring 2010). As demonstrated in Chapter 0 of this thesis, the providers' IT security risk management (i.e., the implementation of safeguard in the Cloud services), and subsequently their capability to answer the (potential) customers' expectation on the IT security of the Cloud services, is predominately determined by the subjective ITSR perceptions of the providers' decision makers.

In this regard, the (potential) customers' IT managers are typically directly confronted with the ITSR perception of the Cloud providers, for example, by customer communication, security whitepapers, or at the latest during the sales pitch (Ackermann et al. 2012). At this point, they are enabled to estimate the ITSR perceptions of the providers, for instance, by reference to the implemented safeguarding measures (e.g., if the providers' decision makers assess a certain ITSR to be a serious threat, there will be adequate safeguards installed in the service) along with statements of the providers' staff and their reactions to expressed security concerns of the customers' IT managers. However, the higher the perceptual incongruences between the providers and the (potential) customer companies concerning the ITSRs, the more likely the customers' expectations regarding the protection of the services are not fulfilled by the provider. For example, a Cloud service might not offer the encryption of the stored data that may be expected by a (potential) customer company's IT manager, because the provider's decision maker does not perceive the possibility of their employees looking at sensitive data to be a serious risk. As a result of the expectation gap fueled by the disagreement regarding this ITSR, the customer company's IT manager will perceive the adoption of this Cloud service to be associated with a higher overall ITSR. Further theoretical support for this association comes from CDT, which suggests that users experience cognitive dissonance or psychological tension if their preceding perceptions are disconfirmed. Accordingly, the (potential) customer company's IT manager will attempt to remedy the dissonance by distorting or modifying his or her perception of the ITSR in order to be more consistent with reality (Bhattacherjee 2001; Brown et al. 2012). Hence, we expect that:

H2.3:   The higher the perceptual incongruence between providers and their (potential) customers regarding the IT security risks, the higher the customers' perceptions of the IT security risks associated with the Cloud services.

4.1.5   Cloud Adoption

Perceived risk (see also Subsection 2.2.1) is formally defined as the expectation of losses associated with a purchase and frequently acts as an inhibitor to purchase behavior (Peter and Ryan 1976). It is relevant in decision-making when the circumstances of the decision create uncertainty, discomfort and/or anxiety, and conflict in the decision maker (Bettman 1973). In general, the perceived risk is conceptualized as a multi-dimensional construct with six sub-dimensions (i.e., performance, economic/financial considerations, opportunity/time, safety, social factors, and psychological risk) (Cunningham 1967).

Conversely, Ackermann et al. (2012) demonstrated that a more technological-orientated conceptualization (i.e., confidentiality risks, integrity risks, availability risks, performance risks, accountability risks, and maintainability risks) is necessary in the context of service-based IT systems (see also Subsection 2.2.2). In particular, the authors found in their empirical study that the customers' perceptions of the ITSRs explain the predominant part of the variance of their overall perception of the Cloud services' risk. Similarly, other studies revealed the perceived ITSRs to be the most salient factor in the formation of (potential) customers' perception of the overall risk associated with the adoption of Cloud services (e.g., Benlian and Hess

2011; Gewald and Dibbern 2009). In line with the results of prior research, we hypothesize that:

H2.4:   *The higher the IT security risk perception of the customers the higher their perception of overall risks associated with the adoption of the Cloud services.*

The combination of uncertainty (probability of loss) and danger (cost of loss) caused by risks have been conclusively demonstrated to strongly inhibit people's intention to adopt a product or service (Dowling and Staelin 1994). Similarly, the negative influence of the perceived risk on IT adoption decisions in general and on IT outsourcing decisions in particular is widely supported. For example, perceived risks have been demonstrated to strongly influence users' intention to adopt Internet-based applications at the end-user level (e.g. Kim et al. 2008). At the organizational level, perceived risk has been found to negatively affect IT executives' intention to increase the level of business process outsourcing (BPO) (e.g., Gewald and Dibbern 2009; Gewald et al. 2006) and to use of Cloud services (e.g., Ackermann et al. 2012; Benlian and Hess 2011). Featherman and Pavlou (2003) proposed and empirically tested an e-service adoption model, which integrates perceived risk in an extended version of TAM. Results of the empirical test of the proposed variance model indicated that intentions to adopt service-based IT systems are adversely affected by (potential) users' perception of the risk associated with the services. Based on the theoretical underpinnings and empirical evidence presented above, we expect that the (potential) customers' IT managers' perceptions of the overall risk associated with the adoption of the Cloud services will significantly reduce their intention to use Cloud services. Accordingly, we hypothesize that:

H2.5:   *The higher the customers' perception of the overall risk associated with the adoption
of the Cloud services, the lower their intention to adopt the Cloud services.*

The expected opportunities of an IT system is most frequently theorized as "perceived usefulness", which is defined as "the prospective user's subjective probability that using a specific application system will increase his or her job performance within an organizational context" (Davis 1989, p. 4). Armbrust et al. (2010) and Cusumano (2010) posit that the adoption of Cloud leads to major operational improvements through cost reduction, standardization and strategic flexibility (see also Section 2.1). For example, Cloud services typically run on shared infrastructure and provide multiple users with a single instance of a highly standardized service, which runs on a scalable and cost-efficient platform. Thus, the Cloud providers can usually provide IT services at lower costs than the customers companies. These improved economics in the providing of services will be (at least partly) passed on to customers, who thus also benefit from the lower total ownership costs. Strategic flexibility may additionally arise because, in comparison to traditional forms of IT service provision, customers of Cloud services are generally more flexible regarding the switching of IT providers (e.g., Lacity et al. 1995; Whitten et al. 2010).

The technology acceptance model (TAM) has been utilized in many studies to gauge user perceptions of system use and the probability of adopting an IT system (e.g., Gefen and Straub 2000; Mauricio et al. 2010; Pavlou 2003). In particular, TAM theorizes that perceived usefulness and perceived ease of use predict a person's intention to use a system with intention to use serving as a mediator of actual system use (Davis 1989). Previous perceptual congruence and expectation confirmation research in the IT context frequently utilizes a TAM-based theoretical model to explain the behavioral consequences of congruence and confirmation (e.g., Brown et al. 2012; Lin et al. 2005; Venkatesh and Goyal 2010). Although attitudes and expectations may theoretically be a broader construct encompassing many beliefs, previous studies suggest that perceived usefulness is an adequate anticipation in the IT adoption context. In particular, empirical studies comparing their relative effects found that the perceived usefulness is the only belief that consistently influences IT system usage intention, whereas ease of use was found to have inconsistent effects on users' attitudes and behavioral intent (e.g., Bhattacherjee 2001; Karahanna et al. 1999; Schepers and Wetzels 2007).

In the context of service-based IT systems, previous studies found that the perceived overall usefulness is the most important expectation of (potential) users' attitudinal appraisals towards e-services and the Cloud (e.g.,Benlian and Hess 2011; Mauricio et al. 2010). Featherman and Pavlou (2003) even found no significant effects of the e-services' ease of use on the users' attitudes and behavioral intentions. Accordingly, we expect the perceived usefulness is the most salient facet of the attitudinal appraisal of Cloud services by (potential) customers' IT managers. Hence, we expect that:

H2.6:   The higher the customers' perceived usefulness of the Cloud services, the higher their intention to adopt the Cloud services.

Drawing on perceived risk literature, Featherman and Pavlou (2003) operationalized and integrated the specific facets of perceived risk and the TAM to propose an e-services adoption model. The results of the empirical tests conducted by the authors indicated, that perceived risks not only inhibit users' intentions to adopt e-services but also lower their expectations regarding the benefits of e-service adoption (e.g., through vanishing cost advantages in the case of performance problems) (Featherman and Pavlou 2003; Mauricio et al. 2010). A similar causal relationship between perceived risks and perceived usefulness was revealed by Benlian and Hess (2011) in an empirical study of (potential) customer companies' intention to use Cloud services. Accordingly, we assume that the (potential) customers' IT managers' perception of the overall risk associated with the Cloud services plays a significant role in the formation of their beliefs regarding the overall usefulness of the Cloud services. Therefore, we hypothesize that:

H2.7:   The customers' perceived overall risk of the Cloud services is negatively related to their perception of the usefulness of the Cloud services.

4.2   Research Methodology

In this section, we first present the measurement models of the empirical surveys of Cloud providers' and (potential) customer companies' ITSR assessments (Subsection 4.2.1). Next, we describe the administration of the two studies (Subsection 4.2.2) and show the characteristics of the obtained sample of Cloud providers' decision makers as well as IT managers of their (potential) customer companies (Subsection 4.2.3). Lastly, we present the data analysis techniques used in this part (Subsection 4.2.4).

4.2.1   Measurement Model

We conducted two empirically studies with Cloud providers' decision makers and their (potential) customers' IT managers to test our hypotheses regarding the existence of perceptual incongruences concerning the ITSR of Cloud services. Therefore, we developed two different questionnaires. In order to ensure the construct and content validity of the measurement model we adopted indicators and scales from preceding research studies with minor wording changes (see Table A-5). Each of the questionnaires was pretested with cognitive interviews (Bolton 1993). More precisely, the questionnaire of the customer study was presented to five IS researchers and three IS professionals. The provider study questionnaire was pretested with four IS researchers and seven IS professionals. The pretests resulted in minor wording changes of the indicators and scales.

In the first part of the customer questionnaire, we presented the details of those Cloud services to the (potential) customers' IT managers, which we found to be offered by the Cloud provider companies (see Cloud service types as shown in Table 4-1). In order to determine the estimation targets of the (potential) customers' IT managers, which, in the following, enabled us to match the responses of providers with that of the (potential) customer companies, we asked the participants to select one of these Cloud services (i.e., the service that is in general interesting for their organization) and answer all questions in the questionnaire regarding this service type. Then, the questionnaire of the customer study contained socio-demographics followed by questions regarding their intention to adopt the selected Cloud service, perceived usefulness of the selected Cloud service, perceived overall risk of the selected Cloud service, and constructs to measure the ITSR perception regarding the selected Cloud service. The ITSR perception was thereby measured based on Ackermann et al. (2012)'s framework with

31 ITSR items, 6 ITSR sub-dimensions, and one overall ITSR construct (see a detailed description of the framework in Subsection 2.2.2).

Since we aimed to investigate the effects of the disagreement regarding the ITSRs on the attitudes and adoption intention of (potential) customers' IT managers, the provider questionnaire only contained socio-demographics, questions regarding the characteristics of the provided Cloud services, and constructs to measure the providers' decision makers assessment of the ITSR of their Cloud services. Therefore, we also used Ackermann et al. (2012)'s framework and measured the providers' decision makers' ITSR perceptions based on the 6 sub-dimensions of perceived ITSRs in the context of the Cloud.

As shown in Table A-5, each construct was measured by 3 indicators.

4.2.2   Survey Administration

In the course of our empirical study, we distributed the developed questionnaires to Cloud providers, which are active in the German market, and their (potential) customer companies. We offered both a printed version and an online version of the questionnaire to the participants. In particular, as the sequences of the indicators of each construct were randomized in order to minimize response-set biases, we also distributed two versions of the printed customer questionnaire with altered arrangement of the indicators (Andrews 1984). The data collection of the study took place between June 10 and July 30, 2012.

First, the provider questionnaire was distributed to all Cloud providers, which are active in the German market.[8] A total of 247 Cloud providers were hereby identified in corresponding databases and publications (Velten and Janata 2011). As far as information was available, we directly contacted the CIO or IT security manager of the Cloud providers. In all remaining cases, we contacted the CEO and asked to forward the study to the responsible manager. Anyway, the executives were motivated by offering a detailed result report including an overview of the risk assessments of their competitors and their (potential) customers. After completion of the first half of the data collection period, all known contact persons were called and reminded of the study. Additionally, a reminder was sent via mail. At the end of the two month study period, we had received 84 completed questionnaires (response rate: 34%) of which 11 had to be excluded due to poor data quality or missing information.

Afterwards, the customer questionnaire was distributed to 6,000 companies, randomly drawn from the Hoppenstedt database, which is a German firm database holding more than 300,000 companies. In order to support the external validity of our study, we did not constrain the sample to specific industries or to firms of a specific organizational size. Whenever possible, we directly contacted the (potential) customer companies' CIO. However, particularly in the

---

[8]   Please note: The providers are not necessarily located in Germany.

case of rather small companies, only the CEO of the companies was listed in the database, whom we contacted in these cases. The customers' IT managers were encouraged to participate in the study by offering an individualized management report, which compare their answers against companies of the same industry. Additionally, we have sent reminders via email to all customer companies and randomly called approximately 50% of the 6,000 companies for follow-up reminders. As shown in Table 4-1, at the end of the two month study period, a total of 472 completed questionnaires were received (response rate: 7.87%). This response rate is still acceptable in the view of the fact, that it is typically very difficult to survey executives and corporate-level managers in the IT context (Poppo and Zenger 2002). Due to missing data and low data quality, we had to exclude some of these responses from the sample. In particular, all questionnaires that were not fully completed by the participants were excluded and only data sets without missing values were used for calculations (51 excluded). Since we sought to investigate the inhibitory role of perceptual incongruence between (potential) customer companies and providers regarding the ITSRs in a pre-adoption stage (see also Section 4.3.1), we selected those companies as (potential) customers of the providers' Cloud solutions, which already grappled intensively with the considered Cloud service (79 excluded) but have not yet adopted Cloud services (38 excluded). In this regard, we argue that only the (potential) customers' IT managers who had previously a critical look at the Cloud services can adequately evaluated whether the IT security level of the considered services satisfies their expectation on the protection of their systems and data (Huisman and Iivari 2006). Hence, the presented results of this study are based on a final sample size of 304 valid responses.

4.2.3 Sample Characteristics

The final data set of participants yielded the descriptive details shown in Table 4-1. The ITSR of the Cloud services were evaluated from the provider and the customer perspective. Therefore, the table first shows the distribution of customer and provider organization sizes (i.e. the number of employees in the organizations). Approximately 45% of the customer companies were corporations with more than 249 employees. In contrast, only 28.8% of the provider organizations in the sample had more than 249 employees. Conversely, there are many rather small Cloud providers active in the market (Velten and Janata 2011), so that the distribution of the provider organization sizes points to a good representative status of the sample. Furthermore, the distribution of the application types of the provided services in the sample underscores its good representative status. Specifically, communication and collaboration applications (23.3%) and customer relationship management applications (13.7%) were the most prevalent service offered by the providers in the sample. However, the customers' IT managers were often interested in obtaining enterprise resource planning services (24.8%) and online storage services (19.1%). As shown in Table 4-1, 65% of the customer study participants were CEOs or CIOs and 87% of the respondents answered that they are directly responsible for the decisions regarding the adoption of Cloud services in their organization. About 65% of the provider participants were CEOs, CIOs, or IT security managers and 39.6% stated that they were directly responsible for their organizations' IT security risk management and 47.9% stated that they are at least partially involved in the decision process. On average, the survey respondents had 10 years of professional experience.

Table 4-1: Sample Characteristics of the Perceptual Incongruence Study		
Category	Customer study	Provider study
Size of organization (employees)	%	%
Small (< 50)	16.4	49.3
Medium (50 - 249)	39.0	21.9
Corporation (> 249)	44.6	28.8
Participant position	%	%
CEO	13.5	24.7
CIO	48.6	23.3
IT security manager	3.1	16.4
IT manager	27.7	15.1
Business manager / COO	4.0	12.3
Other manager	3.1	8.2
Participant experience	%	%
1 year or less	5.4	6.8
2 - 5 years	28.5	27.4
6 - 10 years	37.8	26.0
11 years or more	28.3	39.7
Type of Cloud application	%	%
Communication and collaboration	16.4	23.3
Customer relationship management	11.4	13.7
Content management system	4.5	4.1
Office application	10.5	9.6
Enterprise resource planning	24.8	9.6
Development / execution environment	3.3	9.6
Online storage	19.1	13.7
Computing power on virtual servers	7.7	12.3
Other applications	2.3	4.1

Please note: Customer study n=304; Provider study n=73.

Although the comparison of the respondents' characteristics with those of the original target samples did not show major differences, we conducted further analysis of possible non-response-bias. Therefore, according to Armstrong and Overton (1977), we compared the first 25 % with the last 25 % of the received answers in order to examine if the interest of participants in the topic has any effects. In both samples, we could not identify significant differences among the responses in the considered variables utilizing t-tests. Additionally, we performed a series of chi-square comparisons, which also showed no significant differences between early and late responses. During the phone calls, we asked for the reasons, why some organizations were not willing to participate. Most often, the IT managers of (potential) customer companies told that they do not see themselves as the target group for the offered Cloud services, because they run highly specifically IT systems or the existing IT infrastructure is too small. The Cloud providers' decision makers most frequently told us that because of security reasons the organization's policies forbid taking part in surveys or the contacted person was too busy to participate.

Given the single method used to collect the data, we conducted a series of tests to analyze common method bias (CMB) in our datasets. We performed Harman's single factor test with principal axis factoring and restricted the factors to extract to one. The results showed that a single factor accounted only for 32% of the variance which is below the critical value of 50% (Podsakoff et al. 2003). In addition, we followed Rönkkö and Ylitalo (2011)'s PLS marker variable approach and included two marker items in each questionnaire, which are unrelated to our research model but are subject to the same measurement effects (e.g., "my needs and desires are taken into account in planning the company's benefit program"). The marker variables thereby showed the smallest correlation with all other manifest measures. All tests suggest that CMB is unlikely to be a problem in our analyses and results.

4.2.4 Data Analyses

Our main hypothesis concerning the existence of a significant perceptual incongruence between providers and their (potential) customer companies regarding the ITSRs of the Cloud (H2.1) was tested with descriptive analyses of the ITSR assessments of providers' decision makers and those of (potential) customers' IT managers.

Based on the matched survey responses of Cloud providers' decision makers and (potential) customers' IT managers, we calculated 18 new variables (i.e., one variable for each of the 3 indicators of the 6 dimension of perceived ITSRs) for each of the 304 customer company records, containing the differences between the (potential) customer company's assessment of an ITSR dimension and the corresponding assessment of the provider, which offer the Cloud service, that the customer company's IT manager had selected at the beginning of the study. In the following, these variables functioned as indicators of the perceptual incongruence dimension constructs (i.e., perceptual incongruence on the confidentiality, integrity, availability, performance, accountability, maintainability risks). In line with Ackermann et al. (2012)'s conceptualization of perceived ITSRs and drawing on perceptual incongruence research (Benlian 2011; Huisman and Iivari 2006), we argue that the overall perceptual incongruence concerning the ITSR will be predicted by the sum of all perceptual incongruences on the ITSR dimensions between a customer and the provider of the selected Cloud services. In other words, the higher the disagreement on each ITSR dimension, the higher the overall disagreement between a provider and its (potential) customer on the ITSRs associated with the Cloud service. Accordingly, we operationalized the overall perceptual incongruence as a multidimensional – formative first-order, reflective second-order – construct. In this form of multidimensional constructs, the perceptual incongruence dimension constructs function as indicators of the overall perceptual incongruence construct. Thus, these dimensions are different manifestations of the same higher-order concept but the indicators of each dimension combine to form their respective dimensions (Polites et al. 2012). All other constructs were operationalized directly in a reflective manner and linked as hypothesized (see Figure 4-1).

The hypotheses regarding the effects of perceptual incongruences on the customers' IT managers' adoption intention of Cloud services (H2.2 - H2.7) were tested collectively with a partial least squares (PLS) analysis approach. PLS works by maximizing the explained variance of the dependent variables by estimating partial model relationships in an iterative series of ordinary least squares regressions (Hair et al. 2012). It is well-suited when the focus is on theory development, whereas covariance based approaches (e.g., LISREL) are preferred for confirmatory testing of the fit of theoretical models to observed data and therefore require "stronger theory" than PLS (Ringle et al. 2012). Accordingly, the PLS technique is appropriate and better suited for this study because of its explanatory character (e.g., Chwelos et al. 2001). Additionally, the perceptual incongruence construct are operationalized as multidimensional – formative first-order, reflective second-order constructs – which cannot be adequately estimated using covariance based structure analysis techniques due to their underlying assumptions (Polites et al. 2012).

With n=304, the obtained sample clearly exceeds the rule of thumb for robust PLS calculations that suggests a minimum sample size of ten times the maximum number of paths pointing at any variable (Barclay et al. 1995; Hair et al. 2012). As this rule of thumb is controversially discussed in IS literature, we additionally followed recommendations of Goodhue et al. (2012) and used Cohen (1992)'s statistical power approach to determine the minimum necessary sample size: Based on an expected average effect size of $\beta > 0.15$, a minimum significance level of $\alpha = 0.05$, and 10 independent variables, we would require a minimum sample size of n=147 in this study in order to achieve sufficient statistical power (Cohen 1992). In this study, we were able to obtain a sample size of n=304, which is very well above this recommended threshold. Altogether, the estimated parameters are unlikely to suffer from an unsufficient statistical power of the obtained sample due to too small sample size.

A PLS bootstrapping approach with no sign changes and 5,000 resamples that consisted of the same number of cases as the original sample was used to determine the statistical significance of the estimations (Hair et al. 2012). In contrast to its covariance-based counterpart, PLS does not impose any assumptions regarding the distribution of the indicators in the obtained sample and has been shown by previous studies to be robust in situations where data are non-normal (e.g., Reinartz et al. 2009). Nonetheless, guidelines for PLS recommend to check data distribution for extreme values of non-normality (e.g., Hair et al. 2012; Ringle et al. 2012). In general, absolute skew value of >2 and kurtosis value >7 are viewed as an evidence for substantial deviation from normality (West et al. 1995). In our sample, we found only rather small skew or kurtosis values (up to skew 1.2 and kurtosis 5.1). Thus, the deviation from a normality distribution is not very likely to negatively affect the data analyses in this study.

4.3   Results

The results of the analyses of the data collected in the two empirical studies are presented in this section. We first demonstrate the existence of a large perceptual incongruence between the Cloud providers and their (potential) customer companies regarding the ITSR associated with the Cloud services (Subsection 4.3.1). Second, we present the results of the analyses regarding the effects of the perceptual incongruence on (potential) customer companies' intention to adopt Cloud services (Subsection 4.3.2). By combining the results of Subsection 4.3.1 and Subsection 4.3.2 we show the implications of the disagreement among the Cloud providers and their (potential) customer companies regarding the ITSRs for the sales of Cloud services in the market.

4.3.1   Existence of Perceptual Incongruences between Providers and Customers regarding the IT Security Risks

In the first step of our analysis, we compared the ITSR perceptions of Cloud providers' decision makers with those of (potential) customers' IT managers in order to reveal possible disagreements regarding the ITSRs in the context of the Cloud. Therefore, we matched the ITSR perceptions of (potential) customers' IT managers to the ITSR perception of those providers' decision makers, whose organizations supply the Cloud service that was selected by the customers at the first part of the questionnaire (see above). For example, if a (potential) customer companies' IT manager stated that his or her organization had considered to obtain a customer relationship management (CRM) service, the ITSR perception will be compared to those providers, which provide the selected CRM Cloud service. Two-sided t-tests were thereby used to test the statistical significance of the perceptual differences between the providers' decision makers and the (potential) customers' IT managers concerning the ITSRs of the Cloud services. As shown in Figure 4-2, the results reveal a significant perceptual incongruence between the providers and their (potential) customers regarding all risk items that cover the ITSR in the context of the Cloud exhaustively and mutually exclusively (Ackermann et al. 2012).

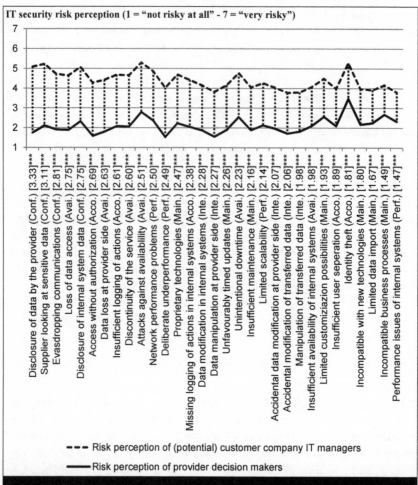

Figure 4-2: Perceptual Incongruences regarding the IT Security Risk Items

Please note: Customer study n=304; Provider study n=73. The average difference between the ITSR perceptions of Cloud providers' decision makers and (potential) customers' IT managers is in brackets. Risk dimensions: Acco. = Accountability risks, Avai. = Availability risks, Conf. = Confidentiality risks, Inte. = Integrity risks, Main. = Maintainability risks, Perf. = performance risks. Significance levels: ***p=<0.001, **p<0.01.

The most striking result to emerge from the data is that providers and their (potential) customers are in agreement about the relative risk of all ITSR items. From the parallel curves in the graph above, we can, for example, see that there is an agreement that insufficient user separation is substantially less risky than identity theft, or that limited scalability is slightly more risky than accidental data modification at the provider side. This relative agreement among customers' IT managers and the Cloud providers' decision makers indicate a shared understanding of the nature of the risks (i.e., validity of the used framework).

Nevertheless, the results also demonstrate that the providers assess all ITSRs items significantly lower than the (potential) customers.

Furthermore, comparisons of the overall perceived ITSRs as well as its six sub-dimensions, as presented in Table 4-2, revealed that the (potential) customers' IT managers estimate the confidentiality risks ($\Delta=3.53$; $p<0.001$), integrity risks ($\Delta=2.40$; $p<0.001$), availability risks ($\Delta=2.88$; $p<0.001$), performance risks ($\Delta=2.51$; $p<0.001$), accountability risks ($\Delta=2.87$; $p<0.001$), and maintainability risks ($\Delta=2.64$; $p<0.001$) to be significantly more risky than the Cloud providers' decision makers. For these comparisons we utilized mean scores of all comparative and absolute risk indicators. Therefore, we conducted several tests to confirm that the indicators measure the underlying ITSR perception constructs (see Table 4-3). In particular, Cronbach's alpha values of all scales concerning decision makers' ITSR perceptions were above 0.92, pointing to the constructs' excellent internal consistency (MacKenzie et al. 2011).

Table 4-2: Perceptual Incongruences regarding the IT Security Risk Dimensions

IT security risk dimension	Average standard deviation	T-value	Average difference
Confidentiality	1.32	54.9	3.53***
Integrity	1.51	32.7	2.40***
Availability	1.44	40.5	2.88***
Performance	1.42	35.7	2.51***
Accountability	1.39	40.9	2.87***
Maintainability	1.32	39.8	2.64***

Please note: Customer study n=304, Provider study n=73. Analyses based on differences of the average of all 3 indicators that measure the ITSR risk dimension. Significance levels: ***p=<0.001.

Overall, the results consistently indicate that there is a considerable perceptual incongruence regarding the ITSRs associated with Cloud services between providers and their (potential) customer companies. Accordingly, Hypothesis H2.1 is strongly supported.

4.3.2 Impacts of Perceptual Incongruences between Providers and Customers regarding the IT Security Risks on Cloud Adoption

In this subsection, we present the assessment of measurement model (Subsection 4.3.2.1) followed by the results of the structural model testing concerning the effects of perceptual incongruences between providers and their (potential) customers regarding the ITSRs on the customers' intention to adopt Cloud services (Subsection 4.3.2.2).

4.3.2.1 Assessment of Measurement Validation

Based on established guidelines for PLS, we first assessed our measurement model's validity and reliability at the construct level (MacKenzie et al. 2011). As shown in Table 4-3, all reflective constructs met the recommended threshold value for the average variance extracted (AVE) of greater 0.5 (MacKenzie et al. 2011). The Construct Reliability (CR) values for all constructs ranged from 0.867 to 0.979, which is significantly above the recommended threshold of 0.7 thus indicating a good internal consistency of indicators (Fornell and Larcker 1981).

Table 4-3: Assessment of the Perceptual Incongruence Measurement Model				
Constructs	Factor loadings	Cronbach's alpha	AVE	CR
Intention to adopt services	0.851 - 0.932	0.921	0.863	0.950
Perceived overall usefulness of service	0.799 - 0.896	0.829	0.704	0.867
Perceived overall risk of service	0.735 - 0.891	0.786	0.744	0.878
Perceived IT security risk	0.844 - 0.925	0.937	0.888	0.961
Incongruence confidentiality	0.904 - 0.931	0.946	0.905	0.966
Incongruence integrity	0.922 - 0.981	0.968	0.939	0.979
Incongruence availability	0.868 - 0.896	0.927	0.872	0.954
Incongruence performance	0.881 - 0.934	0.945	0.901	0.965
Incongruence accountability	0.857 - 0.931	0.947	0.904	0.967
Incongruence maintainability	0.892 - 0.947	0.960	0.926	0.974

Please note: n=304. AVE = Average Variance Extracted, CR = Composite Reliability.

The validity of the individual indicators was assessed by analyzing the relationships between each indicator and its latent construct. All completely standardized factor loadings were found to be large and statistically significant at the $p<0.001$ level (Chin 1998). We also relied on the recently proposed heterotrait-monotrait (HTMT) ratio. All estimated absolute HTMT values (see Subsection 3.3.1 for a detailed description of the HTMT approach) were thereby significantly below the recommended conservative cut-off value of 0.85 (no value greater than 0.47), pointing to the latent variables' excellent divergent validity (Henseler et al. 2014). Moreover, the factor loadings of our reflective indicators were higher with regard to their conceptually corresponding constructs than with regard to any other construct, indicating the latent variables' discriminant validity (MacKenzie et al. 2011). In addition, all constructs fulfilled Fornell and Larcker (1981)'s criterion for discriminant validity. As shown in Table A-6, the square roots of AVE (see Table 4-3) of the constructs' indicators were always higher than their correlation with any other construct in the model.

4.3.2.2   Results of the Structural Model Testing

In order to test our remaining hypotheses, we examined the path significance of each hypothesized association in the research model together with the construct's explained variance (R^2 value) (Ringle et al. 2012). As presented in Figure 4-3, not all disagreements between the providers and their (potential) customer companies regarding the ITSRs have equally strong effects on important downstream customer beliefs. While the perceptual incongruence about confidentiality risks ($\beta=0.561$; $p<0.001$), availability risks ($\beta=0.213$; $p<0.01$), and performance risks ($\beta=0.315$; $p<0.001$) have been revealed to have significant effects on the perceptual incongruence between providers and their (potential) customers concerning the Cloud's ITSRs, weak or non-significant effects of accountability risks ($\beta=0.145$; $p<0.05$), integrity risks ($\beta=0.065$; $p\geq0.05$), and maintainability risks ($\beta=0.032$; $p\geq0.05$) were found. In this regard, the sub-dimensions confidentiality, availability, and performance largely cover risks that ascribe opportunistic behavior or a carefree attitude of the providers towards protection to the Cloud services, such as unintentional downtimes. Hence, the providers' decision makers are likely to assess these ITSRs as rather uncritical. At the same time, for (potential) customer companies, the protection against these ITSR is typically difficult to monitor, such as a supplier looking at sensitive customer data. As such, the (potential) customers' IT managers are likely to be more suspicious regarding the IT security of the Cloud service when there are larger disagreements with the providers on these ITSR dimensions. As a result, these ITSR dimensions are likely to have stronger influence on the formation of the overall perception of the (potential) customers' IT managers that there is a considerable difference of the own ITSR assessments to those of the providers of the Cloud services. Altogether, while Hypotheses H2.1b and H2.1f had to be rejected, we found strong support for Hypotheses H2.1a, H2.1c, H2.1d, and H2.1e.

Conversely, as presented in Figure 4-3, the (potential) customer companies' perception that their ITSR perception falls short of the providers' ITSR assessment (e.g., during the sales pitch) were found to directly decrease their intentions to adopt the Cloud services ($\beta=-0.209$; $p<0.01$), thereby supporting Hypothesis H2.2.

At the same time, the expectation gap regarding the protection of the Cloud services (i.e., the (potential) customer company's IT manager expects safeguarding measures, which are not implemented in the Cloud service), fueled by the perceptual incongruence was found to significantly increase the perceptions of the ITSR associated with the adoption of the Cloud services by (potential) customers' IT managers ($\beta=0.526$; $p<0.001$). Hence, Hypothesis H2.3 is supported. Moreover, with an R^2 value of 0.226, the results point to the high impact of perceptual incongruences on the formation of customers' overall ITSR perception in the context of the Cloud.

In sum, the results demonstrate that the perceptual incongruence between providers and their (potential) customers regarding the ITSRs not only has strong adverse effects on the customer IT managers' perceptions of the ITSR associated with the Cloud services but also directly reduces their intention to adopt the Cloud services.

Beyond that, we confirmed findings of previous studies (e.g., Ackermann et al. 2012; Benlian and Hess 2011) and showed that the ITSR perception has a strong effect on the (potential) customers' perception of the overall risk of the Cloud services ($\beta=0.689$; $p<0.001$). The considerably high variance explained in (potential) customer companies' overall risk assessments ($R^2=0.474$) underscores that the perceived ITSR is an important factor in (potential) customers' risk perception in the context of Cloud adoption decisions. As such, Hypothesis H2.4 is confirmed.

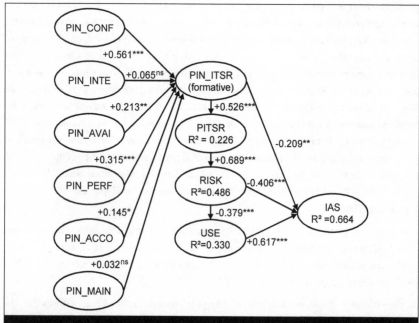

Figure 4-3: Empirical Testing of Perceptual Incongruence Model

Please note: n=304. Measurement model not shown for purposes of clarity. Path significance: ***$p<0.001$; **$p<0.01$; *$p<0.05$; $^{ns}p\geq0.05$. Constructs: IAS = Intention to adopt service, PIN_ACCO = Perceptual incongruence on accountability risks, PIN_AVAI = Perceptual incongruence on availability risks, PIN_CONF = Perceptual incongruence on confidentiality risks, PIN_INTE = Perceptual incongruence on integrity risks, PIN_ITSR = Perceptual incongruence on IT security risk of service, PIN_MAIN = Perceptual incongruence on maintainability risks, PIN_PERF = Perceptual incongruence on performance risks, PITSR = Perceived IT security risk of service, RISK = Perceived overall risk of service, USE = Perceived overall usefulness of service.

Furthermore, in support of Hypothesis H2.5, the overall perception of the risk associated with the adoption of the Cloud services was found to significantly reduce the intention of (potential) customers' IT managers to use the Cloud services (β=-0.406; p<0.001).

Additionally, perceived risk was confirmed to negatively affect customer companies assessment of the usefulness of the Cloud services (β=-0.379; p<0.001), which in turn significantly facilitates the decision of (potential) customer companies to adopt the Cloud services (β=0.617; p<0.001). Accordingly, the Hypotheses H2.6 and H2.7 are supported. Additionally, the squared multiple correlation for the intention to adopt the Cloud services by (potential) customers' IT managers (R^2=0.661) point to the model's strong explanatory power.

As described above, the perceptual incongruence between providers and their (potential) customers regarding the ITSR was found to directly as well as indirectly inhibit the customers' IT managers' intention to adopt Cloud services. In particular, the perceptual incongruence was also revealed to increase the ITSR perception, which, in turn, negatively influences downstream beliefs of IT managers and subsequently affects the customer companies' decisions to use Cloud services. In order to test the joint statistical significance of the direct (β=-0.209) and indirect (β_{ind}=-0.232) effects, we utilized Preacher and Hayes (2008)'s bootstrapping based approach with no sign changes and 5,000 re-samples, consisting of the same number of cases as in the original sample (see a detailed description of Preacher and Hayes (2008)'s bootstrapping approach in Subsection 3.3.1). We thereby found that the perceptual incongruences regarding the confidentiality (β_{ind}=-0.247; p<0.01), availability (β_{ind}=-0.094; p<0.05), and the performance risks (β_{ind}=-0.139; p<0.01) have significant indirect effects on the customer companies' intention to adopt Cloud services. However, the indirect effects of the perceptual differences between the providers and their (potential) customers on the integrity (β_{ind}=-0.029; p≥0.05), accountability (β_{ind}=-0.064; p≥0.05), and the maintainability risks (β_{ind}=-0.014; p≥0.05) were found to be non-significant. We also followed MacKinnon et al. (2007)'s recommendation and tested the distribution of the indirect effects in terms of normality. Since the calculated z-value of 3.04 is way above 1.65, a potential non-normality of the data is not likely to affect the estimated parameter of the indirect effect. Taken together, we showed that the perceptual incongruence regarding the ITSR has significant direct and indirect effects on the customer companies' decision to adopt the Cloud services (overall effect size: β_{over}=-0.441; p<0.001), supporting the dual inhibitory role of perceptual incongruence in Cloud adoption.

Moreover, the combination of the results regarding the average perceptual differences between the providers and their (potential) customers on the relevant ITSR dimensions (i.e., confidentiality, availability, and performance), as shown in Table 4-2, with the estimation of the structural model enabled us to demonstrate that the perceptual incongruence averagely reduces the intention of the customers' IT managers to adopt Cloud services by 21.4%.

4.4   Discussion of Study Findings

Based on the theories of cognitive dissonance and risk perception, this study investigated the nature and dual inhibitory role of perceptual incongruence between providers and their (potential) customer companies in Cloud services adoption. In support of our basic hypothesis, the results of a dyadic empirical study with Cloud providers and their (potential) customers revealed that the perception of the ITSR associated with the use of the Cloud substantially differ among providers' decision makers and customers' IT managers. In particular, we found that the (potential) customer IT managers on average assess all relevant ITSR items to be significantly more risky as the Cloud providers' decision makers evaluate these risks. Especially the assessments of those ITSR which are caused by opportunistic or careless behavior of the providers (e.g., disclosure of data by the provider and supplier looking at sensitive data) were revealed to largely differ among Cloud providers and their customers. On the one hand, these ITSRs are difficult to monitor and control for customers, what may increase the risk perception of (potential) customers' IT managers. On the other hand, since these ITSR are predominately based on misconduct of the employees and insufficient IT security risk management of the providers, their decision makers are more likely to underestimate these risks in their own organizations' Cloud services. In particular, as shown in Chapter 0, the ITSR perceptions of the Cloud providers' decision makers were revealed to be in many cases subject to systematical errors in terms of UO. In this context, the providers' decision makers' underestimation of the own services' exposure to the ITSR inevitably diverges their ITSR assessments and those of their (potential) customers.

Drawing on cognitive dissonance theory, expectation confirmation, and technology acceptance research, we proposed a variance model that explicates the effect of the perceptual incongruence between the providers and their (potential) customer companies concerning the ITSRs on (potential) customers' decisions to adopt Cloud services. We demonstrated that especially the differences in the perceptions of confidentiality risks and the availability risks intensify the perception of the (potential) customers' IT managers that there is a serious disagreement with the Cloud providers. Since the IT security of customer companies' system and data depends on the effectiveness of the IT security risk management of the providers when the Cloud is used as a delivery model, a high level of trust in the service providers is generally a central factor in adoption decisions. In this context, previous research also demonstrates that a disagreement between IT providers and their (potential) customer companies in many cases shakes the customers' confidence in the providers' capabilities (e.g., Tesch et al. 2005). Similarly, a loss of trust associated with the feeling of (potential) customers' IT managers that the providers do not understand their IT security concerns is likely to have strong adverse effects on the customers' decisions to adopt Cloud services.

Beyond that, we found that the disagreement between providers and their (potential) customers to elevate customers' IT managers' perception of the ITSR that is associated with the adoption of Cloud services. In this regard, as presented in Chapter 0, the ITSR perception of the Cloud providers' decision makers largely predicts the outcome of the providers' IT security risk management processes and thus the implementation of safeguards in the services. Hence, if the ITSR assessment of a given Cloud provider is not in congruence with those of the (potential) customer's IT manager, the service of this provider will most likely not have the safeguard measures installed that are expected by the customer. As a result of the expectation gap in terms of missing safeguarding measures, the (potential) customer company's IT manager will assess that the Cloud service is exposed to a higher ITSR.

Although risk perception may generally be a broad construct, encompassing many different factors (i.e., performance, economic/financial considerations, opportunity/time, safety, social factors, and psychological risks), we confirmed findings of previous studies in the context of Cloud adoption at the organizational level (e.g., Ackermann et al. 2012; Benlian and Hess 2011) and demonstrated that the customers' perception of the ITSR is the most important factor in the formation of customer assessments of the overall risk associated with the Cloud adoption.

Moreover, we demonstrated that an extended version of Featherman and Pavlou (2003)'s e-service adoption model is also a valid theoretical lens to analyze customer companies' decisions to adopt Cloud services. In particular, we revealed that the perceived usefulness of Cloud services (e.g., cost savings and strategic flexibility) is an important driver of the intentions of (potential) customers' IT managers to use the Cloud. In this context, we also confirmed findings of previous studies in the context of e-service adoption (Featherman and Pavlou 2003) by showing that the perceived risks significantly reduce the perceived usefulness of Cloud services for the customer companies (e.g., the ITSR associated with the Cloud may vanish the cost savings) (Benlian and Hess 2011). Concurrently, we found that the perceived overall risk is an important inhibitor of the adoption of Cloud services by (potential) customer companies.

Altogether, our findings provide strong empirical support that the perceptual distance between providers and their (potential) customer companies has substantially negative consequences on the customers' decision to adopt the Cloud. Specifically, we found that nearly a quarter of all Cloud sales fail to work out because of the disagreement among the providers and the (potential) customer companies on the ITSR associated with the Cloud services. In this context, our results concurrently make the negative consequences of the Cloud providers' decision makers' underestimation of the own service's ITSR exposure evident. As such, the UO in the ITSR perceptions of the Cloud providers' decision makers does not only inhibit the outcome of the providers' IT security risk management (see Chapter 0) but also has adverse effects on the sales of Cloud services due to an increased perceptual distance between the providers and their (potential) customers.

5 Conclusion and Summary of Key Findings

The purpose of this thesis is to enhance our understanding of the impact of subjective ITSR perceptions on the effectiveness of providers' IT security risk management, which is critical to IT security and the overall success of Cloud services. Specifically, this thesis is aimed at achieving the following three goals by integrating several related but distinct streams of psychological and IS literature and empirical studies with both Cloud providers and their (potential) customer companies (see Section 1.2).

First, this thesis increases our understanding of the nature and the role of decision makers' subjective ITSR perceptions in the context of organizational IT security risk management. Therefore, it introduces absolute and comparative estimates as two independent perspectives of the ITSR perception of decision makers and develops a theoretical model of Cloud providers' IT security risk management that explicates the impact of both perceptual perspectives on the implementation of necessary safeguarding measures.

Second, this thesis reveals that the ITSR perceptions of the providers' decision makers are in many cases subject to UO. Based on the proposed theoretical model, it analyzes the impact of the resulting systematical underestimation of the ITSR on the outcome of Cloud providers' IT security risk management.

Third, this thesis demonstrates that there is considerable disagreement between the providers and their (potential) customer companies regarding ITSRs associated with the Cloud that is fueled by UO. Additionally, our work shows the impacts of this perceptual incongruence on important downstream beliefs of customer companies' IT managers and, ultimately, on the customers' intentions to adopt the services.

The studies presented in this thesis provided several theoretical and managerial-related insights into the role of IT security risk perception and UO in the organizational IT security risk management and Cloud adoption. Section 5.1 presents the theoretical contributions of these studies, while Section 5.2 is devoted to the practical contributions and recommended actions for providers (Subsection 5.2.1) and (potential) customers (Subsection 5.2.2) of Cloud services. The limitations of the studies and avenues for future research are discussed in Section 5.3. In Section 5.4, the thesis concludes with a short résumé of the findings and their implications.

5.1 Implications for Theory and Research

The first part of this thesis makes important theoretical contributions to the emerging body of knowledge about the behavioral and organizational issues of IT security. First, the extant literature has an entirely rational view on organizational IT security risk management, such as, for example, mathematical optimization models based on cost-risk analyses (e.g., Cavusoglu et al. 2004b; Sonnenreich et al. 2006). As such, to the best of our knowledge, this is the first study that offers a theoretical explanation and empirical support for the impact of decision makers' subject risk and coping perceptions on the organizational IT security risk management. In particular, our study confirms key theoretical assumptions on coping perceptions and shows that an adapted version of TTAT can also be used as a valid theoretical lens to explain the outcome of risk and solution analysis phases at the organizational level.

Second, we highlight the importance for researchers to consider decision makers' subjective ITSR perceptions when investigating the ITSR management of organizations. Our study not only enables researchers to better understand the risk analysis phase within organizational IT security risk management but also the results of solution analysis phases by demonstrating that the decision makers' assessment of the avoidability of ITSR is determined by their assessments of the safeguard's effectiveness together with its estimated costs and the perceived feasibility of the organization to implement the safeguard.

Third, based on institutional theory, we demonstrate that the perceived external pressure, such as the expectations and behavior of stakeholders, strongly influences the outcome of providers' IT security risk management. In particular, we were able to demonstrate that external pressure can induce decisions to implement certain safeguards in order to remain competitive, even if the decision makers assessed the ITSR not to be risky or difficult to avoid when it was first evaluated. As such, the extension of TTAT, proposed in this study, enriches our knowledge about IT security risk management of organizations and, in particular, empowers researchers to better comprehend yet unexplained empirical findings in the organizational IT security context. In particular, based on the results of previous institutional research and IT security studies, we matched the providers' relevant stakeholder groups with the institutional pressure dimensions to conceptualize in which way and to what extent the stakeholders eventually affect the providers' IT security risk management. Thus, future research will not only benefit from this conceptualization when studying providers' IT security behavior but also when investigating other strategic decisions of providers, which might be driven by stakeholders' expectations and behaviors, like decisions to increase the array of services or to change the pricing strategies of services offered.

Fourth, following psychological risk perception research, this study offers a deeper understanding of the complex nature and effects of ITSR perceptions and, thus, of the effect mechanisms underlying IT security risk management-related decisions. In this regard, our study offers several avenues for next-generation research to better understand the formation of ITSR perceptions and their behavioral consequences. We demonstrate that there are in general two different perspectives on IT security risk perception, encompassing absolute and comparative risk assessments. Moreover, we show, in particular, that both absolute and relative perceptions are largely independent, thus significantly affecting organizational IT security risk management decisions in different ways. Although previous research has intensively investigated the perception of ITSRs in different contexts, these studies are merely based on absolute ITSR perception measures and thus neglected the implications of comparative ITSR perceptions. In this context, our study also answers calls for research that stress the importance of a deeper understanding of people's subjective ITSR perceptions (e.g., Dillard et al. 2012; Johnston and Warkentin 2010). Even more importantly, since various theoretical models in IS research incorporate the effects of people's ITSR perception, this thesis highlights possibilities to extent these models by adding a new perspective on perceived ITSRs that goes beyond absolute values. This new perspective on ITSR assessments not only advances theory and research but also helps to explain a higher degree of variance in behavioral intentions, like the implementation of safeguarding measures or the adoption of new technologies. The increased extent of explained variance implies that comparative ITSR perceptions not only help to identify new effect patterns between ITSR assessments and downstream beliefs but are also important determinants of IT security-related decisions.

This leads directly to the primary research contribution of the first part of this thesis. In addition to ITSR perception research, this work adds, in particular, to the body of knowledge related to organizational IT security risk management by showing that UO in decision makers' ITSR assessments has significant inhibiting effects on organizations' IT security risk management and ultimately on the security of whole IT systems. As such, the study not only advances our understanding of the formation of IT security-related decisions at the organization level but also offers various opportunities for IS researchers to pick up again as-of-yet largely unexplained behavioral phenomena at the individual level, which might be caused by a systematic underestimation of ITSRs. Examples of such behavioral phenomena would be people's lack of motivation to implement up-to-date anti-malware software or the so-called privacy paradox when disclosing personal information on the Internet (e.g., Jensen et al. 2005; Johnston and Warkentin 2010). In this regard, drawing on psychological research, our study not only highlights the importance of considering possible cognitive errors in terms of UO in ITSR perceptions but could also serve as a basis for future research on how to identify and measure UO in people's ITSR assessments. This is especially important because those studies in the IT security context that have already taken into consideration that respondents may systematically underestimate their own ITSR in comparison to others often have used invalid methods to measure comparative UO (e.g., Krasnova et al. 2009; Nandedkar and Midha 2012). However, IT security researchers could transfer approaches to measure both absolute and comparative UO in the ITSR perceptions developed in this study without substantial changes to various fields of applications, enabling them to effectively test if the ITSR assessments of the respondents in their studies are subject to systematic errors in terms of UO, which is likely to have considerable effects in numerous contexts. Even more importantly, previous IT security studies that examined UO in ITSR perceptions in many cases confused comparative and absolute UO, leading them to eventually draw incorrect conclusions regarding the causes and effects of UO in the IT sector (e.g., Campbell et al. 2007). By clarifying the distinction between comparative and absolute UO and demonstrating different measurement approaches, our study enables next-generation research to better understand the implications of the possibly discovered systematic errors in the ITSR perceptions. Furthermore, our study responds to calls for research demanding differentiated analyses of UO in people's perception of risks other than health risks and its behavioral consequences (e.g., Shepperd et al. 2013) by demonstrating that there is UO in comparative as well as absolute ITSR perceptions, which independently undermine providers' IT security risk management.

The second part of this thesis advances our understanding of how the perceptual incongruence between the providers and their (potential) customers regarding the ITSRs affects customer satisfaction and, ultimately, the sales of Cloud services. First, we contribute to IT security research by transferring the well-known concepts of perceptual concurrence and cognitive dissonance to our discipline. In particular, by applying these theoretical frameworks to the area of IT security, we reveal that the disagreement between providers and their (potential) customer companies regarding the ITSRs has considerable direct and indirect effects on the customers' risk perceptions and their intention to adopt the Cloud. Since users' ITSR perceptions are a fundamental construct in numerous theories and models in IS research (e.g., Featherman and Pavlou 2003; Johnston and Warkentin 2010; Mauricio et al. 2010), these new insights concerning the effects of perceptual incongruences regarding ITSRs offer various opportunities for researchers to better understand the formation of customers' downstream beliefs and the effect mechanisms underlying technology adoption decisions.

Second, on a more abstract level, we highlight the importance for researchers to incorporate both parts of the dyad, i.e. the users and providers of information technology, when studying questions in the context of IT security. Turning away from one-sided studies is especially necessary in view of the fact that modern IT delivery paradigms, such as the Cloud, are becoming increasingly important in IS research and practice, where dyadic customer-provider relationships are an essential characteristic of the IS. Yet, previous research in our discipline is predominantly focused on the risk perception of customers (e.g., Ackermann et al. 2012; Benlian and Hess 2011; Gewald and Dibbern 2009) and has thereby neglected the provider side. Nevertheless, as demonstrated in this thesis, the assessments of the ITSR associated with the Cloud by providers' decision makers also influence the formation of (potential) customers' IT managers' downstream beliefs on adoption of the Cloud (e.g., an unjustifiably low ITSR assessment of the providers is likely to shake the customer companies' confidence in Cloud services protection along with the providers' capabilities).

Finally, we contribute to IS research on perceptual congruence, which is typically focused on the effects of different perceptions regarding the quality factors of IS services (e.g., Benlian 2013; Bhattacherjee 2001; Venkatesh and Goyal 2010) by adding a new perspective of perceptual risk incongruences. In particular, our study demonstrates that different perceptions of IT security risks held by Cloud providers' decision makers and (potential) customers' IT managers can have detrimental effects on customers' satisfaction and other important beliefs in the context of Cloud adoption.

Considered together, we feel that IT security researchers can particularly benefit from our study when examining behaviors which are partly determined by ITSR perceptions because they will not only better understand the formation of ITSR perception and its effects on decision-making but also in which ways cognitive errors can affect these assessments.

5.2   Implications for Practice

The primary practical contributions are based on the empirical evidence that decision makers' subjective assessments of the ITSR significantly affect providers' IT security risk management. In particular, even if providers try to give the impression that their ITSR assessments and, subsequently, the IT security risk management decisions are objectively warranted, we have been able to demonstrate that all relevant phases are largely predicted by the more or less subjective perceptions of the decision makers in charge of IT security. In particular, since there is a lack of quantitative data that allows an objective quantification of the ITSRs in the context of the Cloud, the outcomes of the risk analyses phases in many cases deviate considerably from the actual ITSR exposures of the services. In this thesis, we reveal in particular that the decision makers considerably underestimate the ITSR exposure of the own organization's service due to systematic errors in terms of UO. We thereby showed that these systematic errors often not only inhibit providers' IT security risk management but also intensifies disagreements with the (potential) customer companies regarding the ITSR associated with the use of the Cloud, which has large adverse effects on the sales of Cloud services. However, as systematic errors may prevent the implementation of necessary safeguarding measures by the providers, which also puts the IT security of the customers' systems and data in jeopardy when the Cloud services are used as a delivery model, the results of this thesis have important implications for both providers and (potential) customer companies.

5.2.1   Implications and Recommended Actions for Providers

Already the awareness that they may have unconsciously underestimated the ITSR exposure of their services enables the providers' decision makers to improve the IT security risk management of their organizations' services. Since our results reveal that neither a large professional experience nor a profound IT security knowledge protects the decision makers in unconsciously underestimating the ITSR exposure of the own organizations' Cloud services, the providers should introduce and maintain dedicated procedures in the organizational IT security risk management that mitigate the degree of UO in their decision makers' ITSR perceptions and thus its negative consequences. Appropriate strategies for this mitigation may range from standardized procedures that are implemented in the IT security risk management to informal ones. In this context, this thesis provides information regarding the effect mechanisms and the impact of decision makers' subjective ITSR perceptions, which enable the providers to understand how IT security risk management processes are affected by UO and to develop suitable procedures.

Additionally, providers should develop explicit and measureable parameters (e.g., the number of IT security incidents per month) that would allow the decision makers to monitor the actual protection of the services against certain ITSR and to detect areas where the organizational IT security risk management may function inadequately. In this regard, the implementation of security information and event management (SIEM) tools would enable the providers' decision makers to analyze security alerts generated by network hardware and applications in real-time (Mukhopadhyay et al. 2011). In this regard, the aggregation of data from different sources (e.g., network, security, servers, databases, and applications) provides the ability to consolidate monitored data, which would help the providers' decision makers to avoid missing crucial events. Even more importantly, a variety of correlation techniques is typically implemented in SIEM solutions in order to integrate the events of different sources, turning the data into useful information that may increase the awareness of providers' decision makers regarding the exposure of their organizations' Cloud services to certain ITSR (Kent and Souppaya 2006). Similar to the moderating effects of priory-experienced risks on UO, as revealed by previous psychological research (e.g., Burger and Palmer 1992; Weinstein 1989), the increased awareness of the actual likelihood and damage caused to the own organizations' Cloud service by an ITSR is likely to considerably reduce the UO of the providers' decision makers.

Beyond that, the results of this thesis reveal that decision makers on average display a significantly lower magnitude of UO when providers' IT security risk management is highly formalized (e.g., certified IT security risk management systems). As such, providers might be well advised to clearly and formally define their IT security risk management processes and to consider certifying their IT security risk management (e.g., ISO 27001) in order to reduce the detrimental effects of the decision makers' UO.

Providers' decision makers should also encourage an open information security culture in the organization that not only facilitates the IT security compliance of employees but also enables them to give honest feedback to the decision makers regarding their assessments of the actual effectiveness of the providers' IT security risk management (e.g., when IT security threats are internally discovered) (Siponen 2000). This feedback process can be supported with informal dialogue sessions between the decision makers and the employees (e.g., via corporate internal blogs) or joint round-table sessions. Moreover, the providers' decision makers should consider incorporating external consultants (e.g., independent IT security experts) in key phases of IT security risk management, which can help to detect and correct potentially inaccurate IT security assessments as well as weak points in the providers' IT security risk management.

Additionally, the providers' decision makers should inform themselves of the prevalent safeguarding measures in the Cloud market (e.g., by reference to the published IT security whitepapers of competitors). Decision makers may also be well advised to establish formal or informal contact with the decision makers of other provider organizations in the market (e.g., on industry summits and conferences) to learn more about recent IT security threats and developments in the context of the Cloud. For example, if certain safeguarding measures are implemented in nearly all of the services provided by direct competitors but not in the own organization's service, the rejection of these measures might be caused by the decision makers' underestimation of the ITSR. On top of this, the providers together with branch associations should consider initiating an industry database to centrally collect IT security incidents in the Cloud, which would allow the providers' decision makers to substantiate their risk assessments with quantified data (e.g., Aguirre and Alonso 2012). This would not only reduce the need for the decision makers to rely on subjective ITSR perceptions but also avoid reasons for UO.

The results of the second part not only enable providers to improve their IT security risk management but also to facilitate the sales of their Cloud services. In particular, we found that systematic errors in the ITSR assessment of the providers' decision makers are in many cases likely to fuel perceptual incongruence regarding the ITSR between Cloud providers and their (potential) customers. Therefore, providers' decision makers can learn from this thesis that bringing their ITSR assessments in line with those of (potential) customer companies yields higher satisfaction rates and subsequently increases the (potential) customers' adoption of Cloud services. Specifically, we reveal that almost a quarter of all Cloud sales fail to work out due to the perceptual incongruence between the providers and their (potential) customer companies regarding the ITSR of the Cloud services. Accordingly, providers should introduce and support procedures that ascertain whether the own ITSR assessments agree with that of the (potential) customer companies. Suitable strategies for this facilitation can vary in degree of formality, ranging from standardized, scheduled procedures to informal approaches. For example, in relation to perceptual incongruence regarding ITSR factors examined in this study, the providers can define clear, explicit, and measurable parameters around minimum expected and desired levels of protection against these ITSRs. Afterwards they can decide on ways to track the actual protection in these ITSR dimensions (e.g., IT security-related enquiries of customers per month), which would allow them to identify sources of disagreement with the (potential) customers' IT managers and to discuss how to bridge these perceptual incongruences. In this context, for example, 360-degree feedback regarding perceived ITSRs might be a particularly useful tool to increase perceptual congruence, as our study demonstrated that the ITSR perceptions of providers and their (potential) customers in many cases fall short of the other parties' perceptions, resulting in large detrimental effects on customer companies' satisfaction with Cloud services. Additionally, decision makers might also introduce a feedback process involving informal dialogue sessions with (potential) customers (e.g., via online social business networks or in conferences) or formal retreats (e.g., during the sales pitch) to foster a shared understanding of the ITSR associated with the use of the Cloud. In this regard, the in-depth analysis of the effects of perceptual incongruence dimensions in this thesis reveal that the providers are already able to significantly mitigate the negative effects merely by adequately responding to the customer concerns regarding the confidentiality and performance of the services. Moreover, decision makers should not only pay attention to perceptual congruence between the ITSR assessments but also to the absolute levels of ITSR perceptions. As shown in the second part of this thesis, a high level of perceived ITSR undermines the intention to use Cloud services by (potential) customer companies' IT manager. Conversely, an adequate management of the ITSR to ensure a high level of protection regarding all relevant risk factors, while providing high perceptual congruence, can enable providers' decision makers to achieve higher levels of customer satisfaction and subsequently facilitate the sales of their Cloud services.

Nevertheless, this thesis also highlights that providers' attempts to provide a positive impression of their services by overemphasizing the low level of ITSRs of the Cloud is likely to have contrary effects and undermine the intentions of (potential) customers' IT managers to adopt Cloud services. In particular, controversies between providers and customers regarding an ITSR might be important indicators for the providers' decision makers to reveal systematic errors in the assessment of this risk. Only if it turns out that the ITSR have been assessed correctly and that there are appropriate safeguards in place to protect the services against this risk, the providers should address customer concerns with dedicated marketing measures.

5.2.2   Implications and Recommended Actions for (Potential) Customers

The knowledge that the outcomes of IT security risk management can be predicted by the subjective perceptions of the providers' decision makers and that potential systematic error in the ITSR assessments can inhibit the implementation of necessary safeguards should motivate customers to carefully check the ITSR of the Cloud, for example, by conducting own analyses of the ITSR before a Cloud service is used as delivery model in their organization. In this regard, the customer companies may be well advised to use external expert knowledge, like independent IT security experts, when selecting the appropriate Cloud service for their organization. After customers have adopted a Cloud service, they should be encouraged by our results to continually challenge their providers' security abilities and to perform own regular security tests of the IT security of their services. In this context, the analyses in this study have revealed that the intentions behind decisions to implement certain safeguards in Cloud services are partly influenced by the external pressure exerted on the providers. In particular, even if the dependency on existing customer relationships was assessed to be rather low by the providers' decision makers, expressed customer demands were found to significantly facilitate providers' IT security investment decisions. Accordingly, the findings of this study should encourage customers to proactively request the implementation of certain safeguarding measures from the providers of their utilized service.

Moreover, our results demonstrate that providers' sales staffs, who emphasize the low ITSR of the Cloud, do not necessarily attempt to mislead potential customers by downplaying the ITSRs in order to make their organizations' services seem better protected. Instead, as the providers' decision makers were in many cases found to underestimate the ITSR of their service, these statements might be based on incorrect assumptions regarding the ITSRs. However, based on the approaches used to identify UO in the ITSR perception of the providers' decision makers in this study, the customers can come up with tactics to investigate whether there are inaccuracies in the ITSR analysis processes of the providers. For example, the customers can use the results of this study (e.g., the average IT security investment level of a provider of a given service type) to benchmark a service provider in terms of obvious miscalculations in IT security risk management. Besides, as the findings in this study indicate that the providers' IT security-related decisions are less likely to be affected by UO when the organizational IT security risk management is highly formalized, the customers should prefer the adoption of Cloud services of those providers that have a certified IT security risk management system (e.g., ISO 27001 certification).

5.3   Limitations and Future Research Directions

Five limitations of this thesis merit consideration. First, caution should generally be taken when drawing conclusions from a single study. As such, examining the role of decision makers' subjective ITSR perceptions in organizational IT security risk management and the effects of systematic cognitive errors in their ITSR assessments in terms of UO in other institutional and cultural environments could enrich our study's results. Future research could thus examine the generalizability of our findings in other contexts. In this regard, UO is also likely to have important implications for the IT security behavior on the individual level (e.g., in inhibiting the intention of a user to install anti-malware software on his or her computer due to the systematic underestimation of the ITSR), which should be explored in future research. Furthermore, even if we were in most cases able to gather the ITSR assessments of those decision makers who were ultimately responsible for the IT security of the respective provider's Cloud service, the findings of this study are based on the assessments of one decision maker of each provider. As organizational IT security risk management is often described as strategic decisions, there is usually more than one person involved in the decision-making, which could potentially either intensify or mitigate the effects of UO on the outcome of IT security risk management. Even if previous research results suggest that the biases are stable at the group level (e.g., Hambrick and Mason 1984; Schwenk 1988), studying the existence and the effects of UO on the organizational IT security risk management at different levels of analysis (e.g., including IT security department and business management level) could add to the findings of our study. Likewise, the effects of perceptual disagreement between providers and (potential) customers should be cross-validated in a second set of data. A second empirical study would allow for checking if the ITSR perception of providers and (potential) customers, and thus the perceptual gap, changes over time.

Second, our study is cross-sectional and static; we did not investigate the influence of the decision makers' subjective ITSR assessments on the outcome of the providers' IT security risk management longitudinally. As the decision makers' UO regarding the ITSR exposure of their organization's service was found to be influenced by the structuring of the providers' IT security risk management (e.g., a highly formalized IT security risk management system was demonstrated to eventually reduce the impact of systematic errors in the decision makers' ITSR perceptions), it is conceivable that their degree of UO may vary over time. In particular, since UO was found to significantly inhibit future IT security investments, future research should also investigate if the decision makers' UO in their ITSR assessments in fact induces a kind of vicious circle between UO and IT security risk management. Even more importantly, our data can merely ascertain correlations, not causal relationships. Accordingly, some of the findings of this study depend on the theoretical underpinnings regarding the nature and effects of UO as provided by the psychological literature in different research fields. Even if we conducted various analyses of our data to confirm the theoretical assumptions about how UO influences ITSR assessments and ultimately IT security risk management-related decisions, experimental work (e.g., studies that systematically manipulate the decision makers' UO regarding the ITSR and observe the impacts on their intention to increase the IT security level of their organization's service) could enhance the results of this study. Besides, additional research on moderators and behavioral consequences that goes beyond behavioral intentions to increase the organization's IT security level (e.g., the actual implementation of certain safeguarding measures in the next year) could considerably improve our knowledge about which ways and to what degree UO negatively affects organizational IT security risk management. In this context, current psychological research also calls for experimental work regarding absolute and comparative UO as well as its effects on people's protection behavior in different areas (e.g., Shepperd et al. 2013).

Third, the ways in which people's comparative risk perceptions influence their security behavior are controversially discussed in parts of the psychological research. Even if the major stream in the literature argues that comparative risk assessments do not directly influence the formation of risk perceptions and have thus more indirect effects on the precautionary adoption process (e.g., Dillard et al. 2011; Lipkus et al. 2000; Shepperd et al. 2013), some of the literature questions this assumption (e.g., Craciun et al. 2010). In our study, drawing on previous IS research and theoretical considerations, we argue that the ITSR assessments of the own organization's service in comparison to average competitors mainly determines the competitive pressure to increase the IT security level, which is exerted on the providers. Even though we estimated two alternative models, and the analyses in our study also indicated that the decision makers' comparative ITSR assessment is strongly correlated with their assessment of the competitive pressure, we cannot completely rule out that the comparative ITSR perceptions may (additionally) affect IT security risk management in other ways. In this case, our results would be slightly upwardly deferred through the divergences between the direct and indirect effects of the decision makers' ITSR perceptions. As such, the minor uncertainty that is left regarding the way comparative ITSR assessments affect the decision makers' intentions to increase the IT security level does not impair the basic statement of this thesis. Thus, even more importantly, our results in fact constitute a lower bound of the inhibiting effects of decision makers' UO regarding the ITSR exposure of their service on the provider's IT security risk management. However, future research should integrate additional measures in their study designs that avoid this doubt and that ensure that formation of the overall ITSR assessments is comprehensively captured. Therefore, future research will not only enrich the findings of this study but also advance knowledge of the way comparative risk perceptions in general influence protection behavior. In this context, recent psychological research calls for studies that conduct in-depth investigations of the relationship between absolute and comparative risk perceptions and their behavioral consequences in different fields of application (e.g., Dillard et al. 2012).

Fourth, based on the data obtained in this study, we were primarily able to demonstrate the existence of UO and its negative effects on the providers' IT security risk management. However, our results demonstrate that research on the possibilities of reducing the negative consequences of UO in the IT security context is sorely needed. In this regard, previous psychological research in the health sector has been in many cases able to reduce people's UO with the help of appropriate debiasing interventions, which ultimately facilitate precautionary actions (e.g., Rose 2012; Weinstein and Klein 1995). As such, future research should transfer the established debiasing attempts to the IT security context and empirically test their abilities to reduce both the UO in the absolute and the comparative ITSR perceptions in experimental environments. Moreover, future research may also conduct experimental work in cooperation with providers to develop dedicated debiasing tools that would be geared to the needs of the organizational IT security risk management processes.

Finally, since we sought to investigate the consequence of disagreement regarding ITSRs on (potential) customer companies' adoption decisions, we were not able to observe existing provider-customer relationships. Although previous cognitive dissonance research and perceptual congruence theory strongly support our research methodology, we do not know with absolute certainty that this is the mechanism that in fact determines the empirical results. Future research could enrich the findings of this thesis by investigating the impact of the perceptual incongruence regarding the ITSR in later stages of Cloud adoption, such as the intentions of (potential) customers' IT managers to continue the use of the Cloud. In particular, this research design would allow for a direct observation of the dyadic relationship between Cloud providers and their customers. Moreover, the effects of perceptual incongruence between providers and (potential) customer companies regarding other perceived risk dimensions and IS service quality factors on the adoption of Cloud services should also be examined. Beyond that, the consequences of risk controversies in the context of the Cloud could be investigated with the proposed variance model by replicating the study among IT security experts and comparing the perceptions of IT security experts with that of (potential) customers' IT managers.

5.4   Résumé

This thesis stresses the need to take into account the nature and effects of decision makers' ITSR perception to fully comprehend the complex IT security risk management at the organizational level, thus offering new insights on the complex socio-cognitive ITSR assessment processes and how they shape organizational decisions in the IT security context. Therefore, this study aims to sensitize academics and managers in organizations to become more aware of the role of systematic cognitive errors and their influence on the ITSR assessment of decision makers and ultimately the IT security risk management of organizations. Unfortunately, the rapid technology development inherit in the IT sector today brings about fast changing IT security requirements. As a side product, there is in many cases a lack of historical data regarding the likelihood and damage of ITSRs, so that decision makers must often build on their expertise and knowledge to assess the criticality of ITSRs, which is typically the most important phase of the IT security risk management. However, when estimating the ITSRs of their organizations' services they fail to reflect on the impact of cognitive errors on their ITSR assessment and its potentially devastating effects on the outcome of the organizational IT security risk management.

To overlook or ignore the fact that the decision makers' ITSR perceptions may be subject to UO, means that an organization may pay a significant price, when it comes to an IT security incident, which might have been prevented by a correct assessment of the ITSRs, resulting in an appropriate IT security risk management.

Beyond that, provider decision makers should become more aware of the importance of the individual ITSR perceptions and concerns of (potential) customers' IT managers and its influence on customer companies' decisions to use Cloud services. In particular, our results emphasize the importance of a shared understanding of ITSR to respond to customers' concerns and expectations, which were revealed to be essential in terms of satisfaction with Cloud services. In this context, especially providers' attempts to make ITSRs appear harmless to provide a positive impression of the Cloud may have a contrary effect and significantly undermine the sales of Cloud services.

Appendix

A.1 Supporting Material for Part I (Chapter 3)

A.1.1 *Measurement Items*

Construct	Item / Scale	Source
Table A-1: Measurement Items of the IT Security Risk Management Study		
IT security risk	• Considering the overall financial loss, a compromise of the IT security of the customers' systems and data when our Cloud Computing service was used as delivery model poses a risk to our organization. • With regard to the overall financial loss, a compromise of the IT security of the customers' systems and data when our Cloud Computing service was used as delivery is a danger for our organization. • It is likely that the IT security of the customers' systems and data will become negatively affected when our organization's Cloud Computing service is used as delivery model. ○ 1 = absolutely disagree - 7 = absolutely agree [each]	Based on Liang and Xue (2010)
IT security risk severity (own orga. / avg. comp.)	If the IT security of the customers' system and data was negatively affected when the Cloud Computing service was used as delivery model, … • … it would create a significant financial loss for (our organization / the average competitor). • … it would cause a serve financial damage to (our organization / the average competitor). • … (our organization / the average competitor) would be in serious financial trouble. ○ 1 = absolutely disagree - 7 = absolutely agree [each]	Based on Johnston and Warkentin (2010); Witte et al. (1996), modified to Perloff and Fetzer (1986)'s method to indirectly measure CO
IT security risk susceptibility (own orga. / avg. comp.)	• It is likely that the IT security of the customers' systems and data will become negatively affected when (our organization's / the average competitors') Cloud Computing service is used as delivery model. • The IT security of the customers' systems and data is at risk to be negatively affected when (our organization's / the average competitors') Cloud Computing service is used as delivery model. • It is possible that the IT security of the customers' systems and data will become negatively affected when (our organization's / the average competitors') Cloud Computing service is used as delivery model. ○ 1 = absolutely disagree - 7 = absolutely agree [each]	Based on Johnston and Warkentin (2010); Witte et al. (1996), modified to Perloff and Fetzer (1986)'s method to indirectly measure CO
Comparative IT security risk susceptibility	• In comparison to the Cloud Computing service of an average competitor, ____ that the IT security of the customers' systems and data will become negatively affected when our organization's Cloud Computing service is used as delivery	Based on Johnston and Warkentin (2010); Witte et

Construct	Item / Scale	Source
	model. o 1 = it is much less likely - 7 = it is much more likely o 1 = there is a much lower risk - 7 = there is a much higher risk o 1 = it is much less probable - 7 = it is much more probable	al. (1996), modified to Weinstein (1980)'s method to directly measure CO
Comparative IT security severity	▪ If the IT security of the customers' system and data was negatively affected when the Cloud Computing service was used as delivery model, it would cause a ____ to our organization than to the average competitor. o 1 = much less significant financial loss - 7 = much more significant financial loss o 1 = much less serve financial damage - 7 = much more serve financial damage o 1 = much less serious financial trouble - 7 = much more serious financial trouble	Based on Johnston and Warkentin (2010); Witte et al. (1996), modified to Weinstein (1980)'s method to directly measure CO
Effectiveness of increased IT security level	▪ Increasing the IT security level of our organization's Cloud Computing service in the next year will keep negative influences on the IT security of the customers' system and data down. ▪ If we increase the IT security level of our organization's Cloud Computing service in the next year, negative influences on the IT security of the customers' system and data will be scarce. ▪ Increasing IT security level of our organization's Cloud Computing service in the next year will help avoid negative influences on the IT security of the customers' system and data. o 1 = absolutely disagree - 7 = absolutely agree [each]	Based on Vance et al. (2012)
Feasibility to increase IT security level	▪ We have the necessary knowledge to increase the IT security level of our organization's Cloud Computing service in the next year. ▪ We have the necessary competencies to increase the IT security level of our organization's Cloud Computing service in the next year. ▪ We have the necessary resources to increase the IT security level of our organization's Cloud Computing service in the next year. o 1 = absolutely disagree - 7 = absolutely agree [each]	Based on Vance et al. (2012)
Costs to increase IT security level	▪ There are high costs associated with increasing the IT security level of our organization's Cloud Computing service in the next year. ▪ Increasing the IT security level of our organization's Cloud Computing service in the next year would require considerable financial investment. ▪ The cost of increasing the IT security level in the next year would significantly decrease the profitability of our organization's Cloud Computing service. o 1 = absolutely disagree - 7 = absolutely agree [each]	Based on Vance et al. (2012)
Intention to increase IT	▪ We intend to increase the IT security level of our organization's Cloud Computing service in the next year.	Based on Johnston and

Construct	Item / Scale	Source
security level	▪ We would like to increase the IT security level of our organization's Cloud Computing service in the next year. ▪ We plan to increase the IT security level of our organization's Cloud Computing service in the next year. o 1 = absolutely disagree - 7 = absolutely agree [each]	Warkentin (2010); Venkatesh et al. (2003)
IT security investment level	▪ What percentage of the primary Cloud Computing service's IT budget does your organization (plan to) invest in that service's IT security (ratio of IT security budget / IT budget)? o This year: 0% - 100% o Next year: 0% - 100%	Own development based on Cavusoglu et al. (2004b)
Dependency on existing customer relationships	▪ Please rate the importance of existing customer relationships to the success of your organization's Cloud Computing service. o 1 = not important at all - 7 = extremely important ▪ Please rate your organization's dependence on the existing Cloud Computing service's customer relationships. o 1 = not dependent at all - 7 = extremely dependent ▪ Please make a rough estimate what the percentage of the market does your organization's Cloud Computing service account for (market share of your organization's primary Cloud Computing service)? o 0% - 100%	Based on Chwelos et al. (2001)
Competitive pressure to increase IT security level	▪ In the Cloud Computing market, is a high IT security level helpful in enabling an organization to remain competitive? o 1 = not at all helpful - 7 = extremely helpful ▪ Please make a rough estimate what percentage of your average competitors has got a higher IT security level than your organization? o 0% - 100% ▪ Please rate the pressure to increase the IT security level of its Cloud Computing service in the next year placed on your organization by the actions taken by your average competitors. o 1 = no pressure at all - 7 = extreme pressure	Based on Chwelos et al. (2001)
Enacted customer power to increase IT security level	▪ Please attempt to classify the strength of the encouragement or pressure put on your organization by customers to increase the IT security level of your Cloud Computing service in the next year. o 1 = No encouragement or pressure (Customers did not attempt to encourage or put pressure on the IT security level of our organization's Cloud Computing service), 2 = Information exchange (Customers provided information regarding their IT security concerns when using our organization's Cloud Computing service as delivery model), 3 = Recommendation (Customers recommended that we should increase the IT security level of our organization's Cloud Computing service), 4 = Request (Customers demanded that we should increase the IT security level of our organization's Cloud Computing service), 5 = Promise (Customers made	Based on Chwelos et al. (2001)

Construct	Item / Scale	Source

	promises to raise the adoption level when we increase the IT security level of our organization's Cloud Computing service), 6 = Threat (Customers made threatened to discontinue service if we do not increase the IT security level of our organization's Cloud Computing service)
	• Please rate the amount of influence that customers have in your organization's decisions whether or not to increase the IT security level in the Cloud Computing service in the next year.
	  o 1 = no influence - 7 = strong influence
	• Please rate the pressure to increase the IT security level of the Cloud Computing service in the next year placed on your organization by customers
	  o 1 = no pressure at all - 7 = extreme pressure	

Industry pressure to increase IT security level	• How often does your organization on average receive IT security risk information and alerts from industry sources that urge it to increase the Cloud Computing service's IT security level in the next year?
	  o 1= not at all - 7 = frequently
	• Please rate the pressure to increase the IT security level of the Cloud Computing service in the next year placed on your organization by industry sources.
	  o 1 = no pressure at all - 7 = extreme pressure
		Based on Chwelos et al. (2001)

IT security risk management formalization	• How is the IT security risk management of your organization's Cloud Computing service organized? o 1 = Event triggered information security management (Information security management decisions are typically triggered by past events, like requests of stakeholders, security incidents, etc.), 2 = Best practice information security management (Information security management decisions are predominately based on knowledge and experience of decision makers), 3 = Corporate information security management procedures (Information security management decisions are based on a set of in-house policies), 4 = Corporate information security management system (Operation of an uncertified information security management system that is based on in-house developed framework), 5 = Uncertified information security management system (Operation of an uncertified information security management system that is based on ISO/IEC 27001 or equivalent), 6 = Certified information security management system (Implementation of a formally audited and certified information security management system that is based on ISO/IEC 27001 or equivalent)	Own development based on Kankanhalli et al. (2003)
Number of employees of provider	• How many employees does your organization currently have? o Integer value	Based on Benlian and Hess (2011)
Revenue of provider	• What is your organization's approximate overall annual revenue? o Real value	Based on Benlian and Hess (2011)

Construct	Item / Scale	Source
Involvement of decision maker	▪ I am ____ involved in decisions regarding the IT security of our organization's primary Cloud Computing service. o almost never - almost always	Based on Bulgurcu et al. (2010)
Responsibility of decision maker	▪ I am ____ responsible for the IT security of our organization's primary Cloud Computing service. o not at all - fully	Based on Bulgurcu et al. (2010)

Experience of the decision maker (self-reported)	▪ I have ____ in the area of the IT security of our organization's primary Cloud Computing service.
	  o 1 = very little expertise - 7 = very much expertise
	  o 1 = very little knowledge - 7 = very much knowledge
	  o 1 = very little competencies - 7 = very high competencies
		Based on (Vetter et al. 2011)

A.1.2   *Validity Analysis*

Table A-2: Correlation Statistics of the IT Security Risk Management Study

Construct	1	2	3	4	5	6	7	8	9	10	11	12	13	14	15	16
1 AVOID	1.00															
2 AVOID_COST	0.28	1.00														
3 AVOID_EFF	0.67	-0.09	1.00													
4 AVOID_FEA	0.59	-0.07	-0.06	1.00												
5 CITSR_SEV	0.03	0.14	-0.09	0.06	1.00											
6 CITSR_SUS	-0.20	-0.04	0.08	-0.36	0.01	1.00										
7 EP	0.20	-0.18	0.25	0.13	-0.01	0.09	1.00									
8 EP_CDEP	0.21	0.01	0.11	0.19	-0.12	-0.13	0.69	1.00								
9 EP_COMP	0.17	-0.07	0.29	-0.04	0.10	0.35	0.61	0.12	1.00							
10 EP_CPWR	0.12	-0.30	0.19	0.13	-0.05	0.03	0.84	0.51	0.34	1.00						
11 EP_IND	0.11	-0.14	0.16	0.06	0.03	0.07	0.75	0.34	0.38	0.51	1.00					
12 IIITSL	0.18	-0.23	0.28	-0.12	0.11	0.11	0.37	0.08	0.46	0.32	0.23	1.00				
13 ITSR	-0.11	-0.05	0.22	-0.28	0.11	0.24	0.24	0.04	0.45	0.15	0.11	0.35	1.00			
14 ITSR*AVOID	0.00	-0.24	-0.13	0.30	0.08	-0.27	-0.03	0.02	-0.27	0.00	0.15	-0.35	-0.37	1.00		
15 ITSR_SEV	-0.07	-0.07	0.10	-0.19	-0.58	0.10	0.23	-0.03	0.28	0.12	0.03	0.20	0.61	-0.14	1.00	
16 ITSR_SUS	-0.18	0.03	0.01	-0.30	-0.09	0.41	-0.05	-0.26	0.24	-0.03	-0.09	0.24	0.64	-0.26	0.27	1.00

Please note: n=177. Constructs: AVOID = IT security risk avoidability through an increased IT security level, AVOID_COST = Costs to increase IT security level, AVOID_EFF = Effectiveness of increased IT security level, AVOID_FEA = Feasibility to increase IT security level, CITSR_SEV = Comparative IT security risk severity, CITSR_SUS = Comparative IT security risk susceptibility, EP = External pressure to increase IT security level, EP_CDEP = Dependency on existing customer relationships, EP_COMP = Competitive pressure to increase IT security level, EP_CPWR = Enacted customer power to increase IT security level, EP_IND = Industry pressure to increase IT security level, IIITSL = Intention to increase IT security level, ITSR = IT security risk, ITSR_SEV = IT security risk severity, ITSR_SUS = IT security risk susceptibility.

A.1.3   *Consistency Analysis of the Absolute Unrealistic Optimism Classifier*

Table A-3: Effects of Different Thresholds of Error on the Results of the Classifier

Group	UO					NON-UO				
Threshold	0%	5%	10%	15%	20%	0%	5%	10%	15%	20%
Group n	89	86	75	66	47	88	91	102	111	130
IT security risk management model										
ITSR_SUS	3.12	3.14	3.16	3.07	2.96	4.30	4.24	4.11	4.09	3.98
ITSR_SEV	4.82	4.85	4.93	4.91	4.82	5.33	5.28	5.17	5.17	5.16
ITSR	4.07	4.12	4.11	4.06	3.95	5.12	5.04	4.95	4.91	4.83
CITSR_SUS	2.62	2.62	2.64	2.64	2.72	2.91	2.90	2.85	2.84	2.78
CITSR_SEV	4.03	4.02	4.03	4.03	4.09	4.05	4.07	4.05	4.05	4.02
AVOID_EFF	4.48	4.48	4.51	4.50	4.46	4.28	4.30	4.34	4.39	4.48
AVOID_FEA	4.21	4.20	4.14	4.20	4.13	3.66	3.68	3.78	3.78	3.86
AVOID_COST	3.66	3.65	3.75	3.75	3.72	3.71	3.72	3.63	3.64	3.67
EP_COMP	3.24	3.24	3.22	3.32	3.34	3.32	3.31	3.32	3.25	3.25
EP_CDEP	5.07	5.07	5.04	5.02	4.98	5.28	5.27	5.25	5.23	5.18
EP_CPWR	3.76	3.74	3.67	3.60	3.53	3.82	3.83	3.85	3.86	3.82
EP_IND	3.87	3.85	3.85	3.85	3.74	3.78	3.80	3.80	3.81	3.85
IIITSL	4.79	4.79	4.76	4.76	4.71	5.13	5.11	5.10	5.08	5.05
ITSL	18.52	18.17	16.47	16.06	14.89	30.53	30.46	30.39	29.49	27.94
Control										
EMP	405.3	414.8	465.3	497.9	596.7	554.2	540.45	489.7	468.4	437.0
REV	38.05	38.33	41.15	42.36	40.88	41.78	41.40	38.99	38.44	39.55
EXP	5.79	5.77	5.73	5.62	5.64	5.75	5.77	5.80	5.86	5.82
RESP	6.01	5.98	5.89	5.80	5.85	5.77	5.81	5.89	5.95	5.91
INVOL	5.65	5.63	5.56	5.41	5.49	5.48	5.51	5.57	5.66	5.59
ITSM	3.72	3.69	3.53	3.39	3.15	4.07	4.09	4.16	4.19	4.16

Please note: n=177. Constructs: AVOID_COST = Costs to increase IT security level, AVOID_EFF = Effectiveness of increased IT security level, AVOID_FEA = Feasibility to increase IT security level, CITSR_SEV = Comparative IT security risk severity, CITSR_SUS = Comparative IT security risk susceptibility, EP_CDEP = Dependency on existing customer relationships, EP_COMP = Competitive pressure to increase IT security level, EP_CPWR = Enacted customer power to increase IT security level, EP_IND = Industry pressure to increase IT security level, IIITSL = Intention to increase IT security level, ITSL = IT security investment level (this year), ITSR = IT security risk, ITSR_SEV = IT security risk severity, ITSR_SUS = IT security risk susceptibility. Control constructs: EMP = Number of employees of provider, EXP = Experience of decision makers (self-reported), INVOL = Involvement of decision maker in IT security related decisions of the provider, ITSM = Formalization of provider's IT security risk management, RESP = Responsibility of decision maker for the IT security of the services, REV = Revenue of provider.

A.1.4   Multi-Group Analysis of the Structural Model

Table A-4: Effects of Absolute Unrealistic Optimism on the Structural Model Results				
Relationship β	**Research model with sample**			**Difference between UO and NO-UO**
	Complete (n=177)	**UO (n=75)**	**NO-UO (n=102)**	
AVOID → IIITSL	0.32	0.27	0.26	-0.01
AVOID_COST → AVOID	-0.65	-0.61	-0.51	0.10
AVOID_EFF → AVOID	0.66	0.67	0.57	-0.10
AVOID_FEA → AVOID	0.40	0.51	0.58	0.08
CITSR_SEV → EP_COMP	0.09	-0.01	0.14	0.15
CITSR_SUS → EP_COMP	0.44	0.43	0.46	0.04
EP → IIITSL	0.30	0.27	0.29	0.01
EP_CDEP → EP	0.29	0.27	0.29	0.03
EP_COMP → EP	0.43	0.40	0.40	0.00
EP_CPWR → EP	0.32	0.34	0.32	-0.02
EP_IND → EP	0.31	0.32	0.31	-0.01
ITSR → IIITSL	0.35	0.64	0.45	-0.19*
ITSR*AVOID → IIITSL	0.23	0.49	0.20	-0.29**
ITSR_SEV → ITSR	0.47	0.50	0.48	-0.02
ITSR_SUS → ITSR	0.52	0.40	0.51	0.12

Please note: n=177. Significance levels of differences between effect sizes for UO and NON-UO group estimations with two-tailed t-tests: **$p<0.01$; *$p<0.05$. Constructs: AVOID = IT security risk avoidability through an increased IT security level, AVOID_COST = Costs to increase IT security level, AVOID_EFF = Effectiveness of increased IT security level, AVOID_FEA = Feasibility to increase IT security level, CITSR_SEV = Comparative IT security risk severity, CITSR_SUS = Comparative IT security risk susceptibility, EP = External pressure to increase IT security level, EP_CDEP = Dependency on existing customer relationships, EP_COMP = Competitive pressure to increase IT security level, EP_CPWR = Enacted customer power to increase IT security level, EP_IND = Industry pressure to increase IT security level, IIITSL = Intention to increase IT security level, ITSR = IT security risk, ITSR_SEV = IT security risk severity, ITSR_SUS = IT security risk susceptibility.

A.2 Supporting Material for Part II (Chapter 4)

A.2.1 Measurement Items

Table A-5: Measurement Items of the Perceptual Incongruence Study			
Construct	**Used in**	**Item / Scale**	**Sources**
Perceived IT Security Risk Items	Customer study and Provider study	▪ How does your company assess the risk of *[risk item]* regarding the *(confidentiality / integrity / availability / performance / accountability / maintainability)* of *([1] your / the customers')* systems and data when using *([1] a / [2] your company's)* Cloud service? o 1 = not risky at all - 7 = very risky [31 risk items]	Based on Ackermann et al. (2012)
Perceptual incongruence on IT security risk dimensions	Customer study and Provider study	▪ Regarding the *(confidentiality / integrity / availability / performance / accountability / maintainability)* of the systems and data, it *([1] would be / [2] is)* ... for *([1] your company / [2] a customer)* to use *([1] a / [2] your company's)* Cloud service. o 1 = not risky at all - 7 = very risky o 1 = not dangerous at all - 7 = very dangerous o 1 = associated with very little uncertainty - 7 = associated with great uncertainty	Based on Ackermann et al. (2012)
Perceived IT security risk	Customer study and Provider study	▪ Taking into account all factors that affect the overall IT security of the systems and data, it *([1] would be / [2] is)* ... for *([1] your company / [2] a customer)* to use *([1] a / [2] your company's)* Cloud service. o 1 = not risky at all - 7 = very risky o 1 = not dangerous at all - 7 = very dangerous o 1 = associated with very little uncertainty - 7 = associated with great uncertainty	Based on Ackermann et al. (2012)
Perceived overall usefulness of service	Customer study	▪ Adopting Cloud has many advantages. ▪ Adopting Cloud is a useful instrument to increase operational excellence. ▪ Overall, I consider the adoption of Cloud to be a useful strategic option. o 1 = absolutely disagree - 7 = absolutely agree [each]	Based on Gewald and Dibbern (2009)
Perceived overall risk of service	Customer study	▪ Adopting Cloud is associated with a high level of risk. ▪ There is a high level of risk that the expected benefits of adopting Cloud will not materialize. ▪ Overall, I consider the adoption of Cloud to be risky. o 1 = absolutely disagree - 7 = absolutely agree [each]	Based on Featherman and Pavlou (2003)
Intention to adopt service	Customer study	▪ If there is a superior offer, Cloud Computing should be used for the application domain I am in charge of. ▪ Our company should increase the existing level of adopting Cloud. ▪ I support the further adoption of Cloud Computing. o 1 = absolutely disagree - 7 = absolutely agree [each]	Based on Benlian and Hess (2011)

A.2.2   Validity Analysis

Table A-6: Correlation Statistics of the Perceptual Incongruence Study									
Construct	**1**	**2**	**3**	**4**	**5**	**6**	**7**	**8**	**9**	**10**
1 IAS	1.00									
2 USE	0.76	1.00								
3 PITSR	-0.56	-0.51	1.00							
4 PIN_ITSR	-0.49	-0.42	0.69	1.00						
5 PIN_CONF	-0.41	-0.35	0.42	0.57	1.00					
6 PIN_INTE	-0.36	-0.28	0.31	0.48	0.39	1.00				
7 PIN_AVAI	-0.39	-0.30	0.38	0.56	0.32	0.43	1.00			
8 PIN_PERF	-0.37	-0.38	0.39	0.42	0.21	0.36	0.34	1.00		
9 PIN_ACCO	-0.26	-0.26	0.30	0.49	0.34	0.39	0.22	0.23	1.00	
10 PIN_MAIN	-0.29	-0.32	0.27	0.39	0.16	0.28	0.19	0.44	0.35	1.00

Please note: n=304. Constructs: IAS = Intention to adopt service, PIN_ACCO = Perceptual incongruence on accountability risks, PIN_AVAI = Perceptual incongruence on availability risks, PIN_CONF = Perceptual incongruence on confidentiality risks, PIN_INTE = Perceptual incongruence on integrity risks, PIN_ITSR = Perceptual incongruence on IT security risk of service, PIN_MAIN = Perceptual incongruence on maintainability risks, PIN_PERF = Perceptual incongruence on performance risks, PITSR = Perceived IT security risk of service, USE = Perceived overall usefulness of service.

A.2.3   Formation of IT Security Risk Perceptions in the Context of the Cloud

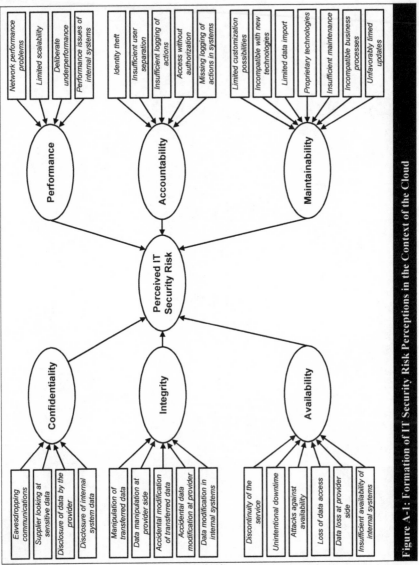

Figure A-1: Formation of IT Security Risk Perceptions in the Context of the Cloud

Please note: Figure is based on Ackermann et al. (2012).

References

Ackermann, T. 2013. *IT Security Risk Management: Perceived IT Security Risks in the Context of Cloud Computing.* Wiesbaden: Springer.

Ackermann, T., Miede, A., Buxmann, P., and Steinmetz, R. 2011. "Taxonomy of Technological IT Outsourcing Risks: Support for Risk Identification and Quantification," in: *Proceedings of the 19th European Conference on Information Systems.* Helsinki: pp. 240-252.

Ackermann, T., Widjaja, T., Benlian, A., and Buxmann, P. 2012. "Perceived IT Security Risks of Cloud Computing: Conceptualization and Scale Development," in: *Proceedings of the 33rd International Conference on Information Systems.* Orlando.

Ackermann, T., Widjaja, T., and Buxmann, P. 2013. "Towards the Optimal Security Level: Quantification of Risks in Service-Based Information Systems," in: *Proceedings of the 46th Hawaii International Conference on System Sciences.* Maui.

Aguirre, I., and Alonso, S. 2012. "Improving the Automation of Security Information Management: A Collaborative Approach," *Security & Privacy* (10:1), pp. 55-59.

Ajzen, I., and Fishbein, M. 1980. *Understanding Attitudes and Predicting Social Behaviour.* Englewood Cliffs: Prentice-Hall.

Al-Roomi, M., Al-Ebrahim, S., Buqrais, S., and Ahmad, I. 2013. "Cloud Computing Pricing Models: A Survey," *International Journal of Grid & Distributed Computing* (6:5).

Allport, F.H. 1955. *Theories of Perception and the Concept of Structure.* New York: Wiley.

Amazon. 2014. "Amazon Web Services: Overview of Security Process." *http://aws.amazon.com/security/*, last accessed: 01/17/2015.

Anderson, C.L., and Agarwal, R. 2010. "Practicing Safe Computing: A Multimedia Empirical Examination of Home Computer User Security Behavioral Intentions," *MIS Quarterly* (34:3), pp. 613-643.

Anderson, R. 2001. "Why Information Security Is Hard-an Economic Perspective," in: *Proceedings 17th Annual Computer Security Applications Conference.* Las Vegas: pp. 358-365.

Andrews, F.M. 1984. "Construct Validity and Error Components of Survey Measures: A Structural Modeling Approach," *Public Opinion Quarterly* (48:2), pp. 409-442.

Armbrust, M., Fox, A., Griffith, R., Joseph, A.D., Katz, R., Konwinski, A., Lee, G., Patterson, D., Rabkin, A., Stoica, I., and Zaharia, M. 2010. "A View of Cloud Computing," *Commun. ACM* (53:4), pp. 50-58.

Armstrong, J.S., and Overton, T.S. 1977. "Estimating Nonresponse Bias in Mail Surveys," *Journal of Marketing Research* (14:3), pp. 396-402.

Aubert, B.A., Patry, M., and Rivard, S. 1998. "Assessing the Risk of IT Outsourcing," in: *Proceedings of the 31st Hawaii International Conference on Information Systems System Sciences.* Maui: pp. 685-692.

Aucote, H.M., and Gold, R.S. 2005. "Non-Equivalence of Direct and Indirect Measures of Unrealistic Optimism," *Psychology, Health & Medicine* (10:2), pp. 194-201.

Aytes, K., and Connolly, T. 2004. "Computer Security and Risky Computing Practices: A Rational Choice Perspective," *Journal of Organizational and End User Computing (JOEUC)* (16:3), pp. 22-40.

Bagozzi, R.P., and Yi, Y. 1988. "On the Evaluation of Structural Equation Models," *Journal of the Academy of Marketing Science* (16:1), pp. 74-94.

Baker, W.H., Rees, L.P., and Tippett, P.S. 2007. "Necessary Measures: Metric-Driven Information Security Risk Assessment and Decision Making," *Communications of the ACM* (50:10), pp. 101-106.

Bandura, A. 1982. "Self-Efficacy Mechanism in Human Agency," *American Psychologist* (37:2), p. 122.

Bandura, A. 2001. "Social Cognitive Theory of Mass Communication," *Media Psychology* (3:3), pp. 265-299.

Bandura, A. 2004. "Health Promotion by Social Cognitive Means," *Health Education and Behavior* (31:2), pp. 143-164.

Barclay, D., Higgins, C., and Thompson, R. 1995. "The Partial Least Squares (PLS) Approach to Causal Modeling: Personal Computer Adoption and Use as an Illustration," *Technology studies* (2:2), pp. 285-309.

Baskerville, R. 1991. "Risk Analysis: An Interpretive Feasibility Tool in Justifying Information Systems Security," *European Journal of Information Systems* (1:2), pp. 121-130.

Baskerville, R. 1993. "Information Systems Security Design Methods: Implications for Information Systems Development," *ACM Computing Surveys (CSUR)* (25:4), pp. 375-414.

Benlian, A. 2011. "Perceptual Congruence between IS Users and Professionals on IS Service Quality – Insights from Response Surface Analysis," in: *Proceedings of the 32nd International Conference on Information Systems.* Shanghai.

Benlian, A. 2013. "Effect Mechanisms of Perceptual Congruence between Information Systems Professionals and Users on Satisfaction with Service," *Journal of Management Information Systems* (29:4), pp. 63-96.

Benlian, A., and Hess, T. 2011. "Opportunities and Risks of Software-as-a-Service: Findings from a Survey of IT Executives," *Decision Support Systems* (52:1), pp. 232-246.

Bernard, H.R., Killworth, P., Kronenfeld, D., and Sailer, L. 1984. "The Problem of Informant Accuracy: The Validity of Retrospective Data," *Annual Review of Anthropology* (13:1), pp. 495-517.

Bettman, J.R. 1973. "Perceived Risk and Its Components: A Model and Empirical Test," *Journal of Marketing Research* (10:2), pp. 184-190.

Bezemer, C.-P., and Zaidman, A. 2010. "Multi-Tenant SaaS Applications: Maintenance Dream or Nightmare?," in: *Proceedings of the Joint ERCIM Workshop on Software Evolution (EVOL) and International Workshop on Principles of Software Evolution (IWPSE)*. Antwerp: pp. 88-92.

Bharati, P., Zhang, C., and Chaudhury, A. 2014. "Social Media Assimilation in Firms: Investigating the Roles of Absorptive Capacity and Institutional Pressures," *Information Systems Frontiers* (16:2), pp. 257-272.

Bhattacherjee, A. 2001. "Understanding Information Systems Continuance: An Expectation-Confirmation Model," *MIS Quarterly* (25:3), pp. 351-370.

Birch, D.G., and McEvoy, N.A. 1992. "Risk Analysis for Information Systems," *Journal of Information Technology* (7:1), pp. 44-53.

Bjorck, F. 2004. "Institutional Theory: A New Perspective for Research into IS / IT Security in Organisations," in: *Proceedings of the 37th Annual Hawaii International Conference on System Sciences*. Maui.

Boehm, B.W. 1991. "Software Risk Management: Principles and Practices," *IEEE Software* (8:1), pp. 32-41.

Bolton, R.N. 1993. "Pretesting Questionnaires: Content Analyses of Respondents' Concurrent Verbal Protocols," *Marketing Science* (12:3), pp. 280-303.

Boyd, M., Huang, S.-M., Jiang, J.J., and Klein, G. 2007. "Discrepancies between Desired and Perceived Measures of Performance of IS Professionals: Views of the IS Professionals Themselves and the Users," *Information & Management* (44:2), pp. 188-195.

Breakwell, G.M. 2000. "Risk Communication: Fators Affecting Impact," *British Medical Bulletin* (56:1), pp. 110-120.

Brown, S.A., Venkatesh, V., and Goyal, S. 2012. "Expectation Confirmation in Technology Use," *Information Systems Research* (23:2), pp. 474-487.

Buehler, R., Griffin, D., and Ross, M. 1994. "Exploring the Planning Fallacy: Why People Underestimate Their Task Completion Times," *Journal of Personality and Social Psychology* (67:3), pp. 366-381.

Bulgurcu, B., Cavusoglu, H., and Benbasat, I. 2010. "Information Security Policy Compliance: An Empirical Study of Rationality-Based Beliefs and Information Security Awareness," *MIS Quarterly* (34:3), pp. 523-548.

Burger, J.M., and Palmer, M.L. 1992. "Changes in and Generalization of Unrealistic Optimism Following Experiences with Stressful Events: Reactions to the 1989 California Earthquake," *Personality and Social Psychology Bulletin* (18:1), pp. 39-43.

Burt, R.S. 1987. "Social Contagion and Innovation: Cohesion Versus Structural Equivalence," *American Journal of Sociology* (92:2), pp. 1287-1335.

Buyya, R., Yeo, C.S., and Venugopal, S. 2008. "Market-Oriented Cloud Computing: Vision, Hype, and Reality for Delivering IT Services as Computing Utilities," in: *Proceedings of the 10th IEEE International Conference on High Performance Computing and Communications*. Zhangjiajie: pp. 5-13.

Buyya, R., Yeo, C.S., Venugopal, S., Broberg, J., and Brandic, I. 2009. "Cloud Computing and Emerging IT Platforms: Vision, Hype, and Reality for Delivering Computing as the 5th Utility," *Future Generation Computer Systems* (25:6), pp. 599-616.

Calderon, T.G. 1993. "Predictive Properties of Analysts' Forecasts of Corporate Earnings," *MidAtlantic Journal of Business* (29:1), pp. 41-58.

Campbell, J., Greenauer, N., Macaluso, K., and End, C. 2007. "Unrealistic Optimism in Internet Events," *Computers in Human Behavior* (23:3), pp. 1273-1284.

Cavusoglu, H., Cavusoglu, H., Son, J., and Benbasat, I. forthcoming. "Information Security Controls in Organizations: Multidimensionality of the Construct and a Nomological Model," in: *Information and Management*.

Cavusoglu, H., Mishra, B., and Raghunathan, S. 2004a. "The Effect of Internet Security Breach Announcements on Market Value: Capital Market Reactions for Breached Firms and Internet Security Developers," *International Journal of Electronic Commerce* (9:1), pp. 70-104.

Cavusoglu, H., Mishra, B., and Raghunathan, S. 2004b. "A Model for Evaluating IT Security Investments," *Communications of the ACM* (47:7), pp. 87-92.

Cavusoglu, H., Raghunathan, S., and Yue, W.T. 2008. "Decision-Theoretic and Game-Theoretic Approaches to IT Security Investment," *Journal of Management Information Systems* (25:2), pp. 281-304.

Chambers, J.R., and Windschitl, P.D. 2004. "Biases in Social Comparative Judgments: The Role of Nonmotivated Factors in above-Average and Comparative-Optimism Effects," *Psychological bulletin* (130:5), pp. 813-838.

Chatterjee, D., Grewal, R., and Sambamurthy, V. 2002. "Shaping up for E-Commerce: Institutional Enablers of the Organizational Assimilation of Web Technologies," *MIS Quarterly* (26:2), pp. 65-89.

Chen, H.H.G., Miller, R., Jiang, J.J., and Klein, G. 2005. "Communication Skills Importance and Proficiency: Perception Differences between IS Staff and IS Users," *International Journal of Information Management* (25:3), pp. 215-227.

Chin, W.W. 1998. "Commentary: Issues and Opinion on Structural Equation Modeling," *MIS Quarterly* (22:1), pp. 7-16.

Choi, N., Kim, D., Goo, J., and Whitmore, A. 2008. "Knowing Is Doing: An Empirical Validation of the Relationship between Managerial Information Security Awareness and Action," *Information Management & Computer Security* (16:5), pp. 484-501.

Chwelos, P., Benbasat, I., and Dexter, A.S. 2001. "Research Report: Empirical Test of an EDI Adoption Model," *Information Systems Research* (12:3), pp. 304-321.

Cloud Security Alliance. 2011. "Security Guidance for Critical Areas in Cloud Computing." *https://cloudsecurityalliance.org/guidance/*, last accessed: 01/17/2015.

Cloud Security Alliance. 2013. "Top Threats to Cloud Computing." *https://cloudsecurityalliance.org/topthreats/*, last accessed: 01/17/2015.

Cloud Showplace. 2014. "Cloud Showplace." *http://www.cloudshowplace.com/*, last accessed: 12/10/2014.

Cloutage. 2013. "Cloud Incidents 2013." *http://cloutage.org/incidents?reported_year=2013*, last accessed: 12/10/2014.

Cohen, J. 1992. "A Power Primer," *Psychological Bulletin* (112:1), p. 155.

Compeau, D.R., and Higgins, C.A. 1995. "Application of Social Cognitive Theory to Training for Computer Skills," *Information Systems Research* (6:2), pp. 118-143.

Craciun, C., Schüz, N., Lippke, S., and Schwarzer, R. 2010. "Risk Perception Moderates How Intentions Are Translated into Sunscreen Use," *Journal of Behavioral Medicine* (33:5), pp. 392-398.

Cremonini, M., and Nizovtsev, D. 2009. "Risks and Benefits of Signaling Information System Characteristics to Strategic Attackers," *Journal of Management Information Systems* (26:3), pp. 241-274.

Cunningham, S. 1967. "The Major Dimensions of Perceived Risk," in *Risk Taking and Information Handling in Consumer Behaviour*, D. Cox (ed.). Havard: Havard University Press, pp. 82-108.

Cusumano, M. 2010. "Cloud Computing and SaaS as New Computing Platforms," *Communications of the ACM* (53:4), pp. 27-29.

Cyert, R.M., and March, J.G. 1963. *A Behavioral Theory of the Firm*. Englewood Cliffs: Prentice-Hall.

Dacin, M.T., Goodstein, J., and Scott, W.R. 2002. "Institutional Theory and Institutional Change: Introduction to the Special Research Forum," *Academy of Management Journal* (45:1), pp. 45-56.

Davis, F.D. 1989. "Perceived Usefulness, Perceived Ease of Use, and User Acceptance of Information Technology," *MIS Quarterly* (13:3), pp. 319-340.

Davis, F.D., Bagozzi, R.P., and Warshaw, P.R. 1989. "User Acceptance of Computer Technology: A Comparison of Two Theoretical Models," *Management Science* (35:8), pp. 982-1003.

Dhillon, G., and Backhouse, J. 2001. "Current Directions in IS Security Research: Towards Socio-Organizational Perspectives," *Information Systems Journal* (11:2), p. 127.

Dibbern, J., Goles, T., Hirschheim, R., and Jayatilaka, B. 2004. "Information Systems Outsourcing: A Survey and Analysis of the Literature," *ACM SIGMIS Database* (35:4), pp. 6-102.

Dillard, A., Ubel, P., Smith, D., Zikmund-Fisher, B., Nair, V., Derry, H., Zhang, A., Pitsch, R., Alford, S., McClure, J., and Fagerlin, A. 2011. "The Distinct Role of Comparative Risk Perceptions in a Breast Cancer Prevention Program," *Annals of Behavioral Medicine* (42:2), pp. 262-268.

Dillard, A.J., Ferrer, R.A., Ubel, P.A., and Fagerlin, A. 2012. "Risk Perception Measures' Associations with Behavior Intentions, Affect, and Cognition Following Colon Cancer Screening Messages," *Health Psychology* (31:1), pp. 106-113.

Dillard, A.J., McCaul, K.D., and Klein, W.M.P. 2006. "Unrealistic Optimism in Smokers: Implications for Smoking Myth Endorsement and Self-Protective Motivation," *Journal of Health Communication* (11:1), pp. 93-102.

Dillard, A.J., Midboe, A.M., and Klein, W.M.P. 2009. "The Dark Side of Optimism: Unrealistic Optimism About Problems with Alcohol Predicts Subsequent Negative Event Experiences," *Personality and Social Psychology Bulletin* (35:11), pp. 1540-1550.

Dinev, T., and Hart, P. 2006. "An Extended Privacy Calculus Model for E-Commerce Transactions," *Information Systems Research* (17:1), pp. 61-80.

Douglas, M. 1985. *Risk Acceptability According to the Social Sciences.* New York: Russell Sage Foundation.

Dowling, G.R., and Staelin, R. 1994. "A Model of Perceived Risk and Intended Risk-Handling Activity," *Journal of Consumer Research* (21:1), pp. 119-134.

Dubendorfer, T., Wagner, A., and Plattner, B. 2004. "An Economic Damage Model for Large-Scale Internet Attacks," in: *Proceedings of the 3th IEEE International Workshops on Enabling Technologies: Infrastructure for Collaborative Enterprises.* Toronto: pp. 223-228.

Dutta, A., and Roy, R. 2008. "Dynamics of Organizational Information Security," *System Dynamics Review* (24:3), pp. 349-375.

Earl, M.J. 1996. "The Risks of Outsourcing IT," *Sloan management review* (37), pp. 26-32.

Ekenberg, L., Oberoi, S., and Orci, I. 1995. "A Cost Model for Managing Information Security Hazards," *Computers & Security* (14:8), pp. 707-717.

Erb, C.B., Harvey, C.R., and Viskanta, T.E. 1996. "Political Risk, Economic Risk, and Financial Risk," *Financial Analysts Journal* (52:6), pp. 29-46.

European Network and Information Security Agency. 2009. "Cloud Computing - Benefits, Risks and Recommendations for Information Security." *https://www.enisa.europa.eu/activities/risk-management/files/deliverables/cloud-computing-risk-assessment*, last accessed: 12/10/2014.

Faisst, U., and Prokein, O. 2005. "An Optimization Model for the Management of Security Risks in Banking Companies," in: *Proceedings of the 7th IEEE International Conference on E-Commerce Technology*. Los Alamitos: pp. 266-273.

Fan, X., Miller, B.C., Park, K.-E., Winward, B.W., Christensen, M., Grotevant, H.D., and Tai, R.H. 2006. "An Exploratory Study About Inaccuracy and Invalidity in Adolescent Self-Report Surveys," *Field Methods* (18:3), pp. 223-244.

Featherman, M.S., and Pavlou, P.A. 2003. "Predicting E-Services Adoption: A Perceived Risk Facets Perspective," *International Journal of Human-Computer Studies* (59:4), pp. 451-474.

Featherman, M.S., and Wells, J.D. 2010. "The Intangibility of E-Services: Effects on Perceived Risk and Acceptance," *SIGMIS Database* (41:2), pp. 110-131.

Federal Office for Information Security. 2011. "Security Recommendations for Cloud Computing Providers." *http://bit.ly/1CAuc6l*, last accessed: 12/10/2014.

Fenz, S., and Ekelhart, A. 2011. "Verification, Validation, and Evaluation in Information Security Risk Management," *IEEE Security & Privacy* (9:2), pp. 58-65.

Festinger, L. 1957. *A Theory of Cognitive Dissonance*. Stanford: Stanford University Press.

Folkman, S. 2013. "Stress: Appraisal and Coping," in *Encyclopedia of Behavioral Medicine*, M. Gellman and J.R. Turner (eds.). Springer New York, pp. 1913-1915.

Forcht, K.A. 1994. *Computer Security Management*. Boston: Course Technology Press.

Fornell, C., and Larcker, D.F. 1981. "Evaluating Structural Equation Models with Unobservable Variables and Measurement Error," *Journal of Marketing Research* (18:1), p. 39.

Foster, I., Zhao, Y., Raicu, I., and Lu, S. 2008. "Cloud Computing and Grid Computing 360-Degree Compared," in: *Proceedings of 7th IEEE Grid Computing Environments Workshop*. Austin: pp. 1-10.

Fouquet, M., Niedermayer, H., and Carle, G. 2009. "Cloud Computing for the Masses," in: *Proceedings of the 1st ACM Workshop on User-Provided Networking: Challenges and Opportunities*. Rome: pp. 31-36.

Freudenburg, W.R. 1993. *Risk and Recreancy: Weber, the Division of Labor, and the Rationality of Risk Perceptions*. Chapel Hill, NC, ETATS-UNIS: University of North Carolina Press.

Garg, A., Curtis, J., and Halper, H. 2003. "Quantifying the Financial Impact of IT Security Breaches," *Information Management & Computer Security* (11:2), pp. 74-83.

Gartner. 2010. "Gartner Says Worldwide SaaS Revenue within the Enterprise Application Software Market to Surpass $8.5 Billion in 2010." *http://www.gartner.com/newsroom/id/1406613*, last accessed: 12/10/2014.

Gartner. 2013. "Gartner Says Worldwide Public Cloud Services Market to Total $131 Billion." *http://www.gartner.com/newsroom/id/2352816*, last accessed: 12/10/2014.

Gaudine, A., and Thorne, L. 2001. "Emotion and Ethical Decision-Making in Organizations," *Journal of Business Ethics* (31:2), pp. 175-187.

Gefen, D., and Straub, D. 2000. "The Relative Importance of Perceived Ease of Use in IS Adoption: A Study of E-Commerce Adoption," *Journal of the Association for Information Systems* (1:1), pp. 1-28.

Gewald, H., and Dibbern, J. 2009. "Risks and Benefits of Business Process Outsourcing: A Study of Transaction Services in the German Banking Industry," *Information & Management* (46:4), pp. 249-257.

Gewald, H., Wüllenweber, K., and Weitzel, T. 2006. "The Influence of Perceived Risks on Banking Managers' Intention to Outsource Business Processes-a Study of the German Banking and Finance Industry.," *Journal of Electronic Commerce Research* (7:2), pp. 78-96.

Gigerenzer, G. 2004. "Dread Risk, September 11, and Fatal Traffic Accidents," *Psychological Science* (15:4), pp. 286-287.

Ginzberg, M.J. 1981. "Earky Diagnosis of MIS Implementation Failure: Promising Results and Unanswered Questions," *Management Science* (27:4), pp. 459-478.

Gold, R.S. 2007. "The Link between Judgments of Comparative Risk and Own Risk: Further Evidence," *Psychology, Health & Medicine* (12:2), pp. 238-247.

Gold, R.S. 2008. "Unrealistic Optimism and Event Threat," *Psychology, Health & Medicine* (13:2), pp. 193-201.

Goodhue, D., Lewis, W., and Thompson, R. 2006. "PLS, Small Sample Size, and Statistical Power in MIS Research," in: *Proceedings of the 39th Annual Hawaii International Conference on System Sciences*. Maui: pp. 202b-202b.

Goodhue, D.L., Lewis, W., and Thompson, R. 2012. "Does PLS Have Advantages for Small Sample Size or Non-Normal Data?," *MIS Quarterly* (36:3), p. 981.

Goodhue, D.L., and Straub, D.W. 1991. "Security Concerns of System Users: A Study of Perceptions of the Adequacy of Security," *Information & Management* (20:1), pp. 13-27.

Goodman, E., Chesney, M.A., and Tipton, A.C. 1995. "Relationship of Optimism, Knowledge, Attitudes, and Beliefs to Use of HIV Antibody Testing by at-Risk Female Adolescents," *Psychosomatic Medicine* (57:6), pp. 541-546.

Gordon, L.A., and Loeb, M.P. 2001. "Using Information Security as a Response to Competitor Analysis Systems," *Communications of the ACM* (44:9), pp. 70-75.

Gordon, L.A., and Loeb, M.P. 2002. "The Economics of Information Security Investment," *ACM Transactions on Information and System Security* (5:4), pp. 438-457.

Grossklags, J., Christin, N., and Chuang, J. 2008. "Security Investment (Failures) in Five Economic Environments: A Comparison of Homogeneous and Heterogeneous User Agents," in: *Proceedings of the 7th Workshop on the Economics of Information Security*. London.

Hair, J., Sarstedt, M., Ringle, C., and Mena, J. 2012. "An Assessment of the Use of Partial Least Squares Structural Equation Modeling in Marketing Research," *Journal of the Academy of Marketing Science* (40:3), pp. 414-433.

Hair, J.F., Tatham, R.L., Anderson, R.E., and Black, W. 2006. *Multivariate Data Analysis*. Englewood Cliffs: Prentice Hall.

Hambrick, D.C., and Mason, P.A. 1984. "Upper Echelons: The Organization as a Reflection of Its Top Managers," *Academy of Management Review* (9:2), pp. 193-206.

Hammitt, J.K. 1990. "Risk Perceptions and Food Choice: An Exploratory Analysis of Organic Versus Conventional Produce Buyers," *Risk Analysis* (10:3), pp. 367-374.

Harris, P.R., and Smith, V. 2005. "When the Risks Are Low: The Impact of Absolute and Comparative Information on Disturbance and Understanding in US and UK Samples," *Psychology & Health* (20:3), pp. 319-330.

Hart, O.D. 1988. "Incomplete Contracts and the Theory of the Firm," *Journal of Law, Economics, and Organization* (4:1), pp. 119-139.

Heart, T. 2010. "Who Is out There? Exploring the Effects of Trust and Perceived Risk on Saas Adoption Intentions," *The Data Base for Advances in Information Systems* (41:3), pp. 49-68.

Helweg-Larsen, M., Harding, H.G., and Klein, W.M.P. 2011. "Will I Divorce or Have a Happy Marriage?: Gender Differences in Comparative Optimism and Estimation of Personal Chances among U.S. College Students," *Basic & Applied Social Psychology* (33:2), pp. 157-166.

Helweg-Larsen, M., and Shepperd, J.A. 2001. "Do Moderators of the Optimistic Bias Affect Personal or Target Risk Estimates? A Review of the Literature," *Personality and Social Psychology Review* (5:1), pp. 74-95.

Heng, X., Dinev, T., Smith, J., and Hart, P. 2011. "Information Privacy Concerns: Linking Individual Perceptions with Institutional Privacy Assurances," *Journal of the Association for Information Systems* (12:12), pp. 798-824.

Henseler, J., Ringle, C., and Sarstedt, M. 2014. "A New Criterion for Assessing Discriminant Validity in Variance-Based Structural Equation Modeling," *Journal of the Academy of Marketing Science* (17:2), pp. 1-21.

Herath, H.S., and Herath, T.C. 2008. "Investments in Information Security: A Real Options Perspective with Bayesian Postaudit," *Journal of Management Information Systems* (25:3), pp. 337-375.

Hong, K.-S., Chi, Y.-P., Chao, L.R., and Tang, J.-H. 2003. "An Integrated System Theory of Information Security Management," *Information Management & Computer Security* (11:5), pp. 243-248.

Hoorens, V., and Buunk, B.P. 1993. "Social Comparison of Health Risks: Locus of Control, the Person-Positivity Bias, and Unrealistic Optimism," *Journal of Applied Social Psychology* (23:4), pp. 291-302.

Hopkin, P. 2012. *Fundamentals of Risk Management: Understanding, Evaluating and Implementing Effective Risk Management.* London: Kogan Page.

Huang, C.D., Hu, Q., and Behara, R.S. 2006. "Economics of Information Security Investment in the Case of Simultaneous Attacks," in: *Proceedings of the 5th Workshop on the Economics of Information Security.* London.

Huber, G.P., and Power, D.J. 1985. "Retrospective Reports of Strategic - Level Managers: Guidelines for Increasing Their Accuracy," *Strategic Management Journal* (6:2), pp. 171-180.

Huisman, M., and Iivari, J. 2006. "Deployment of Systems Development Methodologies: Perceptual Congruence between IS Managers and Systems Developers," *Information & Management* (43:1), pp. 29-49.

IDC. 2014. "Worldwide Procurement Applications 2014-2018 Forecast and 2013 Vendor Shares." *www.idc.com/getdoc.jsp?containerId=249832*, last accessed: 12/10/2014.

Janis, I.L. 1964. "Effects of Fear Arousal on Attitude Change: Recent Developments in Theory and Experimental Research," in *Advances in Experimental Social Psychology*, L. Berkowitz (ed.). New York: Academic Press, pp. 167-225.

Jansen, W., and Grance, T. 2011. "Guidelines on Security and Privacy in Public Cloud Computing," National Institute of Standards and Technology.

Janz, N.K., and Becker, M.H. 1984. "The Health Belief Model: A Decade Later," *Health Education & Behavior* (11:1), pp. 1-47.

Jensen, C., Potts, C., and Jensen, C. 2005. "Privacy Practices of Internet Users: Self-Reports Versus Observed Behavior," *International Journal of Human-Computer Studies* (63:1), pp. 203-227.

Jiang, J.J., Klein, G., and Discenza, R. 2002. "Perception Differences of Software Success: Provider and User Views of System Metrics," *Journal of Systems and Software* (63:1), pp. 17-27.

Jiang, J.J., Klein, G., Tesch, D., and Chen, H.-G. 2003. "Closing the User and Provider Service Quality Gap," *Communications of the ACM* (46:2), pp. 72-76.

Johnston, A.C., and Warkentin, M. 2010. "Fear Appeals and Information Security Behaviors: An Empirical Study," *MIS Quarterly* (34:3), pp. 549-566.

Jurison, J. 1995. *The Role of Risk and Return in Information Technology Outsourcing Decisions*. Basingstoke: Palgrave Macmillan.

Kailay, M.P., and Jarratt, P. 1995. "Ramex: A Prototype Expert System for Computer Security Risk Analysis and Management," *Computers & Security* (14:5), pp. 449-463.

Kaiser, J., Widjaja, T., and Buxmann, P. 2012. "Positioning Clients in Dyadic Dependence Structures of IS Outsourcing Relationships – Conceptualization and Empirical Findings," in: *Proceedings of the 33rd International Conference on Information Systems*. Orlando.

Kankanhalli, A., Teo, H.-H., Tan, B.C., and Wei, K.-K. 2003. "An Integrative Study of Information Systems Security Effectiveness," *International journal of information management* (23:2), pp. 139-154.

Karahanna, E., Straub, D.W., and Chervany, N.L. 1999. "Information Technology Adoption across Time: A Cross-Sectional Comparison of Pre-Adoption and Post-Adoption Beliefs," *MIS Quarterly* (23:2), pp. 183-213.

Karakayali, N. 2009. "Social Distance and Affective Orientations," *Sociological Forum* (24:3), pp. 538-562.

Karofsky, E. 2001. "Return on Security Investment: Calculating the Security Investment Equation," *Secure Business Quarter* (1:2), pp. 16-25.

Kent, K., and Souppaya, M. 2006. "Guide to Computer Security Log Management," Special Publication 800-92, National Institute of Standards and Technology.

Kim, D.J., Ferrin, D.L., and Rao, H.R. 2008. "A Trust-Based Consumer Decision-Making Model in Electronic Commerce: The Role of Trust, Perceived Risk, and Their Antecedents," *Decision Support Systems* (44:2), pp. 544-564.

Kishore, R., Rao, H.R., Nam, K., Rajagopalan, S., and Chaudhury, A. 2003. "A Relationship Perspective on IT Outsourcing," *Communications of the ACM* (46:12), pp. 86-92.

Klein, G., and Jiang, J.J. 2001. "Seeking Consonance in Information Systems," *Journal of Systems and Software* (56:2), pp. 195-202.

Klein, W.M.P. 1997. "Objective Standards Are Not Enough: Affective, Self-Evaluative, and Behavioral Responses to Social Comparison Information," *Journal of Personality and Social Psychology* (72:4), pp. 763-774.

Klein, W.M.P. 2003. "Self-Prescriptive, Perceived, and Actual Attention to Comparative Risk Information," *Psychology & Health* (18:5), pp. 625-643.

Klein, W.M.P., and Weinstein, N.D. 1997. "Social Comparison and Unrealistic Optimism About Personal Risk," in *Health, Coping, and Well-Being: Perspectives from Social Comparison Theory.*, B.P. Buunk and F.X. Gibbons (eds.). Mahwah, NJ US: Lawrence Erlbaum Associates Publishers, pp. 25-61.

Krasnova, H., Kolesnikova, E., and Guenther, O. 2009. "It Won't Happen to Me!": Self-Disclosure in Online Social Networks," in: *Proceedings of the 15th Americas Conference on Information Systems*. San Francisco.

Kreuter, M.W., and Strecher, V.J. 1995. "Changing Inaccurate Perceptions of Health Risk: Results from a Randomized Trial," *Health Psychology* (14:1), pp. 56-63.

Kwok, L.f., and Longley, D. 1999. "Information Security Management and Modelling," *Information Management & Computer Security* (7:1), pp. 30-40.

Lacity, M.C., Khan, S.A., and Willcocks, L.P. 2009. "A Review of the IT Outsourcing Literature: Insights for Practice," *The Journal of Strategic Information Systems* (18:3), pp. 130-146.

Lacity, M.C., Willcocks, L.P., and Feeny, D.F. 1995. "IT Outsourcing: Maximize Flexibility and Control," *Harvard Business Review* (73:3), pp. 84-93.

Lazarus, R.S. 1966. *Psychological Stress and the Coping Process*. New York: McGraw-Hill.

Lazarus, R.S. 1993. "Coping Theory and Research: Past, Present, and Future," *Psychosomatic Medicine* (55:3), pp. 234-247.

Lee, M.-C. 2009. "Factors Influencing the Adoption of Internet Banking: An Integration of TAM and TPB with Perceived Risk and Perceived Benefit," *Electronic Commerce Research and Applications* (8:3), pp. 130-141.

Lee, S.M., Lee, S.-G., and Yoo, S. 2004. "An Integrative Model of Computer Abuse Based on Social Control and General Deterrence Theories," *Information & Management* (41:6), pp. 707-718.

Lenk, A., Klems, M., Nimis, J., Tai, S., and Sandholm, T. 2009. "What's inside the Cloud? An Architectural Map of the Cloud Landscape," in: *Proceedings of the ICSE Workshop on Software Engineering Challenges of Cloud Computing*. Washington: pp. 23-31.

Lerner, J.S., and Keltner, D. 2000. "Beyond Valence: Toward a Model of Emotion-Specific Influences on Judgement and Choice," *Cognition & Emotion* (14:4), pp. 473-493.

Liang, H., and Xue, Y. 2009. "Avoidance of Information Technology Threats: A Theoretical Perspective," *MIS Quarterly* (33:1), pp. 71-90.

Liang, H., and Xue, Y. 2010. "Understanding Security Behaviors in Personal Computer Usage: A Threat Avoidance Perspective," *Journal of the Association for Information Systems* (11:7), pp. 394-413.

Liebermann, Y., and Stashevsky, S. 2002. "Perceived Risks as Barriers to Internet and E-Commerce Usage," *Qualitative Market Research: An International Journal* (5:4), pp. 291-300.

Lin, C.S., Wu, S., and Tsai, R.J. 2005. "Integrating Perceived Playfulness into Expectation-Confirmation Model for Web Portal Context," *Information & Management* (42:5), pp. 683-693.

Lipkus, I.M., Klein, W.M.P., Skinner, C.S., and Rimer, B.K. 2005. "Breast Cancer Risk Perceptions and Breast Cancer Worry: What Predicts What?," *Journal of Risk Research* (8:5), pp. 439-452.

Lipkus, I.M., Kuchibhatla, M., McBride, C.M., Bosworth, H.B., Pollak, K.I., Siegler, I.C., and Rimer, B.K. 2000. "Relationships among Breast Cancer Perceived Absolute Risk, Comparative Risk, and Worries," *Cancer Epidemiology Biomarkers & Prevention* (9:9), pp. 973-975.

Loske, A., Widjaja, T., Benlian, A., and Buxmann, P. 2014. "Perceived IT Security Risks in Cloud Adoption: The Role of Perceptual Incongruence between Users and Providers," in: *Proceedings of the 22nd European Conference on Information Systems*. Tel-Aviv.

Loske, A., Widjaja, T., and Buxmann, P. 2013. "Cloud Computing Providers' Unrealistic Optimism Regarding IT Security Risks: A Threat to Users?," in: *Proceedings of the 34th International Conference on International on Information Systems*. Milan.

MacKenzie, S.B., Podsakoff, P.M., and Podsakoff, N.P. 2011. "Construct Measurement and Validation Procedures in MIS and Behavioral Research - Integrating New and Existing Techniques," *MIS Quarterly* (35:2), pp. 293-334.

MacKinnon, D.P., Fairchild, A.J., and Fritz, M.S. 2007. "Mediation Analysis," *Annual Review of Psychology* (58), p. 593.

Maitlis, S., and Ozcelik, H. 2004. "Toxic Decision Processes: A Study of Emotion and Organizational Decision Making," *Organization Science* (15:4), pp. 375-393.

March, J.G., and Shapira, Z. 1987. "Managerial Perspectives on Risk and Risk Taking," *Management Science* (33:11), pp. 1404-1418.

Marston, S., Li, Z., Bandyopadhyay, S., Zhang, J., and Ghalsasi, A. 2011. "Cloud Computing - the Business Perspective," *Decision Support Systems* (51:1), pp. 176-189.

Mason, D., Prevost, A.T., and Sutton, S. 2008. "Perceptions of Absolute Versus Relative Differences between Personal and Comparison Health Risk," *Health Psychology* (27:1), pp. 87-92.

Mather, T., Kumaraswamy, S., and Latif, S. 2009. *Cloud Security and Privacy : An Enterprise Perspective on Risks and Compliance*. Sebastopol: O'Reilly Media.

Mauricio, S.F., Anthony, D.M., and David, E.S. 2010. "Reducing Online Privacy Risk to Facilitate E-Service Adoption: The Influence of Perceived Ease of Use and Corporate Credibility," *Journal of Services Marketing* (24:3), pp. 219-229.

McFadzean, E., Ezingeard, J.-N., and Birchall, D. 2007. "Perception of Risk and the Strategic Impact of Existing IT on Information Security Strategy at Board Level," *Online Information Review* (31:5), pp. 622-660.

McKenna, F.P. 1993. "It Won't Happen to Me: Unrealistic Optimism or Illusion of Control?," *British Journal of Psychology* (84:1), pp. 39-50.

Mell, P., and Grance, T. 2011. "The Nist Definition of Cloud Computing," Special Publication 800-145, National Institute of Standards and Technology.

Milne, S., Sheeran, P., and Orbell, S. 2000. "Prediction and Intervention in Health-Related Behavior: A Meta-Analytic Review of Protection Motivation Theory," *Journal of Applied Social Psychology* (30:1), pp. 106-143.

Mitchell, V.-W. 1999. "Consumer Perceived Risk: Conceptualisations and Models," *European Journal of Marketing* (33:1), pp. 163-195.

Moss, S., Prosser, H., Costello, H., Simpson, N., Patel, P., Rowe, S., Turner, S., and Hatton, C. 1998. "Reliability and Validity of the Pas - Add Checklist for Detecting Psychiatric Disorders in Adults with Intellectual Disability," *Journal of Intellectual Disability Research* (42:2), pp. 173-183.

Mukhopadhyay, I., Chakraborty, M., and Chakrabarti, S. 2011. "A Comparative Study of Related Technologies of Intrusion Detection & Prevention Systems," *Journal of Information Security* (2:1), pp. 28-38.

Murray, K., and Schlacter, J. 1990. "The Impact of Services Versus Goods on Consumers' Assessment of Perceived Risk and Variability," *Journal of the Academy of Marketing Science* (18:1), pp. 51-65.

Nagpal, J., Kumar, A., Kakar, S., and Bhartia, A. 2010. "The Development of Quality of Life Instrument for Indian Diabetes Patients: A Validation and Reliability Study in Middle and Higher Income Groups," *Journal of the Association of Physicians of India* (58), pp. 295-304.

Nance, W.D., and Straub, D.W. 1988. "An Investigation into the Use and Usefulness of Security Software in Detecting Computer Abuse," in: *Proceedings of the 19th International Conference on Information Systems*. Minneapolis: pp. 283-294.

Nandedkar, A., and Midha, V. 2012. "It Won't Happen to Me: An Assessment of Optimism Bias in Music Piracy," *Computers in Human Behavior* (28:1), pp. 41-48.

Neale, M.A., and Bazerman, M.H. 1985. "The Effects of Framing and Negotiator Overconfidence on Bargaining Behaviors and Outcomes," *Academy of Management Journal* (28:1), pp. 34-49.

Ng, B.-Y., Kankanhalli, A., and Xu, Y. 2009. "Studying Users' Computer Security Behavior: A Health Belief Perspective," *Decision Support Systems* (46:4), pp. 815-825.

Nunnally, J.C. 1978. *Psychometric Theory*, (2nd ed.). New York: McGraw-Hill.

O'Brien, R.M. 2007. "A Caution Regarding Rules of Thumb for Variance Inflation Factors," *Quality & Quantity* (41:5), pp. 673-690.

Oliver, R.L. 1980. "A Cognitive Model of the Antecedents and Consequences of Satisfaction Decisions," *Journal of Marketing Research* (17:4), pp. 460-469.

Owens, D. 2010. "Securing Elasticity in the Cloud," *Communications of the ACM* (53:6), pp. 46-51.

Pang, G., and Whitt, W. 2009. "Service Interruptions in Large-Scale Service Systems," *Management Science* (55:9), pp. 1499-1512.

Parasuraman, A., Zeithaml, V., and Berry, L. 1988. "Servqual: A Multiple-Item Scale for Measuring Consumer Perceptions of Service Quality," *Journal of Retailing* (64:1), pp. 12-40.

Paté-Cornell, M.E. 1996. "Uncertainties in Risk Analysis: Six Levels of Treatment," *Reliability Engineering & System Safety* (54:2), pp. 95-111.

Patterson, D.A. 2002. "A Simple Way to Estimate the Cost of Downtime," in: *Proceedings of the 16th USENIX Large Installation Systems Administration Conference*. Berkeley: pp. 185-188.

Pavlou, P.A. 2003. "Consumer Acceptance of Electronic Commerce: Integrating Trust and Risk with the Technology Acceptance Model," *International Journal of Electronic Commerce* (7:3), pp. 101-134.

Perloff, L.S., and Fetzer, B.K. 1986. "Self-Other Judgments and Perceived Vulnerability to Victimization," *Journal of Personality and Social Psychology* (50:3), pp. 502-510.

Peter, J.P., and Ryan, M.J. 1976. "An Investigation of Perceived Risk at the Brand Level," *Journal of Marketing Research* (13:5), pp. 184-188.

Pfeffer, J., and Salancik, G.R. 2003. *The External Control of Organizations: A Resource Dependence Perspective*. Stanford: Stanford University Press.

Pitt, L., Berthon, P., and Lane, N. 1998. "Gaps within the IS Department: Barriers to Service Quality," *Journal of Information Technology* (13:3), pp. 191-200.

Podsakoff, P.M., MacKenzie, S.B., Lee, J.Y., and Podsakoff, N.P. 2003. "Common Method Biases in Behavioral Research: A Critical Review of the Literature and Recommended Remedies," *The Journal of Applied Psychology* (88:5), pp. 879-903.

Polites, G.L., Roberts, N., and Thatcher, J. 2012. "Conceptualizing Models Using Multidimensional Constructs: A Review and Guidelines for Their Use," *European Journal of Information Systems* (21:1), pp. 22-48.

Poppo, L., and Zenger, T. 2002. "Do Formal Contracts and Relational Governance Function as Substitutes or Complements?," *Strategic Management Journal* (23:8), pp. 707-725.

Powell, W.W., and DiMaggio, P.J. 2012. *The New Institutionalism in Organizational Analysis*. Chicago: University of Chicago Press.

Preacher, K.J., and Hayes, A.F. 2008. "Asymptotic and Resampling Strategies for Assessing and Comparing Indirect Effects in Multiple Mediator Models," *Behavior Research Methods* (40:3), pp. 879-891.

Pring, B. 2010. "Cloud Computing: The Next Generation of Outsourcing," Gartner Group.

Prodan, R., and Ostermann, S. 2009. "A Survey and Taxonomy of Infrastructure as a Service and Web Hosting Cloud Providers," in: *Proceedings of the 10th International Conderence on Grid Computing*. Washington: pp. 17-25.

Radcliffe, N.M., and Klein, W.M.P. 2002. "Dispositional, Unrealistic, and Comparative Optimism: Differential Relations with the Knowledge and Processing of Risk Information and Beliefs About Personal Risk," *Personality and Social Psychology Bulletin* (28:6), pp. 836-846.

Ranby, K.W., Aiken, L.S., Gerend, M.A., and Erchull, M.J. 2010. "Perceived Susceptibility Measures Are Not Interchangeable: Absolute, Direct Comparative, and Indirect Comparative Risk," *Health Psychology* (29:1), pp. 20-28.

Reason, J.T. 1997. *Managing the Risks of Organizational Accidents*. Ashgate: Aldershot.

Reinartz, W., Haenlein, M., and Henseler, J. 2009. "An Empirical Comparison of the Efficacy of Covariance-Based and Variance-Based Sem," *International Journal of Research in Marketing* (26:4), pp. 332-344.

Rhee, H.-S., Ryu, Y.U., and Kim, C.-T. 2012. "Unrealistic Optimism on Information Security Management," *Computers & Security* (31:2), pp. 221-232.

Ringle, C.M., Sarstedt, M., and Straub, D.W. 2012. "Editor's Comments: A Critical Look at the Use of PLS-Sem in MIS Quarterly," *MIS Quarterly* (36:1), pp. 3-14.

Ringle, C.M., Wende, S., and Will, A. 2005. "Smartpls 2.0 M3." Hamburg.

Rogers, R.W. 1975. "A Protection Motivation Theory of Fear Appeals and Attitude Change," *Journal of Psychology* (91:1), p. 93.

Rönkkö, M., and Ylitalo, J. 2011. "PLS Marker Variable Approach to Diagnosing and Controlling for Method Variance," in: *Proceedings of the 32th International Conference on Information Systems*. Shanghai.

Rose, J.P. 2010. "Are Direct or Indirect Measures of Comparative Risk Better Predictors of Concern and Behavioural Intentions?," *Psychology & Health* (25:2), pp. 149-165.

Rose, J.P. 2012. "Debiasing Comparative Optimism and Increasing Worry for Health Outcomes," *Journal of Health Psychology* (17:8), pp. 1121-1131.

Rose, J.P., and Nagel, B. 2013. "Relation between Comparative Risk, Absolute Risk, and Worry: The Role of Handedness Strength," *Journal of Health Psychology* (18:7), pp. 866-874.

Rosenstock, I.M. 1966. "Why People Use Health Services," *The Milbank Memorial Fund Quarterly* (44:3), pp. 94-127.

Rosenstock, I.M., Strecher, V.J., and Becker, M.H. 1994. "The Health Belief Model and HIV Risk Behavior Change," in *Preventing AIDS: Theories and Methods of Behavioral Interventions*, R. DiClemente and J. Peterson (eds.). New York: Plenum Press, pp. 5-24.

Rotchanakitumnuai, S., and Speece, M. 2003. "Barriers to Internet Banking Adoption: A Qualitative Study among Corporate Customers in Thailand," *International Journal of Bank Marketing* (21:6), pp. 312-323.

Rothman, A.J., Klein, W.M.P., and Weinstein, N.D. 1996. "Absolute and Relative Biases in Estimations of Personal Risk," *Journal of Applied Social Psychology* (26:14), pp. 1213-1236.

SAP. 2014a. "Cloud Strategy: Disrupt the Market, Not Your Business." *http://www.news-sap.com/cloud-strategy-disrupt-the-market-business/*, last accessed: 01/17/2015.

SAP. 2014b. "Sap Product and Cloud Security Strategy." *http://www.sap.com/pc/tech/security/software/cloud.html*, last accessed: 01/17/2015.

Schelling, T.C. 2006. *Micromotives and Macrobehavior.* New-York: WW Norton & Company.

Schepers, J., and Wetzels, M. 2007. "A Meta-Analysis of the Technology Acceptance Model: Investigating Subjective Norm and Moderation Effects," *Information & Management* (44:1), pp. 90-103.

Schlaak, B., Dynes, S., Kolbe, L.M., and Schierholz, R. 2008. "Managing of Information Systems Risks in Extended Enterprises: The Case of Outsourcing," in: *Proceedings of the 14th American Conference on Information Systems.* Chicago: p. 280.

Schwenk, C.R. 1985. "Management Illusions and Biases: Their Impact on Strategic Decisions," *Long Range Planning* (18:5), pp. 74-80.

Schwenk, C.R. 1988. "The Cognitive Perspective on Strategic Decision Making," *Journal of Management Studies* (25:1), pp. 41-55.

Scott, W.R. 1995. *Institutions and Organizations.* Newbury Park: Sage.

Sharot, T., Korn, C.W., and Dolan, R.J. 2011. "How Unrealistic Optimism Is Maintained in the Face of Reality," *Nat Neurosci* (14:11), pp. 1475-1479.

Sheetz, S.D., Henderson, D., and Wallace, L. 2009. "Understanding Developer and Manager Perceptions of Function Points and Source Lines of Code," *Journal of Systems and Software* (82:9), pp. 1540-1549.

Shepperd, J.A., Carroll, P., Grace, J., and Terry, M. 2002. "Exploring the Causes of Comparative Optimism," *Psychologica Belgica* (42:1), pp. 65-98.

Shepperd, J.A., Klein, W.M.P., Waters, E.A., and Weinstein, N.D. 2013. "Taking Stock of Unrealistic Optimism," *Perspectives on Psychological Science* (8:4), pp. 395-411.

Simon, H.A. 1960. *The New Science of Management Decision.* New-York: Harper & Brothers.

Singh, J.V. 1986. "Performance, Slack, and Risk Taking in Organizational Decision Making," *Academy of management Journal* (29:3), pp. 562-585.

Siponen, M.T. 2000. "A Conceptual Foundation for Organizational Information Security Awareness," *Information Management & Computer Security* (8:1), pp. 31-41.

Siponen, M.T. 2005. "An Analysis of the Traditional IS Security Approaches: Implications for Research and Practice," *European Journal of Information Systems* (14:3), pp. 303-315.

Siponen, M.T., and Willison, R. 2009. "Information Security Management Standards: Problems and Solutions," *Information & Management* (46:5), pp. 267-270.

Sjöberg, L. 1998. "Worry and Risk Perception," *Risk Analysis* (18:1), pp. 85-93.

Slovic, P. 1987. "Perception of Risk," *Science, New Series* (236:4799), pp. 280-285.

Slovic, P., Fischhoff, B., and Lichtenstein, S. 1982. "Why Study Risk Perception?," *Risk Analysis* (2:2), pp. 83-93.

Smith, D.M. 2014. "Hype Cycle for Cloud Computing," Gartner Group.

Smith, H.J., Dinev, T., and Xu, H. 2011. "Information Privacy Research: An Interdisciplinary Review," *MIS Quarterly* (35:4), pp. 989-1016.

Sonnenreich, W., Albanese, J., and Stout, B. 2006. "Return on Security Investment (ROSI): A Practical Quantitative Model," *Journal of Research and Practice in Information Technology* (38:1), pp. 45-56.

Srinivasan, N., and Ratchford, B.T. 1991. "An Empirical Test of a Model of External Search for Automobiles," *Journal of Consumer Research* (18:2), pp. 233-242.

Srull, T.K., and Wyer, R.S. 1988. *Advances in Social Cognition.* Hillsdale, New Jersey: Lawrence Erlbaum Associates.

Starr, C. 1969. "Social Benefit Versus Technological Risk," *Science* (165:3899), pp. 1232-1238.

Stoneburner, G., Goguen, A., and Feringa, A. 2002. "Risk Management Guide for Information Technology Systems," Special Publication 800-30, National Institute of Standards and Technology.

Straub, D.W., and Nance, W.D. 1990. "Discovering and Disciplining Computer Abuse in Organizations: A Field Study," *MIS Quarterly* (14:1), pp. 45-60.

Straub, D.W., and Welke, R.J. 1998. "Coping with Systems Risk: Security Planning Models for Management Decision Making," *MIS Quarterly* (22:4), pp. 441-469.

Strecher, V.J., Kreuter, M.W., and Kobrin, S.C. 1995. "Do Cigarette Smokers Have Unrealistic Perceptions of Their Heart Attack, Cancer, and Stroke Risks?," *Journal of Behavioral Medicine* (18:1), pp. 45-54.

Sun, L., Srivastava, R.P., and Mock, T.J. 2006. "An Information Systems Security Risk Assessment Model under the Dempster-Shafer Theory of Belief Functions," *Journal of Management Information Systems* (22:4), pp. 109-142.

Swanson, E.B., and Ramiller, N.C. 2004. "Innovating Mindfully with Information Technology," *MIS Quarterly* (28:4), pp. 553-583.

Szajna, B., and Scamell, R.W. 1993. "The Effects of Information System User Expectations on Their Performance and Perceptions," *MIS Quarterly* (17:4), pp. 493-516.

Takabi, H., Joshi, J.B., and Ahn, G.-J. 2010. "Security and Privacy Challenges in Cloud Computing Environments," *IEEE Security & Privacy* (8:6), pp. 24-31.

Tanner, J.F., Hunt, J.B., and Eppright, D.R. 1991. "The Protection Motivation Model: A Normative Model of Fear Appeals," *Journal of Marketing* (55:3), pp. 36-45.

Taylor, S., and Todd, P.A. 1995. "Understanding Information Technology Usage: A Test of Competing Models," *Information Systems Research* (6:2), pp. 144-176.

Teo, H.H., Wei, K.K., and Benbasat, I. 2003. "Predicting Intention to Adopt Interorganizational Linkages: An Institutional Perspective," *MIS Quarterly* (27:1), pp. 19-49.

Teo, T.S.H., and King, W.R. 1997. "An Assessment of Perceptual Differences between Informants in Information Systems Research," *Omega* (25:5), pp. 557-566.

Tesch, D., Miller, R., Jiang, J.J., and Klein, G. 2005. "Perception and Expectation Gaps of Information Systems Provider Skills: The Impact on User Satisfaction," *Information Systems Journal* (15:4), pp. 343-355.

Thompson, S.C. 1999. "Illusions of Control: How We Overestimate Our Personal Influence," *Current Directions in Psychological Science* (8:6), pp. 187-190.

Turban, D.B., and Jones, A.P. 1988. "Supervisor-Subordinate Similarity: Types, Effects and Mechanisms," *Journal of Applied Psychology* (73), pp. 228-234.

Tversky, A., and Kahneman, D. 1973. "Availability: A Heuristic for Judging Frequency and Probability," *Cognitive Psychology* (5:2), pp. 207-232.

Van Niekerk, J.F., and Von Solms, R. 2010. "Information Security Culture: A Management Perspective," *Computers & Security* (29:4), pp. 476-486.

Vance, A., Siponen, M.T., and Pahnila, S. 2012. "Motivating IS Security Compliance: Insights from Habit and Protection Motivation Theory," *Information & Management* (49:3), pp. 190-198.

Vaquero, L.M., Rodero-Merino, L., Caceres, J., and Lindner, M. 2008. "A Break in the Clouds: Towards a Cloud Definition," *ACM SIGCOMM Computer Communication Review* (39:1), pp. 50-55.

Vaquero, L.M., Rodero-Merino, L., and Morán, D. 2010. "Locking the Sky: A Survey on IaaS Cloud Security," *Computing* (91:1), pp. 93-118.

Velten, C., and Janata, S. 2011. "Cloud Vendor Benchmark 2011," Experton Group.

Venkatesh, V., and Goyal, S. 2010. "Expectation Disconfirmation and Technology Adoption: Polynomial Modeling and Response Surface Analysis," *MIS Quarterly* (34:2), pp. 281-303.

Venkatesh, V., Morris, M.G., Davis, G.B., and Davis, F.D. 2003. "User Acceptance of Information Technology: Toward a Unified View," *MIS Quarterly* (27:3), pp. 425-478.

Vetter, J., Benlian, A., and Hess, T. 2011. "Overconfidence in IT Investment Decisions: Why Knowledge Can Be a Boon and Bane at the Same Time," in: *Proceedings of the 32nd International Conference on Information Systems.* Shanghai.

Von Solms, B., and Von Solms, R. 2004. "The 10 Deadly Sins of Information Security Management," *Computers & Security* (23:5), pp. 371-376.

Von Solms, R. 1999. "Information Security Management: Why Standards Are Important," *Information Management & Computer Security* (7:1), pp. 50-58.

Vroom, V.H. 1964. *Work and Motivation*. Oxford: Wiley.

Wang, J., Chaudhury, A., and Rao, H.R. 2008a. "Research Note: A Value-at-Risk Approach to Information Security Investment," *Information Systems Research* (19:1), pp. 106-120.

Wang, L., Tao, J., Kunze, M., Castellanos, A.C., Kramer, D., and Karl, W. 2008b. "Scientific Cloud Computing: Early Definition and Experience," in: *Proceedings of the 10th IEEE International Conference on High Performance Computing and Communications*. Dalin: pp. 825-830.

Wang, Z.H., Guo, C.J., Gao, B., Sun, W., Zhang, Z., and An, W.H. 2008c. "A Study and Performance Evaluation of the Multi-Tenant Data Tier Design Patterns for Service Oriented Computing," in: *Proceedings of the 8th International Conference on e-Business Engineering*. Xi'an: pp. 94-101.

Warkentin, M., and Johnston, A. 2008. "IT Governance and Organizational Design for Security Management," in *Information Security: Policies, Processes, and Practices*, D.W. Straub, S. Goodman and R. Baskerville (eds.). Amonk: M.E. Sharpe, pp. 46-68.

Waters, E.A., Klein, W.M.P., Moser, R.P., Yu, M., Waldron, W.R., McNeel, T.S., and Freedman, A.N. 2011. "Correlates of Unrealistic Risk Beliefs in a Nationally Representative Sample," *Journal of Behavioral Medicine* (34:3), pp. 225-235.

Watson, R.T., Pitt, L.F., and Kavan, C.B. 1998. "Measuring Information Systems Service Quality: Lessons from Two Longitudinal Case Studies," *MIS Quarterly* (22:1), pp. 61-79.

Weinhardt, C., Anandasivam, A., Blau, B., Borissov, N., Meinl, T., Michalk, W., and Stößer, J. 2009. "Cloud Computing – a Classification, Business Models, and Research Directions," *Business & Information Systems Engineering* (1:5), pp. 391-399.

Weinstein, N.D. 1980. "Unrealistic Optimism About Future Life Events," *Journal of Personality and Social Psychology* (39:5), pp. 806-820.

Weinstein, N.D. 1982. "Unrealistic Optimism About Susceptibility to Health Problems," *Journal of Behavioral Medicine* (5:4), pp. 441-460.

Weinstein, N.D. 1984. "Why It Won't Happen to Me: Perceptions of Risk Factors and Susceptibility," *Health Psychology* (3:5), pp. 431-457.

Weinstein, N.D. 1987. "Unrealistic Optimism About Susceptibility to Health Problems: Conclusions from a Community-Wide Sample," *Journal of Behavioral Medicine* (10:5), pp. 481-500.

Weinstein, N.D. 1989. "Effects of Personal Experience on Self-Protective Behavior," *Psychological Bulletin* (105:1), pp. 31-50.

Weinstein, N.D. 1993. "Testing Four Competing Theories of Health-Protective Behavior," *Health Psychology* (12:4), pp. 324-333.

Weinstein, N.D. 2000. "Perceived Probability, Perceived Severity, and Health-Protective Behavior," *Health Psychology* (19:1), p. 65.

Weinstein, N.D., and Klein, W.M.P. 1995. "Resistance of Personal Risk Perceptions to Debiasing Interventions," *Health Psychology* (14:2), pp. 132-140.

Weinstein, N.D., and Klein, W.M.P. 1996. "Unrealistic Optimism: Present and Future," *Journal of Social and Clinical Psychology* (15:1), pp. 1-8.

Weinstein, N.D., Kwitel, A., McCaul, K.D., Magnan, R.E., Gerrard, M., and Gibbons, F.X. 2007. "Risk Perceptions: Assessment and Relationship to Influenza Vaccination," *Health Psychology* (26:2), pp. 146-151.

Weinstein, N.D., and Lyon, J.E. 1999. "Mindset, Optimistic Bias About Personal Risk and Health-Protective Behaviour," *British Journal of Health Psychology* (4:4), pp. 289-300.

Weinstein, N.D., and Nicolich, M. 1993. "Correct and Incorrect Interpretations of Correlations between Risk Perceptions and Risk Behaviors," *Health Psychology* (12:3), pp. 235-245.

Weinstein, N.D., Rothman, A.J., and Nicolich, M. 1998. "Use of Correlational Data to Examine the Effects of Risk Perceptions on Precautionary Behavior," *Psychology & Health* (13:3), pp. 479-501.

Weinstein, N.D., and Sandman, P.M. 1992. "A Model of the Precaution Adoption Process: Evidence from Home Radon Testing," *Health Psychology* (11:3), p. 170.

Weinstein, N.D., Sandman, P.M., and Roberts, N.E. 1990. "Determinants of Self-Protective Behavior: Home Radon Testing," *Journal of Applied Social Psychology* (20:10), pp. 783-801.

Weinstein, N.D., Slovic, P., and Gibson, G. 2004. "Accuracy and Optimism in Smokers' Beliefs About Quitting," *Nicotine & Tobacco Research* (6:3), pp. 375-380.

West, S.G., Finch, J.F., and Curran, P.J. 1995. "Structural Equation Models with Nonnormal Variables: Problems and Remedies," in *Structural Equation Modeling: Concepts, Issues, and Applications,* R.H. Hoyle (ed.). Thousand Oaks: Sage Publications, pp. 56-75.

Wetzels, M., Odekerken-Schroder, G., and Van Oppen, C. 2009. "Using PLS Path Modeling for Assessing Hierarchical Construct Models: Guidelines and Empirical Illustration," *MIS Quarterly* (33:1), p. 11.

Wheeler, E. 2011. *Security Risk Management: Building an Information Security Risk Management Program from the Ground Up.* Amsterdam: Elsevier.

Whitten, D., Chakrabarty, S., and Wakefield, R. 2010. "The Strategic Choice to Continue Outsourcing, Switch Vendors, or Backsource: Do Switching Costs Matter?," *Information & Management* (47:3), pp. 167-175.

Willcocks, L., Fitzgerald, G., and Lacity, M. 1996. "To Outsource IT or Not?: Recent Research on Economics and Evaluation Practice," *European Journal of Information Systems* (5:3), pp. 143–160.

Willcocks, L., Lacity, M., and Cullen, S. 2007. "Information Technology Sourcing Research: Critique, Lessons and Prospects," in: *Proceedings of the 13th Americas Conference on Information Systems*. Keystone.

Witte, K. 1992. "Putting the Fear Back into Fear Appeals: The Extended Parallel Process Model," *Communication Monographs* (59:4), pp. 329-349.

Witte, K. 1994. "Fear Control and Danger Control: A Test of the Extended Parallel Process Model (EPPM)," *Communications Monographs* (61:2), pp. 113-134.

Witte, K., and Allen, M. 2000. "A Meta-Analysis of Fear Appeals: Implications for Effective Public Health Campaigns," *Health Education & Behavior* (27:5), pp. 591-615.

Witte, K., Cameron, K.A., McKeon, J.K., and Berkowitz, J.M. 1996. "Predicting Risk Behaviors: Development and Validation of a Diagnostic Scale," *Journal of Health Communication* (1:4), pp. 317-341.

Wolfe, H.B. 1995. "Computer Security: For Fun and Profit," *Computers & Security* (14:2), pp. 113-115.

Woon, I., Tan, G.-W., and Low, R. 2005. "A Protection Motivation Theory Approach to Home Wireless Security," in: *Proceddings of the 26th International Conference on Information Systems*. Las Vegas.

Workman, M., Bommer, W.H., and Straub, D. 2008. "Security Lapses and the Omission of Information Security Measures: A Threat Control Model and Empirical Test," *Computers in Human Behavior* (24:6), pp. 2799-2816.

Youseff, L., Butrico, M., and Da Silva, D. 2008. "Toward a Unified Ontology of Cloud Computing," *Proceedings of 7th IEEE Grid Computing Environments Workshop*, Austin, pp. 1-10.

Zajac, L.E., Klein, W.M.P., and McCaul, K.D. 2006. "Absolute and Comparative Risk Perceptions as Predictors of Cancer Worry: Moderating Effects of Gender and Psychological Distress," *Journal of Health Communication* (11:1), pp. 37-49.

Zhang, Q., Cheng, L., and Boutaba, R. 2010. "Cloud Computing: State-of-the-Art and Research Challenges," *Journal of Internet Services and Applications* (1:1), pp. 7-18.

Zhao, X., Lynch, J.G., and Chen, Q. 2010. "Reconsidering Baron and Kenny: Myths and Truths About Mediation Analysis," *Journal of Consumer Research* (37:2), pp. 197-206.

Some parts, ideas, and figures will appear in the following, currently unpublished articles:

Loske, A., Widjaja, T., Benbasat, I., Cavusoglu, H., and Buxmann, P. "The Inhibiting Role of Unrealistic Optimism in Cloud Service Providers' Information Technology Security Investment Behavior," *Under review*.

Loske, A., Widjaja, T., Benbasat, I., Cavusoglu, H., and Buxmann, P. "Organizational IT Security Risk Management: The Role of External Pressure," *To be submitted*.

Loske, A., Widjaja, T., Benlian, A., and Buxmann, P. "Perceived IT Security Risks in Cloud Adoption: The Role of Perceptual Incongruence between Users and Providers," *To be submitted.*

WITHDRAWN

DATE DUE

NOV 1 4 2019		
GAYLORD		PRINTED IN U.S.A.

CPSIA information can be obtained
at www.ICGtesting.com
Printed in the USA
LVHW01s1430070518
576274LV00001B/218/P